Marine Mammals

Contributors' Biographies

John J. Burns is a biologist with the Alaska Department of Fish and Game in Fairbanks. He has led several scientific expeditions in Alaska and has served on the Committee of Scientific Advisors on Marine Mammals of the U.S. Marine Mammal Commission. He has studied marine mammals throughout Alaska, with most of his work centering on ice-associated species of the Bering, Chukchi, and Beaufort seas. He is presently involved in studies of outer continental shelf development as it may affect marine systems.

Robert L. DeLong is a wildlife research biologist with the Marine Mammal Division of the U.S. National Marine Fisheries Service in Seattle, Washington. He has studied northern fur seals on the Pribilof Islands and on San Miguel Island in California's Channel Islands, and sea lions and elephant seals on islands off California and Mexico. Currently he is involved in a cooperative study of Hawaiian monk seal population biology.

Francis H. ('Bud') Fay has been involved in marine mammal research in Alaska for the past twenty-five years, and is currently an associate professor of marine science at the University of Alaska in Fairbanks. He was employed for nineteen years as a research biologist at the U.S. Public Health Services Arctic Health Research Center in Anchorage and Fairbanks, and was also a member of the U.S. Marine Mammal Council of the International Biological Program.

Clifford H. Fiscus is a wildlife research biologist with the Marine Mammal Division of the U.S. National Marine Fisheries Service in Seattle. Since 1958 he has been involved in research on fur seals and other pinnipeds, including the Steller sea lion, California sea lion, and Hawaiian monk seal. His cetacean studies include work on the white-sided dolphin, Dall's porpoise, and bowhead whale.

Luis A. Fleischer, a biologist from the University of Mexico, is continuing graduate studies on the Guadalupe fur seal at the University of Washington College of Fisheries in Seattle. He has also worked as a professional diver and handler of dolphins in captivity, and has taught classes in marine science at the University of Mexico.

Roger L. Gentry is a wildlife research biologist with the Marine Mammal Division of the U.S. National Marine Fisheries Service in Seattle. His work has included studies of the California sea lion, elephant seal, northern fur seal, and gray whale. Most recently he has investigated diving behavior in the Antarctic Ross seal and surveyed seals and penguins along the Victoria Land coast.

Raymond M. Gilmore has been involved in biological research for more than fifty years, and marine mammal research since 1946, with the U.S. Fish and Wildlife Service and as professor of comparative anatomy, embryology, and vertebrate zoology at the University of Georgia and at California Western University. He has also spent two years studying marine mammals off southern South America. For the past twenty-five years he has been Research Associate in Marine Mammals at the San Diego Museum of Natural History in California.

Delphine Haley is a free-lance writer and editor, based in Seattle. Her articles on natural science subjects have appeared in many regional and national publications. Former associate editor of *Pacific Search* magazine, she is currently a staff writer for *Pacific Search* and field correspondent for *Defenders of Wildlife*. She is also author of a book on mustelids—*Sleek & Savage: North America's Weasel Family*.

Karl W. Kenyon, now retired and living in Seattle, was a wildlife research biologist with the U.S. Fish and Wildlife Service for twenty-six years, and specialized in marine wildlife, especially the sea otter, northern fur seal, Steller sea lion, Hawaiian monk seal, and Pacific walrus. He is periodically involved with monk seal and sea otter field studies, and serves on the Committee of Scientific Advisors on Marine Mammals of the U.S. Marine Mammal Commission.

Stephen Leatherwood is a marine biologist with the U.S. Naval Ocean Systems Center Marine Mammal Research Unit in San Diego, and an instructor in natural history at the University of California (Berkeley). He has traveled extensively, studying and photographing marine mammals, and is the coauthor of two field identification guides to cetaceans. His numerous published articles focus on population assessment, behavior, and acoustics of cetaceans.

Jack W. Lentfer is currently regional supervisor of the Game Division of the Alaska Department of Fish and Game in Juneau. Since 1966 he has studied polar bears and has participated as a U.S. delegate in all international polar bear meetings. He has also served as a member and chairman of the international Polar Bear Specialist Group affiliated with the International Union for the Conservation of Nature and Natural Resources (IUCN) and as a member of the Committee of Scientific Advisors of the U.S. Marine Mammal Commission.

Willman M. Marquette is a fishery research biologist with the Marine Mammal Division of the U.S. National Marine Fisheries Service in Seattle. He has investigated the sea lamprey problem in the Great Lakes, salmon passage at dams on the Columbia and Snake rivers in the western U.S., and since 1974 has studied subsistence harvest of bowhead whales by Alaskan Eskimos in the Arctic.

Bruce R. Mate is an assistant professor of oceanography at the Oregon State University Marine Science Center in Newport, Oregon, where he is involved in pinniped population assessment studies in Mexico, the U.S., and Canada. He is also active in research on gray whales and marine mammal–fisheries conflicts, and has recently created an international marine mammal information exchange.

Edward Mitchell is a research biologist with the Canadian Department of Fisheries and Environment at the Arctic Biological Station near Montreal, studying the ecology and population dynamics of North Atlantic whales. He serves on the Scientific Committee of the International Whaling Commission, and works with other organizations concerned with marine mammal conservation and management. He has published numerous articles on fossil marine mammals.

Terrell C. Newby, a graduate student in fisheries and wildlife management at the University of Washington College of Fisheries in Seattle, has been studying the harbor seal, killer whale, and seabirds since 1964. His studies have centered on Washington State harbor seals, particularly at Gertrude Island in Puget Sound, and he has also spent two seasons studying northern fur seals on the Pribilof Islands.

Murray A. Newman, director of the Vancouver Public Aquarium in British Columbia, studied zoology at the universities of Chicago, Hawaii, and California (Berkeley), and fisheries biology at the University of British Columbia. With the capture of a killer whale in 1964, he became interested in cetaceans and has worked with white-sided dolphins, killer whales, belugas, and narwhals in the wild and in aquariums.

Randall R. Reeves left a position as director of Urban Activities at Princeton University in 1975 to pursue an interest in marine mammal conservation. Under contract to the U.S. Marine Mammal Commission and the U.S. Fish and Wildlife Service, he has completed studies on the Atlantic walrus, harp and hood seal hunting in eastern Canada, and gray whale harassment. His articles on arctic sea mammals have appeared in many publications.

Stephen B. Reilly is a graduate student at the University of Washington College of Fisheries in Seattle, while also working for the U.S. National Marine Fisheries Service, studying the California gray whale. Prior to this, his studies have centered on pilot whale distribution in the eastern Pacific. He has also worked for the U.S. Naval Ocean Systems Center and for the National Marine Fisheries Service porpoise program.

Dale W. Rice is a wildlife research biologist with the Marine Mammal Division of the U.S. National Marine Fisheries Service in Seattle. For the past twenty years, he has conducted studies on all the species of great whales. He has frequently served on the Scientific Committee of the International Whaling Commission, and is a member of the Whale Specialist Group of the IUCN's Survival Service Commission, and the Marine Mammal Committee of the American Society of Mammalogists. He is coauthor of *The Life History and Ecology of the Gray Whale.*

Victor B. Scheffer, now retired and living in Bellevue, Washington, was chairman of the U.S. Marine Mammal Commission from 1973 to 1976 and was a naturalist with the U.S. Fish and Wildlife Service from 1937 to 1969. He also taught zoology at the University of Washington and the International College of the Cayman Islands. In the course of studying marine mammals, he has visited Siberia, Japan, South America, and Antarctica, and has made fifteen trips to the Pribilof Islands.

David E. Withrow has worked on animal husbandry and training at the Seattle Marine Aquarium and on a United Nations Fishery Development Project in Morocco as a Peace Corps volunteer. In 1974, he was director of Morocco's Casablanca Aquarium, Africa's largest, where he maintained a variety of marine life. Now a graduate student at the University of Washington College of Fisheries in Seattle, he is also employed by the U.S. National Marine Fisheries Service, studying sea lions.

Allen A. Wolman has been a wildlife research biologist at the Marine Mammal Division of the U.S. National Marine Fisheries Service in Seattle since 1965. His studies have involved the biology of cetaceans, especially the sperm, humpback, gray, and killer whales of the eastern North Pacific. He is coauthor of *The Life History and Ecology of the Gray Whale.* He is now involved in fieldwork on the humpback in Hawaii and fin and humpback whales in Alaska.

Marine Mammals

of Eastern North Pacific and Arctic Waters

Edited by Delphine Haley

Pacific Search Press

Pacific Search Press, 715 Harrison Street, Seattle, Washington 98109
©1978 by Pacific Search Press. All rights reserved
Printed in the United States of America

House Editor: Betsy Rupp Fulwiler
Designer: Paula Schlosser
Maps by Judy Petry

Cover: A humpback whale and her calf in waters off Hawaii's island of Maui, an area that has been designated the first whale reserve in the United States. (James Hudnall)

Library of Congress Cataloging in Publication Data

Main entry under title:

Marine mammals of eastern North Pacific and Arctic
    waters.

    Bibliography: p.
    Includes index.
    1. Marine mammals—North Pacific Ocean.
2. Marine mammals—Arctic Ocean. 3. Mammals—
North Pacific Ocean. 4. Mammals—Arctic Ocean.
I. Haley, Delphine.
QL713.2.M36   599'.09'263   78-16859
ISBN 0-914718-35-5

Contents

To the many creative people who contributed to this book,
and to the remarkable marine creatures that inspired them.

Preface

M any people believe that between man and the whales and dolphins there is a mystical bond, an inexplicable kinship that has been recognized and celebrated in art, legend, and literature since earliest times. This book is concerned with a bond of a different type, one shared by all mammals—a biological bond fused by warm blood; mother's milk; hair, fur, or the vestiges of it; and a high order of intelligence.

Although a mammalian status links us biologically to the marine mammals, we are separated from them by the mysterious environment to which they are so well adapted—the sea. Consequently, much of their biology, behavior, and distribution is still unknown, and the study of whales and seals in their natural habitat is recognized as one of the most difficult efforts in all of field biology. On land, the seals, sea lions, walrus, and sea otter occupy some of the most isolated, least hospitable coastlines of the world; even those animals that live near populated areas are extremely wary and difficult to approach for study. As for the whales and dolphins, little time has been spent studying them in their marine environment; instead biologists have had to settle for observing them on the surface of the ocean—a costly and sometimes hazardous job. The other alternative has been to study the remains of animals that have been killed or stranded.

The twenty-one authors of this book are well aware of the benefits and burdens of fieldwork with marine mammals. Altogether they represent well over 250 years of biological research on the seals, sea lions, walrus, dolphins, whales, polar bear, and sea otter and they all share a scientific interest and concern for their subjects of study. As a result, much of this book's content is derived from firsthand observation. "Study Nature, not books," nineteenth-century naturalist Louis Agassiz is supposed to have said. The authors herein have done both.

Geographical boundaries for this book have been established roughly from the Gulf of California (lat 22° N) west across the tip of Baja California to the outermost islands of the Hawaiian Leeward chain (long 180°), thence north to the Arctic Ocean, including the entire Bering Sea, and east to the border of Alaska and Canada (long 140° W). Marine mammals, however, have a healthy disregard for such kinds of geography, and, although they may have real environmental boundaries—such as water temperature, salinity, or food sources—such limits are still unknown. Thus the distribution charts included here are merely approximations of species' ranges and should be interpreted as such—keeping in mind, for instance, that the northern elephant seal, whose northerly limit is usually Vancouver Island, has also been seen as far north as the Aleutian Islands and as far west as Midway Island, and that the arctic ringed seal has been known to wander as far south as La Jolla, California. Moreover, although the distribution of some marine mammals, such as that of the northern fur seal, is well known, the movements of others—such as the Guadalupe fur seal, the pilot whale, and the harbor porpoise—are still far from exact.

Introductory sections of this book are taken from information found in classic sources about marine mammals, supplemented by material more specific to the eastern North Pacific and Arctic. They are included to acquaint the reader with some of the basic forms and functions shared by groups of marine mammals.

Measurements cited in this text are presented in the English form. For those who want to know the approximate metric equivalents, the following table is useful:

1 mile = 1.61 kilometers
1 yard = 0.91 meter
1 foot = 0.30 meter
1 inch = 2.54 centimeters
1 pound = 0.45 kilogram
1 ton = 0.91 metric ton

Predictably, compilations like this involve the cooperation of many people, and the editor and publisher are grateful to all of those involved in this effort. As editor, I am grateful to each author in this book, who beyond the tangible necessities of manuscripts and photographs, contributed friendship, interest, humor—and time when uniformly there was none. In particular, I thank Dale Rice of the United States National Marine Fisheries Service in Seattle who—from the seemingly limitless corridors of his memory—furnished references, answered (too) many questions, reviewed portions of the text, recommended changes, and added encouragement. Special thanks are extended to Steve Leatherwood for sharing not only his photographs but additional sources and contacts; to Karl Kenyon, Ken Balcomb, and all others who contributed their extraordinary photos to visually enhance this book; and to Larry Foster and *National Geographic* for permitting us to reprint their cetacean illustrations. I am also grateful to others who kindly furnished information and criticism: Lawrence Barnes, Howard Braham, Michael Bigg, Robert Brownell, Alyn Duxbury, Anne Evely, Stefani Hewlitt, Mack Hopkins, Marion Johnson, James Mead, William Perrin, Aryan Roest, David Rugh, David Sergeant, Michael Tillman, William Walker, and V. A. Zemsky.

This book is factual in approach, centered—within the space available—on what is known of the unique adaptations, biology, and behavior of the marine mammals. It contains no poems, no legends, no mystical stories—only facts. However, a lack of lyric does not mean a lack of love—and facts have a certain practical eloquence all of their own. Surely it is this type of knowledge that will ultimately help us conserve the marine mammals that share our world.

Delphine Haley

Introduction

The World Ocean is immense living space for marine mammals—those warm-blooded, air-breathing, once land-living creatures that eons ago chose to return to the sea. Among them are the largest, swiftest, and most intelligent beings in the oceans—the whales and dolphins, the seals and sea lions. Efficiently adapted to different niches and roles within the marine ecosystem, the sea mammals are positioned at the top of the food chain. Their abundance thus reflects the habitat's ecological health and productivity.

One of the most favored marine mammal habitats exists in the eastern North Pacific—a vast oceanic spread that extends from the Aleutian Islands arc south to the tip of Baja California and west to the Hawaiian Leeward chain. This region, like all oceanic systems, is an immense nutrient solution, energized by the sun, seasoned with mineral salts, stirred by winds and currents, and enriched with the mineral runoff of many coastal rivers. Its basic ingredient is phytoplankton—the sea's green pasturage—the abundance of which influences all forms of marine life. In terms of phyto-plankton, the margins of this nine million square miles of ocean—with gyral currents in the north and nutrient upwellings associated with the cold, south-flowing California Current—are a productive part of the Pacific and of the planet, as well.

To the north lies the shallow bowl of the Arctic Ocean. Its surface is covered by ice throughout the year, except for a brief and explosive period when some of its open, sunlit waters bloom with plankton. This ocean is fed from the Pacific side by the Bering Sea through the narrow Bering Strait. Almost half of the Bering Sea is underlain with shallow continental shelf, a formation that permits intensive nutrient mixing during the sunlit months.

Because of nutrient productivity, the North Pacific and Bering Sea support one of the world's great fisheries. From these waters American and Canadian fishermen take one billion pounds of fish and shellfish each year, and foreign fishermen take three times more. The Bering Sea alone supports such a large biomass that it has been called the richest of all fisheries per unit area. It has the largest known clam beds, one of the largest salmon runs, and one of the largest marine mammal populations in the world.

Throughout this longitudinal sweep, marine mammals have adapted to a multitude of habitats —from landfast ice to mid-ocean depths to subtropical shoals—and live in climates varying from arctic to temperate or subtropical. Within this region, the cetaceans—whales and dolphins—wend their mysterious ways, leaving us with only hints of their habits and migrations. The great baleen whales sieve for crustaceans or small fish in northern waters in summer and travel south in winter to breed or calve in more temperate climes. One of these, the humpback, weaves bubble nets for krill or herring in Alaska's Glacier Bay, and migrates to warm seas off Mexico or the Hawaiian Islands to nurse its young. Another, the gray whale, forages along the bottom of shallow coves on Vancouver Island's rugged outer coast as it travels north to the Arctic each spring. It returns to calving lagoons off Mexico each fall to complete the longest of all mammal migrations.

Among the toothed whales, the mighty cachalot—the sperm whale—plumbs the submarine canyons off California in pursuit of giant squid. Pods of killer whales cruise the salmon-rich straits and island waters of British Columbia and Washington, and schools of dolphins and porpoises, well adapted to exploit the varied portions of the marine environment, feed and frolic from the Gulf of California to the Gulf of Alaska and beyond.

Remote areas of the Arctic and Pacific also serve as haul outs and congregating places for another group, the pinnipeds—the seals, the sea lions, and the walrus. Fast and floe ice, inaccessible rocky shores, and isolated sand beaches provide havens for resting, breeding, and security from predators—all within reach of the sea. The ice-dominated environment of the far north furnishes

varied niches for arctic seals. The rugged coasts of the Pribilof Islands are a breeding place for northern fur seals, which gather yearly and form the world's greatest concentration of large mammals. Quiet, sandy shores of the inland waters of southeastern Alaska, British Columbia, and Washington are resting places for the reticent harbor seal, while caves and cliffs along the wave-battered Oregon coast furnish one of many habitats for the Steller sea lion. California's offshore islands are ideal pinniped habitat: San Miguel Island harbors six species—five of them breeding populations—said to be the highest concentration of pinniped species in the world.

Other mammals have adapted to these waters. The edge of the arctic ice pack is a hunting ground for the wide-ranging polar bear. Kelp-forested waters off the Aleutians and California are homes for the sea otter. And the shallow coastal areas of the Bering Sea's Commander Islands once sheltered the now extinct Steller sea cow.

Marine mammals have become an integral part of human history and culture in this part of the world. Since earliest times, Eskimos and Aleuts have relied on products from whale, walrus, and seal for survival—for food, lamp oil, adornments and implements, waterproof clothing, and coverings for Eskimo umiaks or Aleut bidarkas. Baleen was used in harpoon lines, nets, and baskets; whale jaws and bones framed their winter homes; sea cow ribs or whale jaws served as runners on sledges. Along the more temperate, rain-washed shores to the south, sea mammals were literally carved and woven into the fabric of coastal Indian culture. The intricate masks and totems of the Haida and Tlingit of southeast Alaska depicted legends of the killer whale, seal, and sea lion. The baskets and ceremonial dances of Washington's Makah and British Columbia's Nootka Indians honored the hunt for the seal and the whale. Smiling killer whales were carved from soapstone by California's coastal

Indians. Clubs to kill seals, sea otters, or sea lions were carved from soft cedar or redwood and decorated with sea mammal designs.

The early native's hunt for the seal or the whale was insignificant in light of the indiscriminate exploitation of sea mammals that occurred at the hand of more "civilized" man during the eighteenth and nineteenth centuries. In 1741, the crew of Vitus Bering's second expedition to North America returned to their Russian homeland with news of a North Pacific treasure in the pelts of sea otter and fur seal. This discovery set in motion a sea mammal search that was to extend down the coast to Mexico. In time, the Russians were joined by British and Yankee whalemen and sealers who, having depleted other seas, moved to the North Pacific in an unrelenting quest for fur, ivory, blubber, and baleen. Across the Pacific, they hunted the sperm whale; in the bays of Mexico, California, and Alaska, the humpback; on offshore and mainland rookeries from the Pribilofs to the Channel Islands, the seals and sea otter; in its calving lagoons and along its coastal migration route, the gray whale; on the Kodiak Ground of the Gulf of Alaska, the right whale. Through the Bering Sea and into the Arctic Ocean, they chased and killed the much prized bowhead. With the invention of the harpoon gun in 1868 and the development of faster boats, the pursuit was intensified, and the faster swimming baleen species—the rorquals—became the victims of ever more efficient whaling techniques.

The marine mammal populations plummeted as a result of this intense slaughter. By the beginning of the twentieth century, the once abundant gray whale was nearly extinct, and the northern right whale and the bowhead were depleted to levels from which they have never recovered. The sea otter, Guadalupe fur seal, and elephant seal were commercially, though not biologically, extinct; the sea cow was gone entirely, and the northern fur seal was on its way. With no call for conservation, the days of plenty were obviously numbered.

A record of these early days of abundance has been preserved in the writings of two participants—Georg Wilhelm Steller and Charles M. Scammon. Steller (1709–1746), ship's naturalist and physician for Vitus Bering's second expedition to North America, was among the first Europeans to explore the rugged coasts of Alaska and the Aleutian and Commander islands. His notes, inspired by a single-minded passion for discovery and detail, formed the first substance of the marine biological knowledge of the Bering Sea. *De Bestiis Marinis (The Beasts of the Sea)* is his written record of the marine mammals—a natural history of the sea otter, the sea lion, the sea bear or fur seal, and the Steller sea cow, the only firsthand scientific observation of this vanished species.

Charles M. Scammon (1825–1911), a whaling captain who plied these seas in the mid-nineteenth century, also contributed a valuable history of this period. Although the biological content of his *Marine Mammals of the Northwestern Coast of North America* (1874) has since been expanded, his historical account remains a first person view of marine mammal wealth gone-by: days when the elephant seal hauled out by the multitudes on the California coast and when the sea otter was plentiful along the shores of Washington and Oregon. Observing the decline of some species, Scammon was pessimistic about their future. In the 1860s he wrote of the walrus: "Already the animals have suffered so great a slaughter at [the hunters'] hands that their numbers have been materially diminished... making it difficult for the Eskimaux to successfully hunt them..." And, although there were as many as 25,000 gray whales in the breeding waters when he hunted them, the downward trend was evident: "The mammoth bones of the California Gray lie bleaching on the shores of those silvery waters," he wrote. "[They] are scattered along the broken coasts, from Siberia to the Gulf of California; and ere long it may be questioned whether this mammal will not be numbered among the extinct species of the Pacific."

The California gray did survive. Along with the walrus, elephant seal, sea otter, and northern fur seal, it is numerous once again. The Steller sea cow did not; it was killed off some twenty-seven years after its discovery.

Although marine mammals are now variously protected by domestic and international regulations, it will take many decades, if then, before some of the great whales—the endangered bowhead, northern right, blue, and humpback—are anywhere near their former numbers. In addition, two pinnipeds of this region—the Guadalupe fur seal and the Hawaiian monk seal—are still endangered.

For some species, the hunting continues. Sperm and Bryde's whales are still taken by Soviets and Japanese in the eastern North Pacific. (The minke is hunted only around Japan.) Gray whales are taken by Soviet catcher boats in the northern Bering and southern Chukchi seas to supply native Siberian villages along the coast; gray, bowhead, and beluga whales are taken by Alaskan Eskimos under exclusion provisions for aborigines; narwhals and belugas are hunted by Canadian Eskimos. The smaller cetaceans (including the narwhal and beluga) are neither regulated nor protected under any international management program. Many are caught incidentally in the nets of commercial fisheries: spotted and spinner dolphins are taken by the tens of thousands each year in the tuna fishery; Dall's porpoises are caught annually in numbers estimated between three thousand and fifteen thousand in the North Pacific pelagic salmon fishery. Harbor porpoises and bottlenose dolphins are also incidental victims, as was the rare Gulf of California porpoise until its associated fishery for totoaba became defunct in recent years.

As for the pinnipeds, bull fur seals are culled yearly from the Pribilof Islands under the provi-

sions of international treaty. Walruses and ice seals are hunted by Eskimos of Siberia and Alaska for subsistence; spotted, bearded, and ribbon seals are also hunted commercially by the Soviets. Harbor seals, Steller and California sea lions—the ongoing foes of domestic and foreign commercial fishermen—are killed under permit when there are no other means of driving them away. (Verification of the numbers killed and high seas enforcement of these regulations, however, are virtually impossible.) Each year, an estimated eight thousand fur seals in the North Pacific are the victims of entanglement in castaway debris. Small marine mammals—mainly California sea lions, and bottlenose and white-sided dolphins—are captured under permit for public display in oceanariums, and all species are the subject of scientific research under permit. Although these may appear to be times of relative conservation, the future of marine mammals is the subject of constant and conflicting pressures within and between some nations.

More than any other animal group, the marine mammals attract and command our attention. Few of us can fail to respond to them—to the bright behavior of the dolphin, the awesome power of the great blue whale, the supple efficiency of the sea lion, the playfulness of the sea otter. The attraction has persisted throughout history—sometimes literally fatal, always mysterious and compelling. The haunting song of the humpback in a way reflects the attraction: It is a sound so old, so eerie that it seems to echo over eons—a leviathan chant that has survived the mists of centuries and the shadowy depths of ancient seas. The response in humans who hear it is felt more in the bones than in the brain—as an atavistic hint of origins no longer remembered. We are rulers of separate realms, yet man and the marine mammals are bound in mysterious ways.

Delphine Haley

Origins
of Eastern North Pacific Sea Mammal Fauna

by Edward Mitchell

Marine mammals have been much in the public consciousness of late. In part, this great interest stems from the recent findings that porpoises and dolphins have many unique behavioral and physiological characteristics, including a sophisticated sonar system. There is also increasing appreciation of the intelligence of these animals. This awareness has stimulated an interest in the ancient origins of these creatures, leading to a better understanding of their modern counterparts.

Although the bulk of scientific work on fossil marine mammals was done in Europe during the late nineteenth century, knowledge of species known from North American fossils did not fully develop until the first half of the twentieth century. Most outstanding among the investigators of North Pacific fossil sea mammals was Dr. Remington Kellogg of the United States National Museum. Many of the interpretations in this chapter are based upon his pioneering work, which began in 1921 and continued until his death in 1969.

For the paleontologist, the present is the key to the past. Understandably then, living descendants are the yardstick against which the fossil assemblages may be measured. Among the North Pacific sea mammals, these include: six species of balaenopterine or rorqual whales (blue, fin, sei, Bryde's, minke, and humpback); a balaenid, the right whale; the eschrichtiid, the gray whale, and twenty-two toothed cetaceans, including ten species of delphinids or dolphins, three species of phocoenids or porpoises, about five or six species of ziphiids or beaked whales, and three species of physeterids or sperm whales. This region is also rich in numbers and diversity of pinnipeds, including the odobenine walrus and four species of otariine or eared seals (the northern and southern fur seals, the California and Steller sea lions). Phocid or earless seals are natural residents here, and include the harbor seal and elephant seal. Unrelated to seals or sea lions is the sea otter, a mustelid carnivore endemic to the eastern North Pacific coast.

All in all, this fauna of sea mammals is large and diverse when compared with others throughout the world. It has its own very distinctive aspect:

The middle Miocene sea lion
Allodesmus *had a proboscis,
not developed in living sea
lions. Here two bulls engage in
combat.* Allodesmus *perhaps
grew to lengths as great as any
living pinniped. Some
inferential evidence suggests
that this large beast was
covered not with fur like sea
lions, but with blubber like
elephant seals. (Bonnie Dalzell)*

about one sixth of these thirty-eight species are
found nowhere else in the world but in the North
Pacific.

But it has not always been thus. Many strange
aquatic mammals have inhabited the North Pacific
in the geologic past, the earlier assemblages differ-
ing in both numbers and proportions from the present species makeup. The published fossil record
for these animals extends back about twenty-five
million years to the late Oligocene and early
Miocene epochs.

Before Miocene time, the record in the eastern
North Pacific is scanty, probably in part because few
marine mammalogists have concerned themselves
with it. There is one record of one archeocete, a
primitive toothed whale, as well as some poorly
documented occurrences of small toothed whales,

squalodonts (predaceous sharktoothed whales), and
mysticetes (baleen whales). However, these occurrences are so few and scattered that no unifying
statement can be made about them. So the later
record will be emphasized here.

An excellent sample of early Miocene marine
mammal fossils has been found in rocks at the
south end of California's San Joaquin Valley. At a
site called Pyramid Hill, long-snouted porpoises,
sharktooth whales or squalodonts, a small otterlike
pinniped, large primitive pinnipeds, and other
marine mammals have been found along with hundreds of other marine and terrestrial species of
animals and plants. Although the marine mammals
found here are known from only fragments of bone
and teeth, an accurate picture has been pieced together thanks to more complete skulls and skele-

tons of related species from other areas.

Only one ancient baleen whale, or cetothere, is known from this early Miocene time in California. It is relatively small, only ten or fifteen feet in total length.

A few bones and teeth of squalodont whales have been discovered in the early Miocene, about twenty-three million years ago, of the eastern North Pacific. These were long-snouted, presumably carnivorous whales with long caninelike teeth in the front of their jaws and large bladelike shearing teeth in the back. The back teeth were broad-based and double-rooted, with serrated edges. Their resemblance to the teeth of some sharks gave rise to the name squalodont.

The otterlike pinniped found at Pyramid Hill was an aquatically adapted mammal more closely related to some land carnivores and to sea lions than to otters. It represents a ''missing link'' between the terrestrial ancestors of the bears, and some of the otariid sea lions. With the discovery of this extinct species, a long-continuing scientific debate over whether the otariid sea lions were evolved from the same land ancestors as the phocid seals was resolved. The seals and sea lions, superficially similar, are quite unrelated to one another.

Long-snouted porpoises are perhaps most characteristic of the early Miocene northeast Pacific fauna. They have been found in early Miocene rocks of South America and Europe, as well as in North America. In some species, the beak measured up to five times as long as the braincase. There has been much speculation about the function of the beak in these porpoises, ranging from realistic to ridiculous. One scientist went so far as to suggest that these animals became extinct because their beaks grew so long that they could no longer swim well and got stuck in the muddy bottoms of prehistoric seas!

The middle Miocene fauna in the eastern North

Artist's conception of the head of the otterlike sea mammal, Enaliarctos mealsi, as it would have appeared in life. Notable features are the long, low head with large, dorsally directed eyes and short muzzle. The shape of the ear and nose is conjectural. Enaliarctos mealsi was an early Miocene carnivore of medium size, phyletically related to early bears and pinnipeds. It is a ''missing link'' in the evolution of sea lions or fur seals from land carnivores. (Bonnie Dalzell)

Pacific is better known partly because more rocks of this age (about twelve to sixteen million years ago) are exposed in areas convenient to paleontologists. One of the most famous and best documented of these assemblages is located at Sharktooth Hill in southern California. Considered late middle Miocene in age, the Sharktooth Hill assemblage includes a ziphiid or beaked whale, a platanistoid or long-snouted porpoise, a primitive sperm whale—Aulophyseter—, nine or more species of other porpoises and dolphins, four kinds of cetotheres or baleen whales, a balaenid or right whale, a hippopotamuslike creature called a desmostylian, and more than two sea lions. The Sharktooth Hill assemblage is apparently typical of the middle Miocene epoch in California. However, some evidence suggests that it might be an imbalanced or

Above: Long-snouted porpoises were a common constituent of early Miocene faunas in the eastern North Pacific. This restoration of Eurhinodelphis *shows that the teeth do not run out to the end of the upper jaw. Color patterns of these six- to eight-feet-long extinct species are of course unknown, but that shown here is probably not unrealistic. (Bonnie Dalzell)*

Below: The middle Miocene cetothere Mixocetus *can be compared with the gray whale as far as appearance and habits, as suggested in this reconstruction. It was one of the larger cetotheres, perhaps attaining lengths of almost thirty feet. There may have been only a single pair of throat grooves in this species. (Bonnie Dalzell)*

skewed sampling of the once-living fauna, perhaps containing animals that were transported to the area after their deaths. Nevertheless, it remains the best single representation for this time period in the eastern North Pacific Ocean.

Cetotheres, small-to-medium-sized primitive baleen whales, were among the most common members of the middle Miocene fauna in California. Some cetotheres were large, many were small, but all probably had relatively short baleen. Perhaps some migrated latitudinally as do their modern counterparts. Abundant and slow-moving, these ancient whales were probably good targets for the large predators of Miocene seas.

The sperm whale, *Aulophyseter*, was a medium-sized whale with upper teeth not well rooted in their sockets. In this and other characteristics, it foreshadows the modern sperm whale. *Aulophyseter* occurs profusely at Sharktooth Hill. Evidently, what is now the south end of the San Joaquin Valley was a haunt or calving place for this species during the Miocene. Numerous remains of both adults and juveniles have been found there.

The group of mammals called desmostylians has no common name. No man has ever seen one of these beasts alive, since the last one died more than nine million years ago. Although known in the fossil record since 1888, or earlier, from many occurrences of their peculiar teeth, different species of desmostylians are only lately being recognized with some understanding of their anatomy. Almost all knowledge of these amphibious marine mammals is based on a small number of skulls and skeletons, few of which have been described scientifically. Their precise relationship to present-day subungulate groups of mammals like sea cows and elephants is still a matter of speculation and research. Suffice it to say that they were a group of large quadrupedal mammals that frequented nearshore marine waters around the North Pacific from Japan to Alaska and Baja California. They evidently lived a walruslike or hippopotamuslike mode of life, but scientists have not yet established whether they were clam eaters, or marine plant eaters.

This restoration of Desmostylus *attempts to give an idea of what the animal looked like when foraging for submarine food, but the type of food involved is purposely obscured since there is scientific argument over whether the beast ate clams or seaweed. Indeed, some would suggest that* Desmostylus *came ashore to forage for plants, rather than to feed on the sea bottom. (Bonnie Dalzell)*

How did the northeast Pacific fauna differ between the early and the middle Miocene periods in this part of the world? For the desmostylians during the middle Miocene, there is some evidence of greater numbers and wider dispersal, both of species and possibly of individuals. By this time, if not before, some desmostylians attained lengths of up to ten or more feet and weights of many thousands of pounds. Sea lions too had diversified by the early Miocene or earlier, before seventeen million years ago. Some types were quite common. Two of the best known kinds—and characteristic of middle Miocene assemblages, as well—are *Desmatophoca* and *Allodesmus*. A long-headed, slimly built sea lion, *Desmatophoca* resembled modern sea lions in many ways. Bones of this animal have been found in Oregon and California. *Allodesmus*, better known from numerous sites in southern and central California, was a rather strange kind of "sea lion." Although certainly related to the otariid sea lions, it more closely resembled the elephant seal because of its large proboscis, and also resembled the leopard seal because of certain features of the skeleton and skull.

Mainly then, the few differences between early and middle Miocene assemblages can be attributed to continued ancestor-descendant evolution of the common faunal elements in the same area of the North Pacific. For example, cetotheres, platanistoids, delphinoids, desmostylians, desmatophocids, and otterlike pinnipeds, and other species evolved in this same area throughout early and middle Miocene time.

However, during the late Miocene and early Pliocene—some twelve to five million years ago—greater differences began to appear. The late Miocene marks the first appearance or apparent greater abundance of modern rorquals like the humpback whale, large, modern-appearing sea lions, ancestors of the living fur seals, numerous species of more modern delphinid and phocoenid porpoises, and

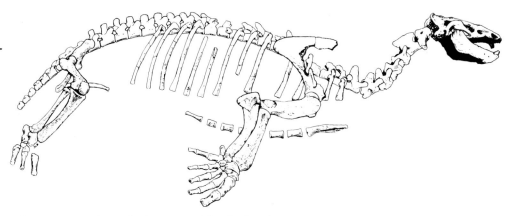

diverse species of physeteroid whales (sperm whales and their allies). Sirenians related to the dugong appeared and were common in the eastern North Pacific by this time; only a few are known before then. Although cetotheres and desmostylians still occurred in the late Miocene, they were approaching the end of their reign in these seas.

By the early Pliocene (about four to five million years ago), the eastern North Pacific fauna was essentially modern. The last of the cetotheres were dying out. Typical walruses had invaded the eastern North Pacific some time previously, or possibly evolved there, but elephant seals and other types of earless or phocid seals had not yet immigrated into the North Pacific. Although there were some aberrant kinds of walruses in the late Miocene and the Pliocene, little is known of them. Fur seals, dolphins and porpoises, most of the whales, and other species were essentially as they are today. Finally, at the end of the Pliocene or in the earliest Pleistocene, about 1.5 million years ago, the sea otter and true seals appeared. An early theory was that the modern sea otter evolved from a North Atlantic species of aquatic mustelid and subsequently immigrated to the North Pacific, but recent findings of sea otter bones and teeth, possibly representing two species, in Pleistocene rocks in California and Ore-

The middle Miocene sea lion Allodesmus was a sea lion by ancestry only, for it evolved in a direction away from typical forms and resembled some Antarctic earless seals like the elephant seal and the leopard seal. This skeleton was of a male, since the baculum was preserved. (Bonnie Dalzell)

gon indicate that the modern sea otter actually may have evolved in this area during Pliocene and Pleistocene time.

Indeed, had one been able to cruise along the reefs and shingles of the California coast in a boat a few million years ago, the marine mammal fauna would have looked different only to a specialist in such matters, who would recognize long-beaked stenodelphinine porpoises, and relatives of the beluga. A dugong or two might spoil the illusion of modernity, but only until one remembered that the

Steller sea cow is actually a part of the modern fauna. (This slow-moving species finally succumbed to man's hunting pressures during the 1760s.)

There is no evidence for extensive Pleistocene extinctions in the sea mammals comparable to the well-known massive changes that took place in the land fauna. But climatic fluctuations probably did affect sea mammals by enforcing separation of some populations, which may have resulted in the evolution of new species.

The modern northeast Pacific fauna is then an

Only a few fossils of this sirenian, Halianassa, are known from California, but the available evidence suggests an animal like the living dugong but with different proportions as shown in this restoration. A true marine herbivore, this sirenian probably frequented inshore waters in association with sea lions and small cetaceans. (Bonnie Dalzell)

agglomeration of species from highly diverse sources. Some, like the harbor seal, are recent immigrants from the Arctic. Others, like the elephant seal, may have immigrated recently from southerly routes. Yet others, like the fur seals, sea lions, and some porpoises, derive from ancestors that lived here from the earliest beginnings of their family lines. The vulnerable Steller sea cow, adapted to feed in quiet inshore waters, would have been one of these but for the immigration of man.

In conclusion, the succession of local faunas or assemblages through time, as recorded in the sequence of rocks along the northeast Pacific coast, clearly shows the greatest change between the assemblages earlier than the late Miocene, and subsequently. In 1966, I suggested that this change in faunal succession existed, with the transition marked by the extinction or emigration of desmostylians, cetotheres, squalodonts, long-beaked porpoises, and some archaic sea lions; and by the origin or immigration of balaenopterine whales, modern sea lions, fur seals and walruses, advanced kinds of dolphins and porpoises, abundant sea cows, elephant and other phocid seals, and the sea otter.

My hypothesis to explain this sequential change in the faunas was that the mid-Miocene and earlier faunas were adapted to warmer water than the late Miocene and subsequent fauna; and I speculated that the late Miocene fauna might be related not only to cold water but might derive in part from the Arctic Basin in earlier times. The closing of the central American seaway connecting tropical Atlantic and Pacific oceans at about nine million years ago, might also have affected Pacific faunal composition. Thus, by this theory, late Miocene and later faunal interchange was enhanced through an Arctic route, and decreased through the tropical Atlantic route.

Subsequent work by Lawrence G. Barnes and myself has shown that this theory of faunal succes-

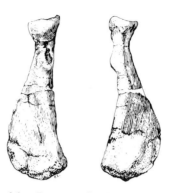

This fossil, a radius or forearm bone, from Pliocene rocks in Alaska, comprises part of the evidence that phocid seals did not evolve in the North Pacific but immigrated here in the Pliocene. (Pamela Immel)

A fossil deciduous tooth of a sea otter Enhydra, *from early Pleistocene rocks of San Pedro, California, indicates that sea otters may have evolved here, and not immigrated from the North Atlantic as one earlier theory proposed. (Mary Butler)*

sion is reasonable. Barnes finds that, if not an artifact of the fossil record, there may have been a lack of extensive cetacean immigration into the North Pacific during the Oligocene, and that the later faunal turnover also included extinction or emigration of primitive delphinoids, as well as evolution or immigration of stenodelphinines, monodontids, eschrichtiids, and phocids. Barnes concludes that climatic fluctuations may influence faunal diversity.

A more general hypothesis developed by Jere H. Lipps and myself in 1976 is that radiations and declines of world sea mammal species were responses to the availability of crops of food, themselves dependent upon climate and oceanic upwelling of nutrient rich waters and the resulting increase of plankton productivity. The peaks in sea mammal species diversity would presumably always follow the opening up of new food resources and other ecological opportunities. The duration of this lag time would depend upon a given species' ability to respond to new opportunities. Thus, there would not be strict coincidence between the first appearance of new, abundant food resources and the peaks in species diversity of an assemblage. Clearly, as the fossil record is further documented, detailed analysis of these patterns will help in interpreting the mechanisms that now, and in the past, regulate sea mammal assemblages and abundance.

Cetaceans
Whales, Porpoises, Dolphins

Cetaceans—the dolphins, porpoises, and whales—are those mammals that took the boldest evolutionary step: They severed all terrestrial ties in favor of a weightless life in water. Over countless ages, they were transformed from four-legged land dwellers to fishlike creatures of the sea, while still retaining warm blood and lungs for breathing atmospheric air. Cetaceans in the North Pacific range in size from the five-foot harbor porpoise to the one-hundred-foot blue whale, a living superlative unsurpassed in size by any other animal. Large or small, all members of this order are the result of the most profound anatomical changes to have occurred in mammalian evolution.

The cetaceans were grouped with the fish by early naturalists because of their streamlined shapes and thorough adaptations to the sea. Aristotle, in the fourth century B.C., recognized their affinity to mammals, and in 1693 British zoologist John Ray was the first to classify them as such. In 1864, British mammalogist William Henry Flower divided the cetaceans further into two suborders: the Mysticeti—those "moustached" or baleen whales that filter food through horny, fringed plates set on either side of the upper jaw; and the Odontoceti—the toothed whales and dolphins that capture their prey by means of numerous conical teeth.

The early evolution of cetaceans is largely unknown due to a lack of fossil evidence. Scientists generally agree, however, that the whales and dolphins are most closely related to the carnivores and ungulates. One theory suggests that their common ancestor was a primitive, wolf-sized, carnivorous mammal (family Mesonychidae) that lived during the Paleocene epoch (fifty-five to sixty-five million years ago). Paleontological and anatomical data accumulated thus far have established three phylogenetic lines: the Odontoceti, the Mysticeti, and the extinct Archaeoceti. Their exact relationship to one another is not known, and no fossil of any of these lines has been firmly established as ancestral to the others. Nor has any fossil yet been found that represents the link between the land-living ancestors and the early cetaceans.

The oldest fossil records of cetaceans are of the archeocetes from the Eocene (about forty-five mil-

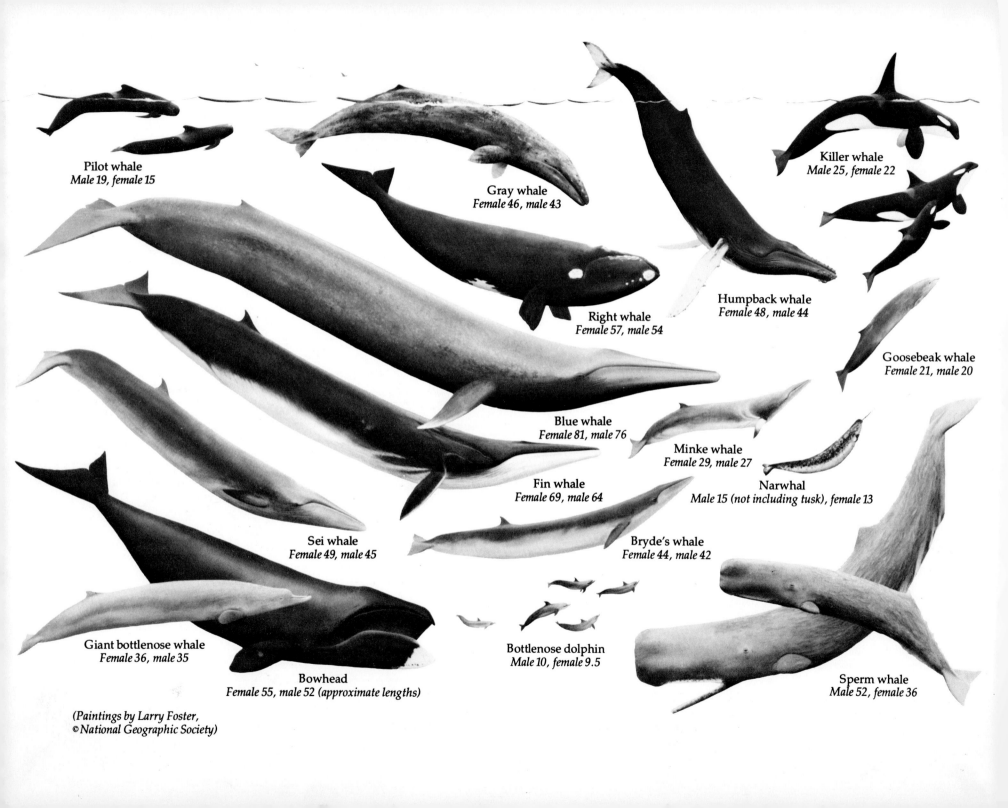

Pilot whale
Male 19, female 15

Gray whale
Female 46, male 43

Killer whale
Male 25, female 22

Right whale
Female 57, male 54

Humpback whale
Female 48, male 44

Goosebeak whale
Female 21, male 20

Blue whale
Female 81, male 76

Minke whale
Female 29, male 27

Fin whale
Female 69, male 64

Narwhal
Male 15 (not including tusk), female 13

Sei whale
Female 49, male 45

Bryde's whale
Female 44, male 42

Giant bottlenose whale
Female 36, male 35

Bottlenose dolphin
Male 10, female 9.5

Bowhead
Female 55, male 52 (approximate lengths)

Sperm whale
Male 52, female 36

*(Paintings by Larry Foster,
©National Geographic Society)*

lion years ago). Some of these aquatic creatures were small and dolphinlike; others were serpent-shaped, measured up to fifty feet in length, and probably moved with vertical undulations of their bodies. Their nostrils were positioned part way back on the head. The archeocetes devoured their prey with curved front teeth and multi-cusped cheek teeth. The largest members of this group were called zeuglodonts, meaning "yoke toothed," because of the shape of their double-rooted cheek teeth. They represented the beginning of the end for this line, and about twenty-five million years ago, the archeocetes became extinct. However, before this time (about thirty million years ago during the Oligocene), the first primitive toothed and baleen whales had made an appearance.

During these and subsequent eons, the cetacean body was evolving for hydrodynamic efficiency. Species appeared and disappeared, replaced by new modifications, until successful evolutionary trends were established. Freed in the water from the size limits imposed by gravity, the cetacean body grew large. Its hairy coat was traded for thick blubber to retain body heat and store energy. Sebaceous and sweat glands were discarded as no longer necessary. The nasal opening gradually shifted from the front of the snout to the top of the head for easier breathing while the whale was horizontally extended. The body became elongated and streamlined for least resistance in water: the neck disappeared and the cervical vertebrae were compressed. The outer form was smoothed by its envelope of blubber, and all projecting parts were either changed or abandoned. External ears were eliminated except for small holes on either side of the head. Nipples and sex organs were withdrawn into slits within the body. The forelimbs became rigid, except at the shoulder, and were changed into paddle-shaped flippers for steering and stability. The posterior limbs were eliminated entirely and replaced by a large, heavy tail with horizontally

flattened flukes. The lumbar region, with massive muscles attached to the vertebrae, became the cetacean powerhouse. The power generated here is transferred to the broad, horizontal flukes, which, by their upward and downward movements, force the water backward. It is a force that, with a few strokes of the tail, can launch forty tons of humpback whale into a full body breach or, if the whale is harpooned, can tow a catcher boat of several hundred tons, or under the most ordinary conditions can move a school of Dall's porpoises along at about twenty miles per hour. Thus equipped, cetaceans are among the swiftest and most powerful creatures in the sea.

A few anatomical traces are reminders that the cetaceans once walked on land. Embryo whales less than one inch long have tiny flaps in place of the hind legs of their ancestors. The fully developed cetacean flippers are composed of arm, wrist, and finger bones, with five fingers for most whale species; they differ from humans only in having more bones in the two central digits. A pair of unattached bones are found embedded in the muscles at the hip site—all that remains of the pelvic girdle. In rare instances, other small bones, thought to be vestiges of leg bones, are found. Even a few hairs persist around the snouts of fetal toothed whales and adult baleen whales as a reminder of their origins.

Baleen whales (Mysticeti) are comprised of three families: Balaenopteridae, Balaenidae, and Eschrichtiidae. All of these whales have double blowholes and baleen or whalebone instead of teeth. Their appearance is characterized by a huge lower jaw, which makes the mouth line appear to lie toward the top of the head. On either side of the mysticete's upper jaw—where teeth would ordinarily be found—are a series of triangular horny plates (baleen). The plates are embedded crosswise in the jaw and hang parallel to each other. The inner margin of each of these plates is fringed with fine or

Relative sizes and body contours of eastern North Pacific cetaceans are illustrated here. Numbers listed with each whale are the mean lengths (in feet) at physical maturity for the male and female of each species. Baleen whales in the Southern Hemisphere generally reach greater lengths than their northern relatives.

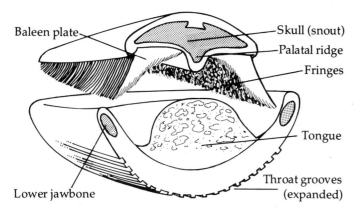

Baleen plate — Skull (snout) — Palatal ridge — Fringes — Tongue — Throat grooves (expanded) — Lower jawbone

coarse hairs, depending on the species. The fringes form a hairy curtain that acts as a sieve to filter the whale's food. When feeding, the mysticete surges after swarms of krill, other zooplankton, or small fish that constitute its diet. It scoops up tremendous amounts of water in the process. The water is then strained out of the mouth through the baleen, while the food is retained.

The family Balaenopteridae has the greatest number of species among the mysticetes. It is comprised of the five finner or finback whales—blue, fin, sei, minke, and Bryde's—and the humpback whale. All have a distinct dorsal fin, from which their common name, "finner," is derived. They vary in size from the minke at about thirty feet to the blue whale at about one hundred feet. The number of baleen plates in these whales coincides roughly with the relative body lengths. For each side of the broad, flat upper jaw, they average: blue, 360; fin, 355; sei, 340; humpback, 330; Bryde's, 300; minke, 280.

These large whales are also called rorquals, an old Norse word meaning "red whale." This term refers indirectly to the many grooves or pleats that extend from the chin almost to and even beyond the navel; more specifically, it describes the pinkish tint of the skin on the bottom of these grooves when the throat of the whale is distended. The throat grooves, probably an adaptation to permit

the enlargement of the mouth during feeding, average from twenty-two in the humpback to eighty in the blue whale. They extend beyond the umbilicus in all rorquals, except in the sei and minke whales in which the grooves stop short of the umbilicus. The rorquals are generally the fastest swimmers among cetaceans: although their normal cruising speed is about five miles per hour, when chased they can maintain a speed of ten miles per hour for over an hour and some are said to attain thirty-five or forty miles per hour in short bursts.

The right whale family (Balaenidae), so called because in the early days of whaling they were the "right" ones to catch, includes two species from the North Pacific and Arctic oceans—the slow-swimming northern right whale and the bowhead. Stockier in shape than the rorquals, these whales lack both throat grooves and a dorsal fin. The upper jaw, from which the long baleen is suspended, is narrow and highly arched. The baleen averages 245 plates on either side of the right whale's jaw and 300 plates in the bowhead. Bowhead baleen, reaching a maximum height of

This cross-section of the snout of a fin whale shows the positions of baleen and the tongue when the mouth is open. After engulfing a school of krill or small fishes, the whale contracts its throat, forcing the water out of its mouth between the baleen plates. The fringes on the inner edges of the plates act as a sieve to retain the food organisms, which are then swallowed. (Dale W. Rice)

Baleen whales (Mysticeti) filter food through horny plates that hang from their upper jaws. The minke whale averages 280 short baleen plates on each side of its upper jaw. Its baleen is yellowish white, turning brown or black on the posterior portions. (W. J. Houck)

fourteen feet, rivals that of the sei whale in the fineness of its fringe.

The gray whale, lone member of the family Eschrichtiidae, is a primitive species having two to four short grooves on the throat and a small dorsal hump instead of a distinct fin. The 160 short baleen plates on either side of its jaw are the coarsest of all species.

Toothed whales (Odontoceti) are divided into four families: Physeteridae, Ziphiidae, Delphinidae, and Monodontidae. As their group name implies, all are equipped with simple conical teeth for seizing fish, squid, or, in the case of the killer whale, small birds and marine mammals. The teeth serve only to capture prey, which is swallowed whole. The dentition of this group is highly variable both within and among families. Toothed whales are also characterized by a single blowhole around which the skull bones are asymmetrically arranged. Air sacs, which probably relate to sound production, are also located near the blowhole.

The family Physeteridae includes the largest toothed whale—the fifty-foot giant sperm whale—and its rare smaller relatives—the ten-foot pygmy sperm whale and the eight-foot dwarf sperm whale. The giant sperm whale's upper jaw, containing a few nonfunctional teeth, extends over the lower jaw, into which are set eighteen to twenty-five pairs of teeth. When the mouth is closed, the lower teeth fit into the sockets of the upper jaw.

The little known beaked whales, family Ziphiidae, with six species in the eastern North Pacific, show a great reduction in teeth to one or two pairs in the lower jaw. Most unique are the two lower teeth of the densebeak whale, which curve out and beyond the upper jaw.

The familiar and successful family Delphinidae is comprised of the most species among toothed whales. They are the dolphins and porpoises, with eight species occurring regularly in the eastern North Pacific and four incidental visitors, and the

killer whale, false killer whale, and pilot whale. For catching fish and squid, there may be as many as two hundred teeth in the upper and lower jaws of the common and spinner dolphins or as few as four to fourteen in only the lower jaw of the Risso's dolphin.

The two species of the family Monodontidae—the beluga and narwhal—are arctic-oriented, pale in color, with blunt-shaped heads. Dentition varies from the beluga, with eight to ten teeth in each jaw, to that oddest of odontocetes—the narwhal, which is essentially toothless except for the male's six-foot spirally twisted tusk that extends from the upper jaw.

To capture prey, cetaceans are well equipped for diving. Because the krill consumed by the rorquals is found in upper water layers, these whales

A right whale skims the surface for food. Its baleen, hanging like vertical venetian blinds from the upper jaw, is clearly shown. The plates, 245 on each side of the mouth, may be eight feet long, with the posterior and anterior plates much shorter. The right whale's long, fine baleen was much sought during the nineteenth century for a variety of uses, from thread to corset stays. (William Watkins, Woods Hole Oceanographic Institution)

usually dive to less than 160 feet and stay submerged between 5 and 15 minutes. They are capable, however, of dives to 1,150 feet and durations of up to 50 minutes. Toothed whales are the deepest divers, the records being held by the sperm and bottlenose whales, which descend regularly to 1,500 feet. Sperm whales have been found entangled in cables on the ocean floor at 3,000 feet and at 3,720 feet. As for duration, sperm whales are known to have submerged for as long as 75 minutes and whalers have reported that the Atlantic bottlenose can remain underwater for 2 hours. Such records make the human's maximum possible dive of about 390 feet, with a maximum breathing interval of 2.5 minutes, seem meager indeed.

Several anatomical and physiological peculiarities combine to permit the larger cetaceans to stay submerged for long durations and at great depths. Although the lung capacity of dolphins and porpoises is one and one-half times larger than that of land mammals, the lung size of large whales relative to their body weight is only about one half that of terrestrial mammals. The smaller lungs may be an advantage to prevent excessive compression of the body at great depths.

Within a few seconds at the surface, the whale can exhale and replace eighty to ninety percent of the air in its lungs (in contrast to land mammals, who replace ten to twenty percent). The most minute passages of the lungs are kept open by cartilaginous rings and elastic tissue in order to effect a rapid and thorough air exchange. Two capillary layers in the walls separating the tiny lung sacs (in contrast to one layer in humans) provide a larger surface area for rapid absorption of oxygen into the blood. Because of these and other modifications, about one half of the oxygen inhaled is absorbed into the blood (one fifth is absorbed by terrestrial mammals). Several other factors contribute to oxygen conservation: cetacean blood contains twice as many red blood cells as in land mammals and thus

can carry twice as much oxygen. The muscles contain up to nine times more myoglobin than in land mammals, enabling the whale to store that much more oxygen. Moreover, cetacean muscles naturally can continue to function for a time without oxygen, and the deficit is replenished when the whale breathes again at the surface.

During the dive, the cetacean's heart rate decreases. Blood bypasses the skin and all nonessential organs, and oxygen is conserved for vital organs—the heart and brain. Because the whale does not breathe underwater, it is free of nitrogen buildup in the blood. At depths greater than about 330 feet, extreme pressure collapses the lungs and forces the air into more rigid bronchial, tracheal, or nasal passages. This prevents nitrogen from being absorbed into the blood and the whale can return

Toothed whales (Odontoceti) have simple conical teeth with sharp points for grasping prey, which is not chewed but swallowed whole. The giant sperm whale has eighteen to twenty-five pairs of teeth in its relatively small lower jaw. When the mouth is closed, the lower teeth fit into corresponding holes in the upper jaw, thereby forming a powerful vise for gripping soft cuttlefish, this whale's principal food. (H. Omura, courtesy of Stephen Leatherwood)

from great depths without experiencing "the bends."

The whale's "blow," a forceful expulsion of compressed air, comes in varying sizes and shapes. The rorquals produce a pear-shaped blow, varying from hardly noticeable for the minke to twenty feet high for the blue whale. The sperm whale, with a forward-set single blowhole, sends its blow diagonally forward some ten to fifteen feet, while the right whale has a double, V-shaped blow ten to fifteen feet high.

Interest in cetacean intelligence has increased in recent years because of knowledge that the whale has an exceptionally large brain and because of the remarkable behavior of dolphins in captivity. Cetaceans are the only animals, other than the elephant, to have a brain larger than man, although the significance of this brain size in terms of "intelligence" is not known. The brain of the sperm whale weighs 20 pounds; the elephant, 10 pounds; the bottlenose dolphin, 3.75 pounds; and man, 3 pounds. The surface of the cetacean brain is highly convoluted with deep and complex folds similar to those in the human brain. Two of the most successfully adapted species—the sperm and killer whales—have unusually large brains with cerebrums more elaborately folded and with greater surface areas than in man. In captivity, dolphins have shown a considerable capacity for learning. They have shown the ability to recognize signals and shapes, to solve problems, to learn by observing, to combine and generalize about new behaviors, even to invent new behaviors of their own. Like some other cetaceans, they communicate with each other and seem to have some social structure. They have a well-developed sense of play and care-giving—not only toward their own kind but toward man. Many aspects of cetacean intelligence are still unknown, perhaps unknowable. Although whales have a large brain capacity and physiologically their brains function basically like those of other animals, their intel-

lectual activity is not necessarily the same. Intelligence in these animals, given the differences in anatomy and environment, is difficult to measure in human terms.

Certain senses have evolved for the cetacean's life in the sea. Smell seems to be of little importance: only in some baleen whales is there a trace of an olfactory mucous membrane and nerve. Taste organs seem to be absent in baleen whales and poorly developed in toothed whales, although some captive dolphins are known to show preferences for certain kinds of fish. Touch is an important sense, as evidenced by the prominence of the trigeminal nerve, the most highly developed of the cetacean's cranial nerves. Among other functions, it transmits sensory impulses from the face and mouth region. In the mysticetes, this paired nerve supplies the

The killer whale has ten to fourteen pairs of sharp teeth in both jaws for seizing fish, birds, or other aquatic mammals. (Vancouver Public Aquarium)

sensory tubercles on the lips and oral cavity and also the bristles on the upper and lower lips. In addition, dolphins in captivity tend to rub and mouth one another, sometimes swimming with flippers touching; killer whales also seek pats or rubbings from their trainers. Live whales stranded on beaches react to touching of their skin.

Cetacean vision above and under water is good, although not without drawbacks among the largest whales because the wide placement of the eyes creates blind spots ahead and behind. There is also some debate about the degree of visual sharpness in cetaceans and whether they can see as well in air as in water. The smaller cetaceans—dolphins and porpoises, which feed on fast-moving fish—are thought to use their eyes most effectively. In general, the eyes are small in relation to body size and have a spherical lens to compensate for the refractive index of the water. The oval eye shape is maintained by a thick, pressure-resistant capsule (sclera). An iridescent layer (tapetum) is located behind the retina; it reflects light and sends it back through the retina a second time for distinguishing objects in dim depths. The pupil may also be greatly enlarged to receive maximum light. Although cetacean eyes lack a lachrymal gland, they are protected by horny outer layers of the cornea and another gland that secretes oily substances.

Hearing is the most important sense. Of the nerves in the cranium, the acoustic nerves are second only to the trigeminal nerve in size and are better developed in toothed whales than in baleen whales. Cetaceans can receive a wide range of frequencies, which extend to around 150 kilohertz (or 150,000 cycles per second) for the bottlenose dolphin. This approximates the frequencies received by bats at 175 kilohertz, and certainly far surpasses the upper limits of humans at 15 to 20 kilohertz.

Exactly how sound is transmitted to the cetacean ear is still unknown. Scientists debate whether the sound passes through the two tubes that extend from the outer to inner ears (even though they are closed for most of their length); whether it is simply transmitted through the head as a whole, as is the case with humans when underwater; or whether sounds are picked up and transmitted through the lower jaw, which extends as far as the ear bones.

Although they lack vocal chords, whales and dolphins produce a variety of sounds. Baleen whales communicate with a repertoire of moans, squeaks, and screams—including "creaking hinge" sounds—which range from 20 hertz to nearly 1,000 hertz. Most famous are the haunting songs of the humpback whale, the most vocal of the baleen species, with varied refrains repeated note for note.

Toothed whales communicate by whistles thought to be produced in the larynx, with sounds usually limited to frequencies between 4 and 20 kilohertz. For most toothed whales, sound also serves as an extension of the visual sense through echolocation. By emitting rapid sounds—clicks or pings ranging between 10 hertz and 120 kilohertz—into blind areas and measuring the time these sounds take to travel to an object, bounce off it and return, the toothed cetaceans locate food and orient themselves. In this way, they "see" with sound waves, interpreting not only distance, but size, shape, and even density. Some investigations show that the echolocation frequencies may go even higher: dolphins have been known to emit sounds up to about 150 to 200 kilohertz. The sound pulses are presumably produced in the nasal sacs of the skull and focused by the melon, a fatty mass situated in the forehead. With this sonar system, a blindfolded bottlenose dolphin can find and catch fish and avoid a variety of obstacles. Obstacles not detected by this sensitive sonar are subtle and sometimes deadly: large-meshed or monofilament nets or gently sloping beaches.

Although much physiological information has been obtained from studying captive and dead animals, many aspects of the cetacean's life in the wild—such as its social behavior—remain a mystery. Unfortunately, few studies have been based on live cetaceans under natural conditions because the extensive fieldwork is physically and financially prohibitive.

Little is known of breeding behavior in the wild, but some elements of the reproductive cycle are known. The highly migratory baleen whales breed in winter. Although breeding seasons for some of the dolphins are not well known, many mate in spring or summer. For the baleen whales, gestation extends ten to thirteen months, and for the toothed whales, ten to sixteen months. The breeding interval is most commonly every two or three years.

A single whale or dolphin calf is born, usually tail first. Birth takes place underwater, and the precocial calf either swims to the surface or is pushed up by its mother or another cow. The young are relatively large—as much as one fourth their mother's length—and immediately begin to acquire insulating fat. This comes from the mother's extremely rich milk, which is higher in protein and fat, and lower in sugar, than the milk of a cow. On this diet, the young cetacean grows quickly. The blue whale calf, measuring twenty-three feet in length and weighing over two tons at birth, doubles its weight within the first week. In seven months, it is fifty feet long and weighs twenty-five tons.

The whale's great size does not necessarily mean that it lives for a long time, for the harpoon has cut short many a cetacean life. The natural life-span of these animals and the mortality factors that terminate it are still matters for study. The age of cetaceans is usually determined by counting dentine layers in the teeth of odontocetes and the rings on the earplugs of mysticetes. Potentially, the natural life-span of the great whales compares to that of man and may be even greater. Several fin whales with earplugs bearing seventy and eighty or more rings have been found. Old Tom, an Australian kil-

ler whale, is said to have lived for at least 50, possibly as long as 80, years. Pelorus Jack, a Risso's dolphin, was known to escort ships into a New Zealand harbor for 24 years. Some maximum recorded ages are: gray whale, 70; blue whale, 110; fin whale, 114; humpback, 77; sei whale, 74; Bryde's whale, 72; minke whale, 47; sperm whale, 77; giant bottlenose whale, 70; killer whale, 50 plus; bottlenose dolphin, 35; striped dolphin, 34; spotted dolphin, 31.

Throughout their lives, cetaceans are besieged by a variety of external parasites. Large barnacles attach themselves to the larger whales, such as the gray and the humpback. One small barnacle, *Xenobalanus globicipitis*, has been found on the flukes, fins, and flippers of a great variety of cetaceans. Lampreys, suckerfish or remoras, and several crustaceans are also known to attach themselves to the large whales.

As for more lethal predators, the killer whale preys on its kin: it will attack the gray whale, the minke, and the smaller dolphins and porpoises. The remains of dolphins have also been found in the stomachs of sharks, but whether the dolphins were taken alive is not known. Very rarely a rogue walrus will kill a narwhal or a beluga, as will the polar bear when these whales are trapped in the ice. All of this predation is insignificant, however, and major mortality factors are still unknown—except for the obvious predation of man, aided by his nets, catcher boats, and harpoon guns.

The story of man's relationship to the whales and dolphins is a long litany of exploitation. Suffice it to say that the cetaceans—having survived evolution's most rigorous challenges—may find the challenge of man insurmountable. It is an all too obvious fact that in human hands rests the doubtful fate of the ocean monarchs, the grandest and most intelligent beings in the seas.

D.H.

Blue Whale

by Dale W. Rice

"*B*allena! Ballena azul!" I had almost dozed off in the warm sun on the flying bridge of the whale catcher *Lynnann* when Ernesto's cry from the crow's nest jerked me to attention. Three miles off our port beam a thin jet of vapor rose from the water, drifted downwind, and dissipated. Then I spotted two great, blue green shadows gliding under the gentle swells. In a moment, they broke the surface and sent up two more plumes of vapor. Ernesto repeated his cry: "Blue whales! Two, maybe three!" With a quick sighting over the compass binnacle, I kicked out the "iron mike" that had been holding us on course and spun the wheel to port. *Lynnann* heeled hard over in a tight turn—a maneuver that brought the rest of the crew scurrying up from the galley. There is no whaler and no whale biologist, no matter how experienced, who is so jaded that his heart does not race at the sight of a blue whale.

Fifteen minutes of hard steaming brought us close to the whales. Captain Bud Newton took the wheel for the stalk. I positioned myself on the gun platform on the bow, but the big ninety-millimeter harpoon cannon remained unloaded and covered. I was armed instead with a twelve-gauge shotgun that fired ten-inch, pointed, stainless steel tubes, each inscribed with a number and the message "Notify U.S. Fish and Wildlife Service." The next time the whales surfaced and blew, the skipper put us on collision course with them. A few minutes later I spotted one of them in the clear water just ahead of us. Powerful rhythmic strokes of its sixteen-foot-wide flukes effortlessly propelled its streamlined bulk through the water. After an eternity, the huge flat head broke the surface and the animal blew with a loud "whoooosh" only twenty-five yards away. Braced on the pitching platform, I fired just as the whale arched its giant back to submerge. It did not even flinch as the marker buried itself in the back muscles—a mere mosquito bite.

These blue whales, which congregate off the coast of Baja California every year from February to June and again in October, represent one of the last sizable stocks of blue whales left on the earth. On several occasions, I have encountered aggregations of as many as fifty to sixty animals. By marking

With its double blowhole wide open, a blue whale surfaces off Baja California. The blue whales in this area represent one of the last sizable stocks left in the world. (Ken Balcomb)

some of these animals, we hoped to trace their migration routes. If any had been killed on the whaling grounds farther north, the marks would have been discovered in their flesh and we could have determined exactly where they spent the summer.

Unfortunately for science—but fortunately for the survival of the species—hunting of blue whales was banned in 1966, shortly after our marking program got under way. Recent observations give some indication of their winter grounds, however. During the 1975 Soviet-American Whale Research Cruise on the catcher boat *Vnushitel'nyi*, we saw several small groups of blue whales about seven hundred miles off the coast of Guatemala (lat 08° N, long 94° W). Another stock of blue whales spends the winter in the western North Pacific from southwestern Honshu to Taiwan, and a few have also been sighted in the mid-Pacific between twenty and thirty-five degrees north latitude.

During the summer, the North Pacific blue whales range in the immediate offshore waters from central California and the northeastern coast of Honshu north to the Gulf of Alaska and the Aleutian chain. They rarely enter the Bering Sea, but have occasionally been observed as far north as the Chukchi Sea.

Besides the North Pacific, blue whales have been found almost everywhere else in the world's oceans at one time or another. They range from the tropics north through the North Atlantic to the Arctic Ocean north of Spitsbergen (lat 85° N), and south throughout the Southern Hemisphere to the Ross Sea of Antarctica (lat 78° S).

The blue whale (*Balaenoptera musculus*) is the largest of the rorquals, a family of baleen (whalebone) whales characterized by their pleated or corrugated throats. The six species of rorquals range in size down to the little minke whale, which is only thirty feet long. Aside from its great size, the blue whale may be distinguished by its blue gray color that is mottled with lighter gray; only the

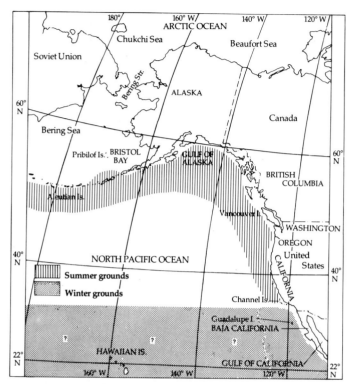

Blue whale distribution

undersides of its flippers are white. The dorsal fin is small—little more than a step in the ridge of its back—and its tongue, palate, and baleen plates are inky black.

Although the blue whale is the largest animal that has ever lived, it is difficult to separate fact from fiction when you try to find out how big it gets. Although blue whales over one hundred feet long have been reported, such measurements have never been properly documented. After combing the literature and questioning whale biologists from all over the world, I find that the longest blue whale (measured in the standard zoological manner—in a straight line from the tip of the snout to the notch between the tail flukes) that can be authenticated was a ninety-eight-foot female examined by Dr. Masaharu Nishiwaki of the

Japanese Whales Research Institute in the Antarctic in the 1946–1947 season. The heaviest blue whale on record is an eighty-nine-foot female that was cut up and weighed, piece by piece, aboard a Japanese floating factory ship in the Antarctic on 27 January 1948. She weighed 285,600 pounds. Allowing for a twelve percent loss of blood and body fluids, she must have weighed about 320,000 pounds when alive. The largest blue whale that I have examined in the North Pacific was an eighty-two-foot female killed off San Francisco on 23 September 1959. This animal weighed 181,200 pounds and must have weighed about 203,000 pounds when alive. She yielded 52,500 pounds of meat.

The blue whale becomes sexually mature at about ten years. From then on, each female gives birth to a calf once every two or three years. The mating season extends over about five months in the late fall and winter, and the gestation period lasts about a year. Because the annual cycles of Southern Hemisphere and Northern Hemisphere blue whales are six months out of phase, they cannot interbreed.

At birth, the blue whale calf is about twenty-three feet long and weighs some 5,500 pounds. During the nursing period, its mother must supply over fifty gallons of milk a day. This milk contains thirty-five to fifty percent fat and enables the calf to gain weight at the prodigious rate of over 200 pounds a day or some 9 pounds per hour. At the age of seven months, when it is weaned, the calf is fifty-two feet long and weighs 50,000 pounds.

Of all the large whales, the blue whale is the most particular about its diet. It is not known to feed on anything other than certain species of krill—small shrimplike crustaceans—from one part of the world to another. In the Antarctic Ocean, blue whales eat *Euphausia superba*, a "giant" species of krill that reaches a length of over two inches. Off California and in other parts of the North Pacific, the main species is *Euphausia pacifica*, which is less

than an inch long; of secondary importance is a slightly larger species called *Thysanoessa spinifera*. In whatever part of the world, all the species of krill that are selected by the blue whale share two characteristics: They congregate in large, dense shoals and they live fairly close to the surface. The only possible exception to this exclusive diet of euphausiids occurs off Baja California, where I have observed blue whales apparently feeding on "red crabs" (*Pleuroncodes planipes*). These look like tiny lobsters and, like the euphausiids, often gather in immense shoals at the surface.

An average blue whale weighing seventy-five or eighty tons probably requires about 1.5 million calories a day. Since it fasts for much of the winter, it must consume about twice this amount—or 3 million calories a day—during the summer months. One pound of *Euphausia pacifica* supplies about 400 calories. This means that the whale must consume about four tons of krill every day. Its stomach holds about a ton, so it eats four full meals daily. Because *Euphausia pacifica* weighs only one tenth of a gram, it takes about forty million of these krill to sustain one blue whale for one day.

To obtain this immense quantity of food, a blue whale must filter thousands of cubic yards of water through the sievelike series of baleen plates—about 360 on each side—that grow in its upper jaw. Most species of baleen whales fall into two groups on the basis of their feeding behavior: the "skimmers"—such as the right whale and the sei whale—which swim along with their mouths wide open, and the "gulpers"—such as the blue whale. When a blue whale encounters a shoal of krill, it rolls on its side, presumably to allow more maneuverability in the horizontal plane. Its huge, U-shaped lower mandible hangs open about fifty degrees and its pleated throat balloons out. It slowly engulfs a mass of krill, closes its mouth, and by tightening its throat muscles, sends the water streaming out through its baleen plates, leaving the krill trapped on the fibrous fringes of the inner edges of the baleen plates. Its huge, fleshy tongue then scrapes the krill back to the gullet. The whale repeats this process, hour after hour, day after day.

Probably because of its fastidious diet, the blue whale is much less prone to infestations of parasitic worms than are other species of baleen whales. In examining stomachs of blue whales, I have never found herring-worms (*Anisakis simplex*), which other species of baleen whales often harbor in great numbers (apparently picked up by eating fish infested with the immature stages). About half the blue

whales taken off California carried thorny-headed worms (*Bolbosoma nipponicum*) attached to the lining of the small intestine. The only other internal parasite I have found was a giant kidney worm (*Crassicauda crassicauda*), which was present in about one quarter of the animals examined.

The blue whale usually does not carry many ectoparasites either. The few it does have are some of the most peculiar creatures in the animal kingdom. *Penella*, a crustacean of the order Copepoda, is so highly specialized that, at first glance, it is not even recognizable as an animal. The female of this

Hitchhiking suckerfish cling to the mottled back of a surfacing blue whale, the largest animal that has ever lived. (Dale W. Rice)

species grows anchored in the whale's blubber by a three-pronged, tripod-shaped "root," between the "legs" of which is the rounded head. Its stemlike "neck," which is several inches long, protrudes from the whale's skin and is terminated by a thickened "trunk," which bears a fringe of gill filaments and two long, threadlike ovipositors. The male (rarely seen by zoologists) is a tiny creature that looks more like a normal crustacean.

A barnacle called *Xenobalanus globicipitis* is another unique ectoparasite. Although a true sessile barnacle, it looks more like one of the stalked or gooseneck barnacles because the shell is reduced to a small, star-shaped structure. Most of its body— which may be over two inches long—protrudes from the shell; it is long and cone-shaped with a downturned "collar" through which its cirri (legs) protrude. This barnacle selects as its habitat the trailing edge of the tail flukes and occasionally the tips of the flippers or dorsal fin. On one whale, I found several hundred forming a solid rank along the hind margin of the flukes; in such a position, they must withstand a terrific water velocity when the whale is swimming fast. These barnacles are not true parasites but filter their own food from the water flowing past the whale. Blue whales rarely carry "whale lice" (really amphipod crustaceans) of the species (*Cyamus balaenopterae*) that also occurs on other species of rorquals.

Just as the barnacles "ride" the whale in order to take advantage of the food-carrying water currents, other fellow travelers have adapted themselves to exploit the tremendous volume of water that flows between the baleen plates. Such uncountable millions of *Balaenophilus unisetus*, an almost microscopic copepod crustacean, live on the baleen plates that these ectoparasites form a whitish scum. "Big fleas have little fleas . . .," and so *Balaenophilus* carries on its body and legs many jug-shaped ciliate protozoans belonging to a still undescribed genus. Another denizen of the baleen

plates is a tiny roundworm called *Odontobius ceti*.

One of the most interesting creatures that makes the blue whale its home is the whale sucker (*Remora australis*), a fish related to the more familiar shark sucker. This fish has been found only on cetaceans of several species—both large and small—but shows a decided preference for the blue whale. I have seen dozens clinging to the sides of a blue whale, but like many of the blue whale's coterie of hangers-on, the whale suckers simply go along for the ride and catch their own food en route (a biological relationship called phoresy). One fish, however, is not such a harmless hitchhiker. This is the Pacific lamprey (*Entosphenus tridentatus*), which uses its suckerlike mouth and sharp teeth to bite into the whale's skin, where it leaves wounds, which become distinctive scars.

The blue whale was too swift and powerful for the nineteenth-century whalers to pursue with their open boats and hand harpoons. But by the early 1900s, following the invention of the harpoon cannon, the blue whale (because of its large size) became the most sought-after target of whalers the world over. Floating factory ships and fleets of catcher boats pursued the whales far into the Antarctic pack ice. The slaughter reached a peak in 1931 when 29,649 blue whales were killed throughout the world. Although there was a brief respite during World War II, the slaughter continued afterward. By 1966, the species was so scarce that it formed an insignificant portion of the world's whale catch. The International Whaling Commission then belatedly afforded the blue whale complete protection throughout the world. The original blue whale population in the early 1900s probably numbered over two hundred thousand. Today, there are only about twelve thousand blue whales left in the entire world—ten thousand in the Southern Hemisphere, fifteen hundred in the North Pacific, and a few hundred in the North Atlantic.

Finner Whales

by Edward Mitchell

Stories abound regarding the size, tenacity to life, speed, and near extinction of the beautiful big whales. However, the nature of the beast alone is so noteworthy that I recount the facts without embellishment. In order to compare and contrast the interesting differences between the superficially similar finner whales, they are described together.

Balaenopterid whales are the most recently evolved and modern type whale now living. The zoological family Balaenopteridae, the rorqual or groove-throated mysticetes, can be divided into the humpback (genus *Megaptera*), and the finner species group (genus *Balaenoptera*). The blue whale, the largest, and the related but superficially different humpback whale are discussed separately in this volume. The remainder of the Balaenopterids comprise the second largest, the fin whale *(Balaenoptera physalus)*; and in order of decreasing size, the sei whale *(B. borealis)*; Bryde's whale *(B. edeni)*; and the smallest of the lot, two species of minke or little piked whales *(B. acutorostrata* and *B. bonaerensis)*. Of these, the minke *(B. acutorostrata)*, fin, and sei whales are those most commonly found in the east-

ern North Pacific, from California north to Alaska. Bryde's whales are more tropical species, and the southern minke *(B. bonaerensis)* is most abundant in the Southern Hemisphere. Only the fin, sei, Bryde's, and minke whales of the North Pacific will be discussed here.

Even whalers have difficulty in distinguishing between these species. Identification of these whales at sea is usually based upon a combination of physical characteristics—size and shape of the dorsal fin, its placement on the body, the shape and color of the head and trunk, and behavioral features—including respiration rate, the nature of the roll at the surface, and the whales' running pattern when chased. Generally, the fin whale has a dorsal fin that is more angular on its leading edge than that of the sei whale, which is more smoothly curved and slightly higher, like a sickle or scimitar. The dorsal fin of the minke whale differs a little, having a broad base.

The position of the fin on the body differs in all these species. The minke whale's dorsal fin is quite far forward on the body, and whenever the whale

A minke whale—sharp-headed little finner whale—shows its acute snout tip, darkened pigmentation, and white patch on the flipper that is visible underwater. (Edward Mitchell)

A sei whale shows the single head ridge, slightly arched rostrum, and pointed snout while "skim" feeding at the surface. The baleen is visible, while the lower jaw is open but below the surface out of sight. (Edward Mitchell)

blows, the dorsal fin is immediately visible as it breaks the surface of the water. The sei whale's dorsal fin is slightly farther aft on the body than that of the minke whale, and the fin whale's dorsal fin is even farther back. That of the blue whale is far back on the tail. Generally, the larger the species of whale, the smaller the dorsal fin, the farther back it is on the body, and the later after the blow it is seen.

Therefore, if the size, shape, and color of head, dorsal fin, and back are known, whales can be identified at sea by noting the time interval between the appearance of the dorsal fin and the head, and when the animal blows. Thus the minke whale's dorsal fin is evident immediately, very often the sei whale's dorsal breaks the water just after the blow, and in the fin whale the wheellike silhouette of the whale shows the blow, then the back of the whale, and finally the dorsal fin. In the blue whale the appearance of the fin is much delayed—first the blow is seen, then the back of the animal, which often disappears beneath the surface, and finally a very small nubbin of a dorsal fin breaks the water just before the flukes lift slightly and the animal dives. These characteristics may differ a little, depending on the behavior of the whale at the time of sighting, and so cannot be taken as absolute. But with an estimate of the size of the whale, its pigmentation pattern, the environmental and zoogeographic context of the sighting, and the general behavioral pattern of the whale, a good final identification can be made, sometimes even at a distance of one or two miles.

The sei whale takes its name from a fish that it accompanies into the fjords of Norway. Known as a "skimmer," the sei feeds near the surface. Its respiratory rate reflects this behavior because the blows are evenly spaced over long intervals. As a shallow diver and skimmer, the sei whale emerges from the water to blow at a shallower angle than the fin whale. Hence, the dorsal fin shows for a much longer time on the sea surface, and the back is often exposed over a longer distance.

The fin whale is reputed to dive to moderate and deep depths, and accordingly its respiratory rate will show unequal spacing. Three or four blows, equally spaced, will be followed by a hiatus of five to ten minutes as the animal dives and surfaces again. Thus even at great distances the blow rate or pattern of a large balaenopterine whale will aid in the identification of the species.

Of these species only the blue whale consistently lifts its flukes slightly above the surface when diving, termed "fluking up" by whalers. This is often not visible at a distance, since the flukes do not come up vertically out of the water as they do with humpback, right, and sperm whales. Instead the flukes are elevated only a few inches above the surface, horizontally, while water spills off slowly. In deeper water the flukes lift slightly more as the whale may descend at a steeper angle.

Bryde's whales differ from sei whales mainly in their accessory head ridges. Two ridges run from near the snout tip back to beside the blowhole, alongside the median head ridge. Thus a whale with three prominent ridges on its head is usually a Bryde's whale; with only one, it is one of the other species of *Balaenoptera*.

Minke whales are not so easily categorized. They have the habit of approaching ships, called "seeking" behavior, and because they are small and somewhat secretive, tend to be sighted only once or twice without a careful watch. The blowing pattern is not as regular or predictable as the sei whale's or the fin whale's, but this may reflect the minke whale's response to an observer. Smallest of the finners, this whale takes its name from the habit of a Norwegian whaleman named Minke of overestimating the length of whales taken by his ship. Thus, all small or undersized whales came to be called "Minke's whales," a name that stuck with the northern species.

Minke whales have a distinct type of pigmentation—the major area of the body and trunk is dark, but the flippers have a white patch. These patches can be seen easily underwater, and can identify this Northern Hemisphere species. The proximal margin of the white band may differ slightly from that in the North Atlantic population.

Pigmentation also affords the best means of identifying the fin whale—a chevron on the neck, and a lower jaw that is completely white on the right and dark on the left. When approaching whales on their right sides, identification can be confirmed by noting the white lower jaw.

Because the particular hue of these whale species may vary among individuals and may appear different under diverse light and weather conditions, the overall pigmentation pattern is also important for their identification. The blue and sei whales, for instance, have darker bellies than the other finners. They are, furthermore, partly covered with large spots and splotches, the resulting pattern resembling the shoals of zooplankton on which

A blue whale shows its mottled pigmentation; wide, broad, and flat rostrum with blunt, rounded tip of snout; and characteristic dense and high blow. (Edward Mitchell)

they feed. The fin and minke whales, on the other hand, are more boldly patterned with blocks or fields of dark gray and white. Their complex pigmentation of stripes, chevrons, and distinctive patches has evolved, I believe, to aid them in camouflaging themselves from fast-moving prey, such as fish. Details of the Bryde's whale's pigmentation are not well known; nor is it clear how this species fits into the above hypothesis.

Of these balaenopterine whales, the one most likely to engage in aerial acrobatics is the smallest—the minke whale—which leaps from the water in a clean breach, sometimes upside down. Frequently a splash at great distances at sea will turn out to be a humpback or minke breaching. The breach of a minke differs from a humpback's—the latter usually comes part way out of the water and

falls sideways, making a big splash; the minke arches more gracefully and its splash is smaller. Its breach is often associated with feeding activities.

All of these whales are worldwide in distribution. Generally the blue and fin whales migrate most poleward during the summer feeding season. The minke occurs broadly over the North Pacific in summer months, but winter sightings are in far lower latitudes, mainly between twenty and twenty-five degrees north latitude. Although the sei whale also migrates, it is a more boreal species than most finners. The more tropically distributed Bryde's whale may not be so migratory as the others.

Unlike the California gray whale, whose circumscribed migration route enters very shallow coastal waters, the fin whale is a more pelagic, open ocean animal with a less restricted migration.

Although populations do occur off coasts, there are open sea populations in the middle of the North Pacific Ocean. All of these populations migrate north and south; hence, there is a limited gene flow among them—east to west and west to east. Two major stocks are presently recognized in the North Pacific.

In most of the world's oceans the blue whale migrates up to the edge of the ice—the case in the North Atlantic Ocean and in the Southern Hemisphere. But in the North Pacific this pattern appears to be reversed—the blue whale does not migrate far into the Bering Sea. The fin whale is found throughout the Bering Sea in the summer feeding season, and many Russian and Japanese kills were from this area.

The minke whale feeds on fish such as sand lance and anchovy, and also on euphausiids and other invertebrates. The fin whale eats small fish when they are in concentrated groups, or euphausiids when they are plentiful. However, the blue whale is adapted to feed only on invertebrates, basically four species of euphausiids. The sei whale feeds mainly on even smaller invertebrate prey species, such as copepods. The baleen plates—especially the differences in length and texture of the bristles and the number of plates—reflect an apparent adaptive spread into a variety of niches throughout the evolution of these balaenopterine whales.

The sei whale appears to be versatile in its feeding habits, mainly using the "skimming" technique but also able to use the "swallowing" method for feeding. Sei whales, on the average, feed on higher trophic levels in the North Pacific than in the Antarctic, but this apparently reflects the fact that the two regions are not trophically equivalent in structure.

Bryde's whales may feed on a more restricted diet, and at a generally higher trophic level than sei whales. Evidence from the North Pacific shows sea-

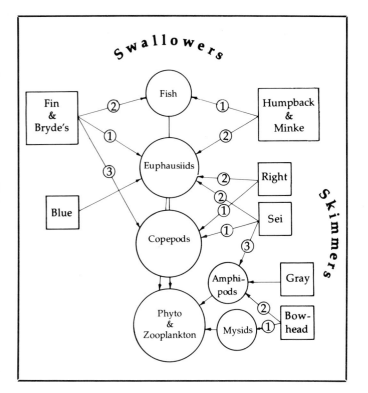

This generalized food web shows predation by swallowing and skimming baleen whales on main food sources. "Skimmers" strain a long column of water with their mouth continuously open, whereas "swallowers" literally gulp a mouthful at a time, then close the mouth, squeeze the water out, and retain the food. The gray whale is intermediate in structure and behavior between specialized skimmers such as the bowhead, right, and sei whales, and the typical swallowers such as the fin and humpback whales. The numbers refer to the order of preference for prey by each whale species. (Edward Mitchell)

sonal fluctuations in the amount and nature of feeding.

Most of these whales school in pods of varying numbers, but little is known of the social structure within schools. In general, one to three minke whales are sighted together in schools or pods, both inshore and offshore. Fin whales usually congregate in groups of three to ten, or twenty, and schools of many more animals are often sighted on the feeding grounds. Sei whales likewise congregate in the tens, and as with fin whales, are apt to be sighted in greater numbers on feeding grounds.

Little is known of fin whale herding behavior or group composition during the reproductive season in the northern winter. Reproduction in the North Pacific fin whales is not completely understood, but they probably breed in the months of

December and January, migrate north after calving, and feed in the northernmost reaches of the Pacific Ocean up to and including the Bering Sea. Gestation is about eleven months; at birth the calf measures some twenty feet in length. The return migration to more temperate waters occurs during October and November; and the cycle starts again. Any individual female fin whale may breed one year and suckle the next; there is often one resting year—sometimes more—between pregnancies. The calves nurse for about six months and are weaned when they reach a length of thirty-six to forty feet.

Sexual maturity is attained long before physical maturity. Females are slightly larger than males, but sexual dimorphism is not otherwise distinct in finners. For example, in the Northern Hemisphere fin whale, sexual maturity is attained at a length of fifty-eight feet for males and sixty feet for females. Physical maturity is attained at sixty-two feet for males and at sixty-seven feet for females. The maximum length for the Northern Hemisphere fin whale is eighty feet.

A fin whale, as it noses up and begins to blow, shows its white, right lower jaw; single head ridge; long, wide, and flat head; light flippers; and distinctive chevron on the thorax and neck. (Edward Mitchell)

However exact these measurements appear, several important biological parameters remain unknown in the smallest of the North Pacific finners, the minke whale. The length at sexual maturity in males is twenty-two to twenty-three feet, in females at twenty-four feet; the length at physical maturity is about twenty-seven feet; and maximum size is about thirty-two feet. But the ovulation rate is not well documented, and the sex ratio in fetuses is unknown, as are the age at sexual maturity and the longevity. The calving interval is approximately one year, length at birth is estimated at nine feet, and the gestation period is about ten months. Breeding apparently peaks in January and June, with calving peaks in December and June. The minke occurs broadly over the North Pacific in summer months, but winter sightings are in far lower latitudes, mainly twenty to twenty-five degrees north.

The North Pacific minke is one of the few mysticete whales ever to have been restrained or captured and held alive for any period. On three occasions, minkes were held in captivity in an aquarium in Japan, for between two weeks and up to three months. One of these escaped after thirty-seven days in captivity.

The North Pacific sei whale may be segregated into three populations: east, central, and west. Migration trends are documented on the east side, as animals marked off California migrated to off Vancouver Island, British Columbia. Male eastern sei whales grow to a maximum length in excess of forty-five feet, females to over forty-nine feet, at ages over twenty-five years. The age at sexual maturity is about ten years. The observed pregnancy rate of sei whales off California was forty percent. Ovulation rates off California are known to be 0.70 ovulation per ear plug growth layer.

There may be two kinds of North Pacific Bryde's whale, an offshore form and a smaller inshore form. Those in the central Pacific are apparently the offshore form. The inshore form occurs on the west coast of Kyushu, Japan, and possibly off Baja California. (Here is where study of even one stranded specimen could help resolve this uncertainty.) Bryde's whales are often, if not commonly, confused with sei whales. Maximum length is forty-two feet in males, forty-four feet in females, at ages greater than fifteen to eighteen years. In the central North Pacific, sexual maturity is attained between seven and ten years of age. The observed pregnancy rate is forty-two percent and the calculated ovulation rate is 0.5 ovulations per year.

Balaenopterine whales live for decades. Estimates of age are subject to various interpretations, and range upward for some species, such as the fin, to many tens of decades.

Although the largest whales are obviously difficult to weigh, some figures are available: an 89-foot blue whale weighed 122 tons, and a 69-foot fin whale weighed 54 tons. (Blue whales in the Northern Hemisphere become sexually mature at 72 to 74 feet, physically mature at 87 feet, and grow to 98 feet.)

None of these finner whales is known to "sing" like the humpback whale. Their acoustic behavior is reputedly limited to the emission of very low-frequency sounds—perhaps as low as twenty cycles per second—which may be propagated over great distances. These repetitive signals have been recorded in many parts of the world, but the attribution of them to specific species of the balaenopterine whales is still being researched. There is evidence that higher frequency signals may be emitted by some of the Balaenopteridae, but this needs corroboration.

The eyesight of whales appears to be quite good, although their main sensory input from their environment is probably acoustic. Their sense of smell has been modified to some degree. The chemoreceptors responsible for taste and smell may be highly specialized and modified.

It has been said that the large whales are

among the most intelligent of mammals, but this needs study and confirmation. Whalemen say finners can be hunted much like the ungulates. Groups can be stampeded, and during the stalking maneuvers individual whales can be tricked into diving and turning in specific directions. The whaler takes advantage of these predictable reactions in order to place his ship near the whale when it surfaces.

Even though these large sleek whales appear very healthy, they carry a parasite burden comparable to land mammals. The most obvious is a parasitic copepod—the female burrows into the blubber of the whale, anchoring itself with three projections from the head region. These animals, called *Penella*, look like pieces of rope or string attached to the whale's skin, projecting about six to ten inches, and can easily be seen at sea on heavily infested animals from distances of 300 or more feet. Barnacles are sometimes found on the finner whales, but are not as common as on the humpback.

The sei whale, migrating to tropical waters in the northern winter, is especially prone to parasitism by lampreys and/or predation by cookie-cutter sharks. Seen at close range sei whales often have small spots, one or two inches in diameter, particularly on their flanks. Some of these spots represent natural pigmentation splotching; others represent scars apparently left by lampreys and/or cookie-cutter sharks.

Many whales, especially the balaenopterines, show green, yellow, or brown colored patches of diatoms on their bodies. These whales have usually just migrated from one region to another, particularly from the temperate to polar waters. Odd scars such as deep gouges, tooth marks, broken jaws, and mutilated fins, flippers, and flukes are fairly common in all whale tribes. Fin whales landed at whaling stations often show scars that may represent the bites of small sharks and killer whales.

The balaenopterine whales were exploited heavily from about 1890. Before this time a suitable technology had not been developed to capture these sleek, large, very fast, and powerful species. Likewise, the market for products had not changed from the earlier demand for sperm whale oil for illumination and whalebone for corset stays. With the drop in population numbers of the bowhead and the right whales, emphasis was placed upon the balaenopterines. After the blue whale, the fin whale was heavily exploited because it was the next largest animal. Then, with heavy catches of fin whales in the world's oceans, the emphasis shifted to the smaller sei whale, which was exploited at a high rate. The exploitation regime has moved down the size range; the smallest species are now being caught, with increasing emphasis on southern minke, tropical Bryde's, and northern minke whales.

Population estimates for some years between 1972 and 1977 of some of these species in the North Pacific are: 1,700 or more of the blue whale; 17,000 fin whales; 9,000 sei whales; 17,800 Bryde's whales (western North Pacific stock only); and an unknown, but low number of minke whales. The blue, then the fin and sei, are now protected in the North Pacific. Recent estimates of abundance of Bryde's whales in this region do not, in my opinion, take full account of the possibilities that inshore and offshore forms may be separate biological entities, and may not completely address the problem of mixing of catch effort statistics, and sighting statistics, between the two forms and the sei whale.

In the North Pacific, the exploitation of minke whales in the coastal waters of Japan began centuries ago. Since the 1920s modern catcher boats have been used in an expanding fishery. At present, the annual catch is 200 to 400 whales. The pelagic catch is smaller. An earlier catch in British Columbia was negligible, and is zero at present. There are no cumulative catch data from the coastal

fishery in Japan for the period before 1948, but for the years 1948 to 1975, the total catch was 4,777 whales.

At this time, Antarctic, North Atlantic, and North Pacific minke whales are being exploited as one of the last of the finner whale fisheries. I am not reassured that this last *Balaenoptera* resource will be managed successfully, so as not to overfish the minke stock.

I have not presented here any distribution map of the North Pacific species of finner whales. Al-though thousands of finner whales have been killed in the last fifteen years, no one has plotted the total known ranges based on hard data from whale kill localities for all species by season. Various small distribution maps exist, but these are scattered and difficult to consolidate. Further, they do not repre-sent the entire species range. The best source for the distribution patterns of North Pacific finners are various maps in reports of the International Whal-ing Commission that show sightings abundance or catch per unit effort by ten degree squares through-out the North Pacific Ocean.

A Bryde's whale shows the auxiliary head ridges that are the main distinctive feature of this close relative of the sei whale, and the characteristic shallow angle of approach to the surface. (Edward Mitchell)

Humpback Whale

by Allen A. Wolman

The humpback whale (*Megaptera novaeangliae*) —with its winglike flippers, agile behavior, and haunting "song"—is one of the most familiar of the large cetaceans. Although generally recognized by a pear-shaped blow some six feet high, it is most specifically identified as it breaches, displaying its unique body contours. In breaching, the humpback leaps clear of the water and spins partially as it falls with a resounding smack. Sometimes it rolls on the surface, slapping the water with its flukes or flippers; occasionally it holds one flipper in the air while lying on one side. It has also been seen, on rare occasions, holding both flippers in the air while lying on its back. The humpback also swims on its back for short periods, and sometimes turns somersaults under and above the water.

This whale's ability to vocalize is outstanding. It has a rich, varied "vocabulary" and a wide range through the tonal scale. Its "song," a long series of varied phrases repeated in sequence over intervals of more than a half hour, has been the subject of scientific study. The songs have been recorded at sea, and were played at the 1970 World's Fair in Japan and incorporated into a "concerto for whale and orchestra" by an American composer. Some scientists, such as Roger Payne of the New York Zoological Society, claim that not only do different stocks of humpbacks have regional "dialects," but they also vary their phrases slightly from year to year, and may be identified by groups over a number of years.

At maturity, the humpback reaches a length of about fifty-one feet and weighs about thirty-five tons. The body color pattern varies with each individual, and is dark on the dorsal surface and lighter on the ventral surface. The body is relatively short and rotund, and is characterized by exceptionally long flippers. The flippers, which are one fourth to one third the total body length, are knobbed on the anterior edges. The span of its symmetrical flukes is one third the length of its body. Vestigial hip bones and femurs are found in the humpback, as in some other species. The late Roy Chapman Andrews, renowned naturalist of the American Museum of Natural History, found traces of a tibia, tarsus, and metatarsus in one animal.

In a stunning display of power and grace, a humpback breaches in Alaska's Frederick Sound. This whale's generic name Megaptera, *meaning "big winged," describes its long, sweeping flippers. (Allen A. Wolman)*

A feeding humpback, straining water through the baleen in its mouth, lunges on the surface of Fitzhugh Sound north of Vancouver Island. Its throat grooves are clearly visible. (Graeme Ellis)

Blubber thickness in the humpback is greater than in other rorqual species, and second only to the blue whale in absolute thickness. Averaging about five inches, the yield of this blubber is three to six tons of oil.

The North Pacific humpback has twelve to twenty-six grooves or pleats in its throat, reaching to the navel or behind it. Wartlike, round protuberances, each containing one hair or hair sac, appear on the skin of the head forward of the blowholes. Large barnacles grow on its chin, along the anterior portion of the grooves, along the anterior edge of the flippers, and on the flukes.

Many of the round scars on the skin of the humpback are caused by the Pacific lamprey (*Entosphenus tridentatus*). The humpback is also heavily infested by commensal barnacles (*Coronula diadema* and *C. reginae*), on which the stalked barnacle (*Conchoderma auritum*) grows, completing the impressive display. Two species of parasitic amphipod crustaceans called "whale lice" make their home on the skin among the barnacles, and a parasitic copepod (*Penella balaenoptera*) is sometimes found attached to the skin. Endoparasites abound, with nematodes in the stomach, kidneys, and ureter, and acanthocephalans in the intestines, but these infestations are rarely debilitating.

The baleen plates in the mouth are about two and one-half feet long, compared with an eight-inch length for the minke whale and a ten-foot length for the Greenland right whale. The 270 to 400 plates attached on each side of the mouth are relatively short and dark, varying in color from ash black to brown, with fairly coarse, gray brown fringes.

Although the humpback feeds mostly on euphausiids (shrimplike crustaceans), it will occasionally eat large meals of fish, such as anchovies, herring, sardines, cod, and salmon. Whale stomachs examined in winter in coastal or subtropical waters of both hemispheres were usually found to be empty, evidence that the humpback whale—like the gray, blue, and fin whales—is a seasonal feeder, obtaining nourishment in polar water and living on body fat reserves in warmer waters during the breeding season.

The humpback feeds in various ways. When food is concentrated, it may open its mouth and, swimming rapidly, plough into the midst of its prey—a technique called "lunge feeding." In what appears to be a more leisurely method, the humpback may roll on its side at the surface and feed laterally. A "bubble net" feeding technique—noted by A. Ingebrigtsen in 1929 and again recently by Charles Jurasz, a biologist in southeastern Alaska—is one of the most interesting methods. This is a process in which one or two whales swim in a ring below the surface, presumably blowing bubbles with their blowholes. The air rises to the surface as a wall of bubbles, forming a coil-shaped "net." When the fish see the bubble wall, they apparently are frightened and compress themselves toward the center. Then the whale rises swiftly to the surface in the center, with its huge mouth open to collect its prey. Jurasz has noted that the bubble nets may be woven as a figure six, a nine, or in a circle.

The North Pacific humpback reaches sexual maturity between six and twelve years. The mating and calving season occurs between October and March when the animals congregate in the warmer coastal waters. At mating time, the humpback's courtship is full of affectionate display. It consists, in part, of stroking the partner with its entire body and flipper, as one animal glides past the other—a behavior similar to that of the bottlenose and pilot whales. The humpback also gives its partner playful slaps with its long flippers, resulting in smacks heard miles away, according to Captain Charles Scammon, the famous whaler.

The gestation period for the humpback is twelve months, with the average interval between

A humpback feeds on its side with its huge mouth wide open. Its knobby snout is seen to the right, along with part of the left baleen row. On the left, the grooved lower jaw is ballooned out as it engulfs its prey. (Dale W. Rice)

This aerial view shows a humpback's bubble net off Cape Fanshaw in southeast Alaska. The bubbles formed by the whale apparently serve as a "net" to contain small fish. After the net is completed, the humpback rises through the center of the circle with its mouth open to collect its prey. (J. M. Olson)

conceptions being about two years. The female rarely bears a calf two years in succession. The percentage of twins is 0.39 percent of total pregnancies, contrasted with 1.3 percent in man. In the Southern Hemisphere, humpback cows are known to have about fifteen calves during their lifetime.

The newborn calf measures up to sixteen feet and weighs about two tons, or five to six percent of its mother's weight. Lactation lasts eleven months, some of which is probably protracted weaning. Care-giving behavior is noted between mother and calf, as it is during courtship. Males and females also are known to assist wounded companions by supporting them under the surface to keep their blowholes clear of the water.

The humpback whale is found in all oceans of the world. Although an oceanic species, it comes inshore for breeding and generally has well-defined migration patterns. The humpback is more segregated into self-contained populations than any other species, with the possible exception of the gray whale. Since the reproductive cycles of Northern Hemisphere and Southern Hemisphere stocks are six months out of phase, the species is divided into three reproductively and geographically isolated populations, one each in the North Pacific, the North Atlantic, and the Southern Ocean.

Unlike most other rorquals, the humpback is mostly confined during winter breeding to shallow waters along the coast or around oceanic islands. This restriction further divides each of the three major populations into several largely discrete breeding stocks, which may broadly overlap on their summer feeding grounds.

Like most baleen whales, the North Pacific humpback spends the summer on high-latitude feeding grounds in the North Pacific, where productive cooler waters provide abundant food. On the Asian side, it ranges south to the Sanriku Coast of Honshu, and ranges south on the American-Canadian side to about Point Conception, California. It is found through most of the Bering Sea where the food is plentiful; a few are found in the Chukchi Sea, as well. Unconfirmed reports suggest that there may also be a small resident population in the Gulf of California.

In winter, the North Pacific humpback migrates long distances to low latitudes and warmer waters, where calves are born and mating occurs. There are three major areas of concentration in the eastern North Pacific. On the Asian side, there is an as yet undetermined stock around the Mariana Islands, the Bonin Islands, the Ryukyu Islands, and Taiwan. Around the main Hawaiian Islands, about five hundred humpbacks winter from Kaula to Hawaii, and especially southwest of Molokai and west of Maui. In Mexican waters, about one hundred humpbacks range along the west coast of Baja

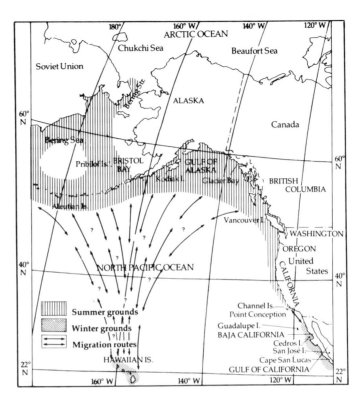

Humpback whale distribution

California, chiefly from Cedros Island south to Cape San Lucas and around the cape at least as far north as San José Island.

There are many gaps in our knowledge of the humpback's movements. Some general trends, however, have been established. The journeys north and south each take about two months, with five and one-half months on the feeding grounds and the remaining time on the breeding grounds. Usually traveling in pods of two to five, the humpback adopts a pattern of spouting three to six times and then submerging for two to six minutes. It averages less than four knots per hour.

The Mexican humpbacks migrate from Mexican and California waters to the Bering Strait and Chukchi Sea. Their northward migration begins in March and April, and they reach Vancouver Island

in May or June. Some humpbacks remain off the coasts of Washington, British Columbia, southeastern Alaska, and the Aleutian Islands, while others move through the Aleutians, reaching the Bering Strait and Chukchi Sea in July and August. The route northward of the Hawaiian humpbacks is unknown; their summer feeding area is possibly along the Aleutian chain west of Kodiak Island.

During the humpbacks' migrations, there is temporal segregation by sex, age, and reproductive state among the whales. The trip north to the feeding grounds is led by newly pregnant females and immatures, followed by mature males and females in early lactation. Females late in their lactation period take the lead south to the breeding grounds, followed by immatures of both sexes, adult males, resting females, and pregnant females. Thus, preg-

The humpback's flukes are as unique as a fingerprint. Photographic fluke files, now being collected for both coasts of the United States, will enable researchers to identify and track individual whales. (Allen A. Wolman)

nant humpbacks arrive early and stay late on the feeding grounds.

Although tagging and tracking the large mysticete whales is a formidable task, it is nevertheless more desirable than recovering implanted tags from dead animals. Radio tags also have the advantage that the animal can be detected remotely. In 1976, Dale W. Rice, Michael F. Tillman, James Johnson, and I radio-tagged a humpback whale in southeastern Alaska and followed it for over six days during a United States National Marine Fisheries Service study. The whale, named "Friendly Fred," showed no antagonism or concern but ignored us and went about its normal behavioral business. While being tracked, Friendly Fred remained within a fifteen-mile radius of the position where he was tagged. Again in 1977, five more whales were tagged; one was tracked for five days. Although there are many technical problems yet to be solved for this type of effort, a satellite tracking program in conjunction with radio tagging eventually may enable continuous monitoring of an animal and the full description of its migratory route—an exciting prospect.

Another method of tracking—photographically identifying individual killer whales by their distinctive dorsal fin and saddle patch markings—was successfully used between 1972 and 1975 by biologist Michael A. Bigg and his associates at the Canadian Department of Fisheries and Environment in Nanaimo, British Columbia. In 1976, using the same methods, the National Marine Fisheries Service contracted for a study of Washington State killer whales. In Alaska recently, Charles Jurasz has been using photography to identify individual humpbacks by their fluke patterns and other pigmentation, among a resident summer group of at least sixty animals that live in the inside waters of southeastern Alaska. In addition, the National Marine Fisheries Service is also in the process of building a "mug shot" file on humpback whales in Alaska, Hawaii, and off the west coast of Mexico.

Human activities are affecting humpback populations in Alaska and Hawaii. There is some concern for the small population of humpbacks in Alaska's Glacier Bay. Under a United States National Park Service grant, Charles Jurasz has collected data on vessel-whale interaction and has noted an increasing number of boats (which include large, oceangoing liners) and some avoidance behavior on the part of the whales.

The humpbacks in Hawaii are attracting scientists, photographers, and curiosity seekers, and this pressure could change the humpback's feeding activities, interrupt the nursing of calves, or even drive the whales away. In addition, conservationists have become concerned over the potential impact of increasing boat traffic and shoreline development, especially off the west side of Maui. A scheduled interisland hydrofoil service also has posed the danger of collisions with whales, with possible tragic consequences.

The history of humpback whaling all over the world has been one of repeated episodes of overexploitation, resulting in the depletion of the local stocks. At present, the world population of these whales is about six thousand. Before 1905, the total population of humpback whales in the North Pacific was probably on the order of 15,000. Between 1905 and 1965, modern whaling killed about 28,000 humpbacks. In recent years—1965 to 1974—the total population on the summer feeding grounds has averaged roughly 850. The number of humpbacks on the three major winter breeding grounds in recent years has been: Mexico—100 plus; Hawaii—500, plus or minus 90; Asian coast—unknown numbers, but few. Of all the great whales, the humpback is now the second rarest of the cosmopolitan species—second only to the right whale. Only the bowhead whale, restricted to arctic waters, may be more rare than either.

Gray Whale

by Dale W. Rice

The annual migration of the gray whales along the west coast of North America is one of the world's outstanding wildlife spectacles. In traveling between their summer grounds in the Bering Sea and Arctic Ocean and their winter grounds along the coast of Mexico, the gray whales may cover ten thousand miles in a year—the longest migration undertaken by any mammal.

From December through January, these huge marine mammals may be seen from almost any headland or point along the western North American coast. They swim steadily southward, maintaining a speed of about five knots day and night. They usually surface and "blow" four or five times in a minute; they then dive and remain submerged for about four minutes. Although single animals and pods of two or three are usually seen, sometimes more than a dozen may travel together. Most of them pass within a mile of the beach—occasionally at the very edge of the kelp beds. However, when crossing long bights and indentations of the coastline (such as southern California below Point Conception), they may take a shortcut and pass far offshore. From certain ideal lookout points (such as Yankee Point south of Monterey, California), as many as two hundred whales may pass in a single day during the middle of January. From late February to early May, they are again seen, this time heading north.

Another population of gray whales lives in the western North Pacific, migrating between summer grounds in the northern Okhotsk Sea and winter grounds along the southern shores of South Korea (and formerly in the Seto Inland Sea of southern Japan). This population is nearly extinct.

Subfossil bones discovered along our middle Atlantic seaboard, and along the shores of the English Channel and the Baltic and North seas, reveal that gray whales lived in the North Atlantic until at least A.D. 500. Historical accounts suggest that they occurred in Iceland as late as the early seventeenth century, and possibly in New England in the early eighteenth century. The reason for their extinction in the North Atlantic is unknown.

Most primitive of the living baleen whales, the gray whale (*Eschrichtius robustus*) is classified in a

A gray whale surfacing off Vancouver Island's west coast reveals the characteristic shape of its head and barnacled snout. (Jim Darling)

When traveling, the gray whale makes four or five shallow dives in quick succession between blows. After the last blow, it raises its flukes and dives deeply, remaining submerged for about five minutes. (Jim Darling)

family by itself—the Eschrichtiidae. It is similar to the extinct whales called cetotheres, which lived from the middle Oligocene to the early Pliocene epochs, ten million to thirty million years ago.

The gray whale is readily recognized by its mottled gray color and lack of a dorsal fin. Instead of this fin, it has a low hump, followed by a series of ten or twelve knobs along the dorsal ridge of the tail stock; these are easily seen when the animal arches to dive. The upper jaw is moderately narrow and arched, and there are two or three grooves on the throat that presumably allow for expansion when the whale is swallowing. The flippers are large and paddle shaped, and the tail flukes are broad. The adult gray whale is thirty-six to fifty feet long and weighs between sixteen and forty-five tons.

Most gray whales spend the summer in the shallow waters of the northern and western Bering Sea and in the adjacent waters of the Arctic Ocean. Some go as far east as Barter Island off Alaska's arctic coast and as far west as Wrangel Island off Siberia's northern coast. A few, however, remain throughout the summer along the Pacific coast as far south as northern California.

Summer is feeding season for the gray whale. Its unique feeding habits explain why it remains in relatively shallow water. Unlike the other baleen whales, the gray whale is a bottom feeder. Amphipods (crustaceans one-third to one inch long that are related to sand fleas) are its main food. To catch these, the whale rolls over onto its side so that one cheek is parallel to, and a few inches above, the bottom. The jaws remain closed, but the lower lip on the bottom side is folded outward. By retracting the large muscular tongue, water and amphipods are sucked into the mouth. The water is then jetted out between the baleen plates that grow in a row along each side of the upper jaw. The coarse fringe on the inside of the baleen plates filters out the amphipods, which are then swallowed.

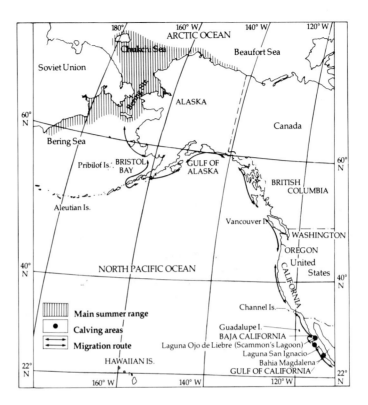

Gray whale distribution

While feeding in this manner, the gray whale does not move along the bottom but surfaces to blow before diving to a new location.

In October, the arctic seas begin to freeze, so the gray whales—fat after a summer of heavy feeding—begin their long southward migration. About Christmas, the first gray whales arrive on the winter grounds along the west coast of Baja California. A few go around Cape San Lucas into the southern end of the Gulf of California. Here they find warm, calm waters, but little if any food. By the time they head north again in February and March, they have lost twenty to thirty percent of their body weight. They are so thin that they bear little resemblance to the plump animals that headed south the previous autumn. When they reach the northern feeding grounds once again, they have fasted for almost six months.

Both male and female gray whales reach sexual maturity when they are between five and eleven years old—with the average being eight years. Their breeding season is limited primarily to a three-week period in late November and early December while they are on their southward migrations, although a few females may breed as late as the end of January on the winter grounds. Usually, the female breeds once every two years. During the following summer, the pregnant females put on twenty-five percent more weight than the nonpregnant animals.

The gray whale calf is born in the winter after a gestation period of about thirteen months. Females ready to give birth resort to certain shallow, protected lagoons in Baja California. The most famous of these is Laguna Ojo de Liebre, often called Scammon's Lagoon. Other major calving areas are farther south in Laguna San Ignacio and in Bahia Magdalena and adjacent waters. A few females give birth each year on the eastern side of the Gulf of

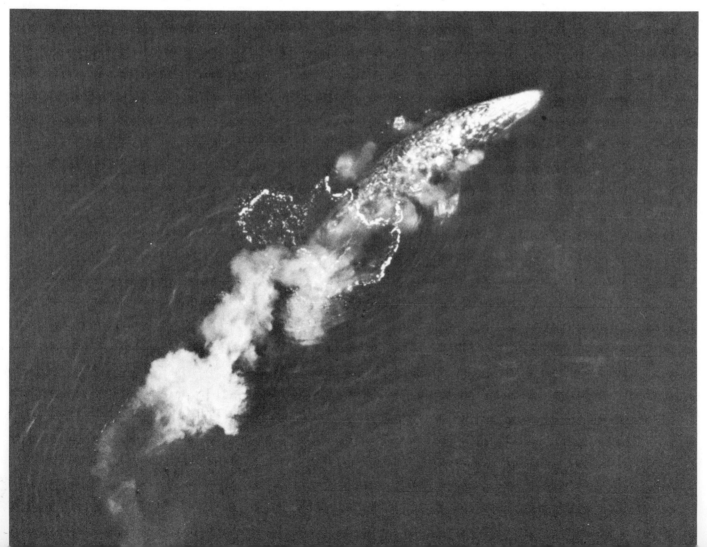

A bottom-feeding gray whale leaves a trail of mud as it surfaces to blow near Saint Lawrence Island in the Bering Sea. (Howard Braham)

California, along the coasts of Sonora and Sinaloa.

At birth, the calf is sixteen feet long and weighs close to one thousand pounds. The mother's rich milk—over fifty percent fat—nourishes the calf for several weeks on the winter grounds and during the long migration to the summer grounds. The calf grows rapidly and by August, when it is weaned, it has attained a length of twenty-eight feet. During its remaining two or three months on the summer grounds, it feeds heavily, and by the time it heads south in late autumn, it is some thirty feet long.

The only predator that threatens the gray whale is the killer whale. Schools of killer whales have been seen attacking gray whales—usually unsuccessfully, although they have managed to kill a few calves. Many gray whales bear the tooth marks of killer whales on their flippers and flukes. The position of these scars suggests that killer whales attempt to catch gray whales by immobilizing them so that they cannot come to the surface and breathe. However, it is doubtful whether killer whales are capable of killing a healthy, adult gray whale. Gray whales may live to be over fifty years old.

On its skin, the gray whale carries large clusters of a unique parasitic barnacle (*Cryptolepas rhachianecti*). The whale is also infested with thousands of parasitic amphipod crustaceans called "whale lice," which belong to three species of the genus *Cyamus*. Two of these lice are unique to this whale. Internal parasites are not common but include tapeworms and thorny-headed worms in the intestine, roundworms in the stomach, and flukes in the intestine and liver.

The Nootka, Makah, Quillayute, and Quinault Indians, who lived on Washington State's Olympic Peninsula and British Columbia's Vancouver Island, were long renowned for their whale hunting ability. Ancient middens excavated at La Push, Washington, have yielded the bones of gray whales. The Indians chased the whales in large dugout canoes and struck them with harpoons that were attached to a line and float. As late as 1928, the Indians still hunted whales on the Washington coast.

In arctic Alaska and the Chukchi Sea of eastern Siberia, the Eskimos have also hunted whales for thousands of years, and still do. In aboriginal times, they chased the whales in frail, skin-covered boats called umiaks and killed the animals with ivory- or bone-tipped harpoons. After contact with American whalers in the late nineteenth century, they ex-

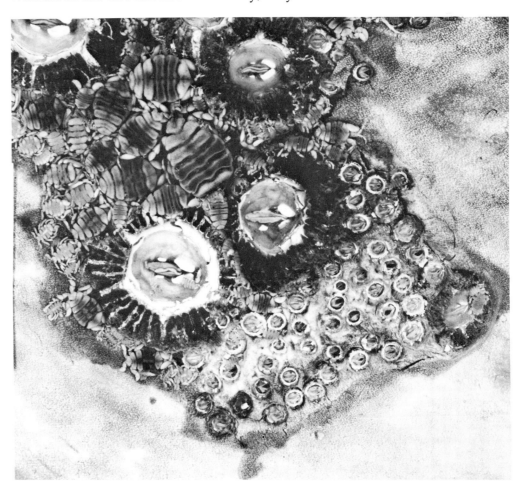

The barnacle Cryptolepas rhachianecti *is unique to the gray whale. In this photo younger specimens surround older ones. Whale lice* (Cyamus scammoni)—*also of a species unique to this whale—cluster around the barnacles. (Dale W. Rice)*

changed the harpoon for the darting gun and bomb lance.

During the mid-nineteenth century, American whalers from New Bedford and other eastern American coast ports scoured the globe in search of sperm whales and right whales, and discovered the gray whales in the North Pacific. Concentrated in their calving lagoons, the whales were easy prey for the whalers, who found that they could get a full load of oil in two or three months, rather than the three to five years required for a sperm whaling voyage. Soon there were dozens of whaling vessels working the lagoons of Baja California, as well as a dozen shore whaling stations along the California coast intercepting the migrating whales. This heavy exploitation rapidly depleted the gray whale stocks. By the year 1900, the once-abundant gray whales were almost extinct, and the last whaling station closed.

The few surviving gray whales were left in peace for a few years, and their numbers presumably began to increase slowly. Soon, however, a new threat to their survival appeared. In 1905, the first modern whaling station was established on the west coast of British Columbia. Using steam-powered catcher boats equipped with harpoon guns, the new breed of whaler was far more efficient than the old-fashioned type, who used open boats and hand harpoons. Other stations soon sprang up in California, Washington, and Alaska. Fortunately for the gray whales, these modern catcher boats were fast enough to hunt the larger and more profitable rorquals—the blue, fin, and humpback whales—which had been too swift for the nineteenth-century whalers to attack and were thus still common during the summer months. Furthermore, the smaller gray whales could be found only in winter when the weather was often rough. Therefore, the whalers made little effort to catch the gray whales.

Another innovation in whaling soon

appeared—the floating factory ship, which enabled whalers to shift operations to any area in which they found whales. Inevitably, expeditions consisting of a factory ship and a fleet of catcher boats attacked the gray whales on their winter grounds and in the calving lagoons in Mexico—first in the winter of 1913–1914, and again in the winters from 1924–1925 to 1928–1929. These whalers turned their attention away from the gray whales when they discovered large numbers of blue and humpback whales along the Mexican coast.

In 1947, seventeen nations ratified the International Convention for the Regulation of Whaling. This convention forbids the killing of gray whales, except by aborigines or by contracting governments when the meat and other products are to be used solely for local consumption by aborigines. Today, under these terms, the Soviet government kills about 160 gray whales each year in Siberia for use by the local villagers. The Alaskan Eskimos also kill a few gray whales.

Under the protection afforded by the international treaty for the past thirty years, the gray whale population has increased substantially. For the years from 1967 to 1978, United States National Marine Fisheries Service personnel have counted the gray whales as they migrate south past Yankee Point near Monterey, California. The census station is manned during all daylight hours throughout the migration period. The counts reveal that the population is now stable or perhaps increasing slowly. Extrapolating for whales passing at night, we calculate the total population to number between ten and twelve thousand. Historical data suggest that the original population, prior to exploitation, was no more than fifteen thousand.

The most famous gray whale was "Gigi," the first baleen whale to be successfully kept in captivity. She was netted in Scammon's Lagoon on 13 March 1971 when she was about six weeks old. When I first saw her a few days after her arrival at

San Diego's Sea World, she was nineteen feet two inches long and weighed forty-three hundred pounds. Whipping cream fortified with protein and fat was fed to her through a tube. At seven months, she was weaned to a diet of squid, which she soon consumed at a rate of eighteen hundred pounds a day.

During Gigi's year in captivity, many investigators studied her physiology and behavior, so she contributed immeasurably to our knowledge of cetacean biology. By March 1972, however, she had grown to twenty-six feet nine inches and weighed thirteen thousand pounds. Although this is near-normal growth for her species, Gigi was obviously getting too big (and too expensive!) to keep. So, she was given a distinctive freeze-brand and fitted with a radio transmitter backpack (designed to fall off within one year). On 13 March, Gigi was released among her wild cousins, who were then migrating northward. She was radio-tracked intermittently until 5 May, when she was off Santa Cruz, 350 miles north of the release site. Although some doubted Gigi's ability to survive in the wild, there were unconfirmed sightings of her during subsequent years. Finally, in February 1977, Gigi was positively identified in Laguna San Ignacio, Baja California.

The west coast of British Columbia's Vancouver Island near Long Beach is the site for a recent research project sponsored by the Vancouver Public Aquarium. Characterized by patches of shallow, sandy beach, this otherwise rugged area apparently provides good feeding for the migrators. A summer resident population of about forty whales also lives off this coast. University of Victoria graduate student Jim Darling and his assistant Cindy Dundon have observed and photographed the gray whales. In 1977, they identified over fifty individuals from three thousand photographs of skin pigmentation patterns on their backs. In the previous year, they identified about thirty-five different whales, over

half of which were seen again in 1977. The researchers hope that, once the whales are photographed and identified by the pigmentation system, some of the whales can then be aged and sexed. This would lead to knowledge of the population's age and sex composition.

For many years, the gray whale has been the object of a popular tour-boat business in southern California. Two- or three-hour cruises enable the passengers to observe and photograph the migrating whales at close range. In recent years, week-long cruises into the calving lagoons have been instituted; they are rapidly gaining in popularity. As a result, conservationists have become greatly concerned about the possible harmful effects of the frequent disturbance of the whales—especially of mothers with newborn calves—by these tour groups. In 1972, the Mexican government declared most of Scammon's Lagoon a whale refuge that vessels are forbidden to enter during the calving season.

Several of the whales in Laguna San Ignacio, however, actually welcome the tourists! During recent seasons, they have approached and played around the inflatable boats that carry the tourists, going so far as to solicit back-scratchings from the occupants.

The California gray whale is the only whale population that, following severe depletion, has recovered to near-original numbers. We cannot be optimistic about its future, however. The new Baja California Highway has made some of the whale's calving lagoons readily accessible to small boats hauled overland. Industrialization and pollution of the lagoons will undoubtedly accelerate as the human population grows. In addition, proposed oil drilling on or adjacent to the lagoons poses another threat to the future of the California gray whale, the great mammalian migrator.

Right Whale

by Raymond M. Gilmore

*I*n the earliest days of commercial whaling, the right whale (*Balaena glacialis*) was the "right" or proper whale to capture because, at that time, it was the most suitable whale to hunt. It yielded large amounts of edible oil, came close to shore in winter when it calved and mated, swam slowly, and could be rather easily—though carefully—approached by rowed boats. Moreover, it usually floated when dead and could be recovered by small boats. In fact, as a result of its relationship with man, this cetacean has been *too* "right" or correct for, in the North Pacific today, the right whale is rare indeed.

It was as long ago as A.D. 1000 that the Basques hunted the right whale along the shores of southwestern France and northeastern Spain, where a population came in winter to calve and mate. In the seventeenth century, the English and Dutch hunted another kind of "right" whale, the arctic right whale or bowhead. And the sperm whale soon was to be considered an even more proper or prized whale to capture. Yet the name "right whale" remains firmly established as the common name for

Balaena glacialis of temperate waters.

The right whale's black color is the basis for another common name—"black whale" or "black right whale." Although it is usually black all over, some individuals do have sharp patches of milk-white on the underside. This ventral white coloration is conspicuous at sea only when the animal rolls on its back or turns when breaching.

Breaching—an impressive display of power and surprising agility—is common with the right whale. It may be either a challenge to an intruder or a response to a challenge from an intruder. Then again it may be purely an expression of animal spirits, especially in the winter breeding season.

The right whale is forty to sixty feet long at maturity. Yet because of its robust body, it can weigh a surprising 25 or 30 to 80 tons, rather than 25 to 60 tons for comparable lengths in other species. One fifty-seven-foot female was described by a Soviet cetologist as weighing 117 tons, but this is excessive and could be a mistake of recordation or transcription.

A strongly down-curved and narrow upper jaw,

A rare northern right whale surfaces near Punta Abreojos, Baja California. Characteristics unique to this species are visible—widely separated blowholes, a highly arched lower lip with scalloped margins, and hardened, raised areas or callosities on the snout. (Dale W. Rice)

which is partly hidden between high walls of the lower lip, is a distinctive feature of the right whale. Also characteristic is a large, raised area called the "bonnet" at the tip of its spatulate or spoon-shaped snout. In adults, this rough, thickened area (or callosity) is covered with amphipod whale-lice and barnacles, which give it a whitish color. Other callosities—some small and pointed, others large, round, and flat—are found on the head and lower jaw. A large callosity is almost always located on each side of the scooplike chin, and over each eye. Small callosities are often randomly situated on the sides of the lower jaw.

The callosities are present at birth as roughened areas, or ridges and depressions, or pits—without lice, of course. The lice quickly transfer from the mother and take up their abode on the calf's callosities. On each one of these areas is a hair or a clump of short, crinkly hairs, reminiscent of the bumps or knobs on the head of the humpback. Other similar hairs are also scattered on the head and jaws.

The function of the callosities is unknown. Although there are other strange adaptations in cetaceans—such as the "case" in the head of the sperm whale or the swollen stink-sac on the underside of the tails of some gray whales—the right whale's callosities remain one of the strangest adaptations. Perhaps they are recognition marks, or just some odd feature that has no survival value. Roger Payne, a New York Zoological Society zoologist who has worked extensively with the southern right whales off Argentina, has found that the arrangements of the callosities are unique and that some individuals can be identified by their callosity patterns.

The right whale has other distinctive characteristics. It has no fin on its broad back, and no grooves on its throat. Its nostrils are widely divergent, which creates the strikingly V-shaped spout or blow by which this whale is readily identifiable.

When it sounds after a series of breaths at the surface, it often throws flukes. These are wide and pointed, measuring thirty to thirty-five percent of its body length. Other slow-swimming whales—such as the gray, humpback, and sperm—also raise their flukes upon diving. The right whale's flippers are short and broad with a shallow notch or indentation at the inner tip.

The sight of the characteristic V-shaped spout, wide, smooth, black back, and high wall of the lower lip caused three of us to hurry with cameras to a skiff at Scripps Institution of Oceanography in La Jolla, California, on 31 May 1955. This was to be my first chance to closely observe a right whale. We finally found the lone animal swimming south about two miles at sea, and watched in wonder as it breached in front of us three times, then five times more. We followed eagerly because the right whale was at that time—and sadly still appears to be—rare in the eastern North Pacific, as it is in many other parts of the world where it was once common.

In fact, it was the right whale's rarity that caused me in 1969 to begin seeking a herd known to feed on the coast of Argentina but whose winter breeding and calving grounds were then unrecorded. Fourteen years after sighting the La Jolla individual, I was rewarded in the Golfo Nuevo on Argentina's Patagonian coast when a giant right whale breached near our ship, the research vessel *Hero*—exploratory ship of the United States National Science Foundation. Within a few moments, we realized that we had found the right whales congregated on their annual winter grounds—a thrilling discovery, hitherto unknown to the scientific world.

By the time international restrictions were first set on the taking of whales in the early 1930s, the right whale had already been depleted. In 1935, Charles H. Townsend and A. C. Watson compiled a now-famous map on which they recorded the cap-

A right whale breaches—its belly turned toward the observer and its huge flippers spread in a swan dive. This rare incident precipitated the author-photographer's hunt for the location of a herd of Argentine right whales that he found fourteen years later. (Raymond M. Gilmore)

tures of 8,415 right whales by nineteenth-century American hand-whalers in the world. It gives us some idea of the right whale's numbers and distribution in the eastern North Pacific and adjacent Bering Sea. The captures occurred primarily in the Gulf of Alaska (north of lat 50° N) and from the Queen Charlotte Islands west to the eastern Aleutians, on what was known as the Northwest, or Kodiak, Ground—the summer feeding grounds of the North Pacific right whale.

These grounds were the last—along with an area around Japan, the Kuril Islands, and the adjacent Okhotsk Sea—of the then untouched populations of right whales. The whaling ships arrived there in the 1840s, after they had hunted other late grounds around New Zealand, south Australia, Tasmania, and Chile. Whaling on these grounds had, in turn, followed the depletion of grounds in the south Indian and Atlantic oceans—an early example of the sad story of whaling.

The right whales in the eastern North Pacific were taken mostly between May and August each year, with a few in April and September. Another author, Heinrich Bolau, estimated that between 1846 and 1851, there were three hundred to four hundred ships taking right whales on the Kodiak Ground. At five whales per boat, these ships could take between fifteen hundred and two thousand whales a year! At that rate, he predicted, the whale would soon be exterminated. He was correct. Based on Japanese sightings between 1965 and 1971, the 1973 Annual Report of the International Whaling Commission lists the estimated population for the North Pacific right whale to be between one hundred and two hundred animals. The only encouragement in these figures is that our famous and badly persecuted whale is still in existence.

Although we have some knowledge of the summer feeding grounds, information about the winter range for calving and mating is almost nonexistent. If the right whale had restricted itself

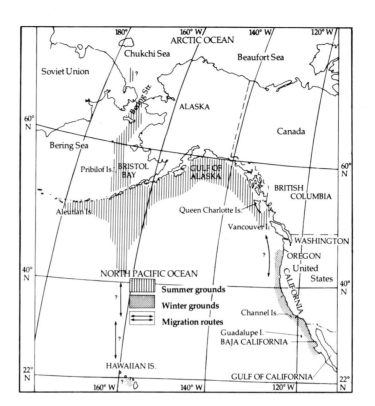

Right whale distribution

to a small area in winter—as it does in the Southern Hemisphere—it would have been seen close to the shores of western North America or its coastal islands. But such coastal winter grounds apparently did not exist, else early whalers would surely have reported them. Moreover, Russian, American, and English sealers and sea otter hunters from the late eighteenth to the late nineteenth centuries explored every inch of the coastline from the Aleutians to midwestern Baja California, and never mentioned the right whale to my knowledge.

Even Charles M. Scammon, the famous literate whaler in the North Pacific during the mid-nineteenth century, was unsure of any wintering ground. He said, "It has ever been a matter of mysterious conjecture with the most philosophical whaleman, where the northern Right Whales go to bring forth their young, and whither they migrate during the winter months . . . But no bay has yet been discovered north of the equator, in the Pacific, where the north-western Right Whales go to calve; and . . . nothing is definitely known of their winter resort.''

Occasionally right whales have been taken or seen along the west coast of the United States. In earlier days, Scammon called these animals "merely stragglers." In my own work, I have collected eighteen reports of right whales, either captured along this area between 1850 and 1953 or sighted between 1955 and 1967. These eighteen sightings involved more than thirty-nine individuals. Could these early "stragglers" along the coast have supplied the known summer population on the Northwest Ground? And can the more recent "stragglers" in this area supply the numbers seen by the Japanese between 1965 and 1971? Although this does not seem likely, it is all we have to go on at present.

There is some vague but tantalizing evidence that some right whales of the eastern North Pacific went toward the Hawaiian Islands in winter and returned from there in spring. This evidence is on Townsend and Watson's famous map. It shows four captures by Yankee whalers of at least three right whales in May, and one in October about one thousand nautical miles north of Hawaii—not quite halfway to the eastern Aleutian Islands and the Alaska Peninsula. There could have been more than one whale taken in each of these recorded captures. The map also shows other capture sites a bit north of those just mentioned, but still southwest of the Alaska Peninsula by one thousand nautical miles. Here whales were taken during the months of April through October and again in December. According to a researcher in this matter—Kenneth Martin, director of the Kendall Whaling Museum in Sharon, Massachusetts—there is simply no clear evidence historically or recently that any right whales have wintered in the Hawaiian Islands. So the location of

a long sought concentrated herd of wintering right whales, calving and breeding in the eastern North Pacific, is still a mystery.

The right whale's continued rarity in the eastern North Pacific invites several possible explanations. One cause may be a slow reproductive rate—so slow that recovery from a depleted population of say a few score or hundred could take many more years than expected, especially if whaling continued to pick off an individual now and then. Another explanation may be that other whales compete with the right whale for the same food on the same summer feeding grounds, with the result that reduced food supply may hold down the population once it was reduced. Both Edward Mitchell of the Canadian Department of Fisheries and Environment and Hideo Omura of The Whales Research Institute in Japan have suggested that the sei whale in both the North Pacific and in the North Atlantic may be a competitor of the right whale.

A third explanation is conjecture. The Soviet whaling fleet that operated in the Gulf of Alaska and off nearby coasts in the summers of the mid-1960s and into the 1970s may have taken a number of right whales that they did not report. This conjecture is based on a similar case that is indirectly known—the decimation by a Soviet fleet of a presumably recovering population of right whales around the Tristan da Cunha Islands in the central south Atlantic Ocean during the southern winter of 1963. Although this was reported in 1967 in *Oryx*, an international conservation journal, the Soviets apparently did not report these captures to the Bureau for International Whaling Statistics, nor did they publish, to my knowledge, a report of their biological findings. Hence, the number of captures and the interesting biological data from this harvest remain unknown to science.

Lack of biological data also leaves many questions unanswered about the right whale's reproductive cycle. Usually once every two years and sometimes one or three, depending on the species, all the larger baleen whales have a single calf for each sexually mature female. In the case of the right whale, breeding and calving may occur every third year. A female right whale observed by Roger Payne and identified by unique markings on her back seems to support this hypothesis. She was seen one winter with a calf and returned two winters later, this time with another calf. It is generally agreed that breeding occurs in winter, and that, after a gestation of about one year, a calf some twenty feet long—large for the mother of fifty to sixty feet—is born.

Social organization in the right whale seems to go little beyond breeding in adults and the special bonding between mother and offspring. The right whales on summer feeding and winter breeding or calving grounds are little more than aggregations of conjugal pairs and mothers with calves. Social organization also includes some form of communication, whether by vocalizing at a distance or by seeing and touching when close. Vocalizations have been recorded for the right whale of the western North Atlantic in spring and for the Argentine right whale in winter. The sounds of the latter—as reported by bioacousticians William C. Cummings, James F. Fish, and Paul O. Thompson—were found to be "belchlike" or were "moans," "pulses," and "miscellaneous low-frequency sounds." All were in the low-frequency range, and the intensity or strength of the belchlike sounds and some pulses was high. The sounds were most frequent and pronounced during courting activities.

Only in recent years—with various research teams on the right whales of Argentina—has the relationship between man and the right whale been friendly and mutually satisfactory. As with most cetaceans, the relationship has otherwise been almost entirely one of the hunter and the hunted. Man has hunted and killed for two whale products: baleen and oil. The edible oil from the right whale

was used in cooking; even more was used for illumination of street-lamps and house-lamps. Later, sperm whale oil—a waxy, inedible oil—proved to be a better illuminant.

Yield of oil was usually measured in barrels, which were formerly wine barrels that held 30 to 33 gallons. High yield from a large, healthy right whale of fifty to sixty feet was said to have been as much as 200 to 290 barrels, an amount equivalent to between 6,000 and 8,700 gallons, an enormous amount, if true. No wonder the right whale was so valuable.

The high yield of oil was not only a result of this whale's large size but also of its thick blubber, which is from six to fourteen inches thick, but averages ten, depending on the size and condition of the animal and the point on the body where the blubber is measured. This thick blubber is what causes the right whale to float when dead.

Baleen was almost as profitable as whale oil. Only its lesser quantity put it in second place. In the later years of whaling, however, when the oil was cheap, baleen became the most valuable product. At that time—when a dollar was worth perhaps twenty times or more what it is today—right whale baleen sold for $5.00 to $7.00 per pound. One or two big right whales, each yielding fifteen hundred to two thousand pounds of baleen, would thus pay for a whaling voyage. It is little wonder that the whalers hunted almost the last right whale they could find.

The right whale's baleen grows in two rows of many transverse plates, one row hanging from each side of its narrow upper jaw. Each row has an average of 225 to 250 plates. The closely set plates diverge at the bottom to fit within the wide lower jaws. Looking at a complete row from the outside, the large triangular wall appears like the slats of a vertical venetian blind. These blades may measure five to eight feet long, measured from the root's base in the gum. The posterior, and especially the anterior blades, are of course much shorter—down to six inches or so from the gum.

Looking at a complete row from the inside of the mouth, this same triangular outline is apparent, but it now appears as a great hairy wall of matted fibers. It is this wall that holds the whale's food while water strains through the baleen to the outside. The two rows, or walls, do not meet in front, where there is a gap of about six inches.

The great length of some plates, and the even greater length and fineness of the fibers, made the right whale's baleen very valuable. The cortex was split into long strips for umbrella ribs, hoops for skirts, buggy whips, and corset stays. The long, fine fibers—about 0.008 of an inch in diameter—are almost as fine and soft as thread. They were removed by retting, and then were woven into fabrics, which lent a stiffness and a sensuous rustle to taffeta and crinoline. Baleen was ideal material for this purpose: it could be washed with the garment without softening or losing its elasticity, and without discoloring the fabric.

It is the fineness and denseness of the right whale's baleen fibers—115 to 140 per inch—that enables this whale to collect its food—the tiny but abundant micro-zooplankton called copepods. These minute crustaceans vary in size from a small pinhead to a grain of wheat. All have characteristic long, partly haired, first antennae (like flexible arms) and a double "tail." Right, bowhead, and sei whales—each with fine baleen fibers—all feed heavily on this abundant food when it is available.

Of course, the right whale can also feed on larger food, which is just as easy to trap in its baleen: small larval crustacea; euphausiid shrimp between one-half and two inches long; small, winged, swimming mollusks; and even small fish—any animal food, in fact, that is up to six inches long and swarms densely enough to provide an easy meal.

Death has come to the right whale not only from the early whalers' heavy hands. A number of natural causes contribute to its mortality. The young or senile may drown during storms, and a difficult or prolonged birth may result in drowning before the calf can take its first breath. Killer whales may take some right whales, although the frequency of predation is unknown. It is probably quite rare and likely to occur mostly with calves. Certainly killer whales are known to harass large whales, the right whale included. In 1972 biologist William Cummings, then with the Naval Undersea Center (in San Diego, California) detailed a rough and potentially dangerous attack in Golfo San José, Argentina. Here, five killers harassed a pair of right whales for twenty-five minutes. The result was a vigorous joint defense by the two right whales—rolling and thrashing with their flukes—and the final retreat of the orcas.

The death of an individual, however sad, is not important in the long run—unless, of course, such mortality exceeds natality and the population declines. And if such imbalance and decline continue long enough, the population becomes extinct. Although the natural death of countless populations has been going on for eons of geologic time, extinction is difficult to excuse when caused by man. We certainly hope that this never happens to the right whale.

Bowhead Whale

by Willman M. Marquette

The bowhead whale (*Balaena mysticetus*)—also known as the Greenland right whale, Arctic right whale, and polar whale—is one of the largest of the baleen or whalebone cetaceans. It is one of a group referred to as "right whales" by the early commercial whalers because these cetaceans were slow moving, yielded large amounts of valuable oil and baleen, floated when dead, and thus were the "right" whales to kill. Yankee whalers referred to *Balaena mysticetus* as the bowhead because of its high-arching mouth, which gives the head a distinctive profile.

Bowheads were hunted nearly to extinction by commercial whalers in the eastern Arctic between 1611 and 1887. In the western Arctic, commercial whaling for bowheads began in 1848 when the vessel *Superior* became the first whaler to pass through the Bering Strait in search of these animals. Other whalers followed, and the fishery peaked between 1850 and 1854 when some fifteen hundred whales were taken. After that, the fishery steadily declined; by 1907, bowheads had become scarce in the western Arctic.

Today, the only significant remaining population of bowheads is found in western arctic waters, which include the Bering, Chukchi, and Beaufort seas. Although the size of the original bowhead population is unknown, the Scientific Committee of the International Whaling Commission has concluded "that initial stock size in 1850 was a minimum of 11,700 (10-year peak catch plus adjustment for losses), and probably approximately 18,000 (adjustment for residual stock). The present size may be about 1,000 bowheads, approximately 6 percent (to 10 percent) of initial size."

Counts of whales migrating past Barrow, Alaska—when they were presumably en route to summer feeding grounds in the eastern Beaufort Sea—indicate that at least 800 bowheads followed the nearshore lead in the spring of 1976 and that about 867 did so during the spring of 1977. These counts provide minimum estimates of the number of whales en route to *only* the eastern Beaufort Sea during the study period, rather than providing a complete population estimate. (Unknown numbers migrated unobserved before and after the study

In what is probably breeding behavior, a couple of bowheads rub heads. Both whales show the white chin patch typical of this arctic species. (Jack W. Lentfer)

period, as well as through offshore leads and along the Siberian coast.) Information about the number of bowheads in Soviet waters is not presently available, but Soviet scientists plan to obtain data on these whales in a cooperative study with the United States.

Following the bowhead population's severe depletion, several conventions and acts gave the whale complete protection from further exploitation: meetings of the International Convention for the Regulation of Whaling held in 1931, 1937, and 1946; the United States Marine Mammal Protection Act of 1972; and the United States Endangered Species Act of 1973. However, these acts do allow for a subsistence harvest of these whales by Indians, Aleuts, and Eskimos.

Hunting bowhead whales for subsistence has been a vital part of Eskimo life since before 1800 B.C. In fact, coastal Eskimos have developed a culture intimately associated with this whale. Historically, they established their villages at locations that were accessible to migrating whales. Eskimos of Saint Lawrence Island and the arctic Alaska coast conduct present-day whaling using a combination of traditional and modern equipment and techniques. In spring, residents of two Saint Lawrence Island villages (Gambell and Savoonga) and the mainland villages of Wales, Kivalina, Point Hope, Wainwright, and Barrow engage in whaling. Ice conditions east of Barrow do not permit spring whaling by residents of Nuiqsut or Kaktovik on Barter Island, but these people participate in the autumn hunt, as do the Barrow whalers. In autumn, only a few villages along the north coast of Alaska are involved in the hunt because most bowheads then cross the Chukchi Sea to the coast of the Soviet Union. The Eskimos of the western Canadian Arctic formerly took an occasional whale and, although the practice continued until the 1940s at Pangnirtung, traditional bowhead whaling is no longer pursued.

Commercial whalers were willing to endure a rugged life for the prized products from the bowhead. The baleen was the finest available, and oil from the carcasses was of high quality. Bowheads yielded an average of fifteen hundred pounds of baleen and 100 barrels of oil per animal. The individual yield varied, however, from as little as 80 barrels to as high as 375 barrels of oil, whereas baleen ranged from a few hundred pounds to a record yield of thirty-one hundred pounds from a single large whale. Prices for whale products fluctuated on the world market. Over a period of one hundred fifty years, the price of oil varied between $0.02 and $0.50 a pound, and baleen prices ranged from $0.10 to $6.70 a pound. When high prices for baleen prevailed, the animals were killed for only their baleen—a single large bowhead was worth up to $10,000 or more. The discovery of petroleum in 1859 and the manufacture of spring steel, celluloid, and other products to replace the diminishing supply of baleen brought an end to the need for these whale products.

Commercially, whale oil was used for illumination, lubrication, tanning of leather, and preparing wool cloth. It was also used in the manufacture of soap, paints, and varnishes. The baleen was valuable for a variety of purposes, including use in the manufacture of watch springs, walking canes, fishing rods, handles, corset stays, skirt hoops, umbrellas, pen holders, paper cutters, shoehorns, combs, and furniture, just to mention a few.

Primitive Eskimos utilized the entire whale for food, clothing, implements, homes, and even toys before the products of civilization became available to them. The first priority was food: a high percentage of the carcass was eaten by the natives; the remainder was fed to the dogs and used as bait for traps. Whale gut was made into waterproof clothing, and was even used for windows. The ear bones are still prized as curios of considerable economic value, and the epithelium of the liver is still used to make drumheads.

Eskimos primarily used the oil rendered from the blubber and bones as fuel for lighting and heating their homes, as dip for food, as cooking oil, and as an ingredient in making dye. The oil was also traded to inland Eskimos to acquire caribou and wolverine skins for clothing and bedding.

Baleen was once used by the Eskimos in a multitude of everyday items: thread, whaling gear, fishing equipment, and lashings. Utensils—such as cups, dishes, buckets, and baskets—were also made. Implements—including knife blades, combs, sinew shuttles, sleds, and water ladles—were made entirely or in part of baleen. Devices for collecting food—such as animal traps and spears—were durable and easily made. The Eskimos also used baleen for making art and craft objects; even toys were devised using this utilitarian substance.

Bones from the whales supplied material for various tools. They were used to shoe the runners of sleds (snow does not stick to such runners). Ribs and jawbones were used in house construction, as clotheslines, as racks for storing many items out of reach of dogs, and as posts for tying up dogs. The cemetery at Point Hope is well known for its fence, constructed of nearly one thousand ribs and jawbones, as well as for the huge jawbones used for gate posts and markers for some of the graves. Years ago, at the village of Gambell on Saint Lawrence Island, ribs and jawbones were even used to erect a barrier to Eskimos invading from Siberia.

Because of its isolation in the harsh arctic environment, the bowhead has been subject to little biological research. Before 1961, the scarce data recorded in the literature were obtained by a few of the early whalers. Between 1961 and 1973, Floyd Durham, a University of Southern California scientist, studied the bowheads harvested by Alaskan Eskimos, and his findings were a major contribution to the biology of this species.

In 1961 and 1962, and from 1973 to the present,

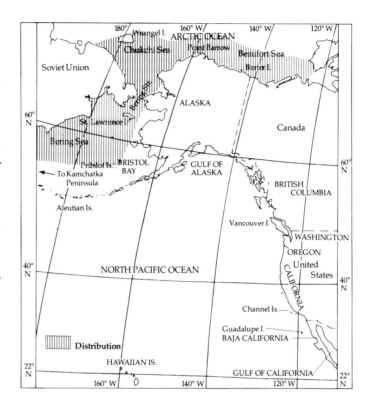

Bowhead whale distribution

the United States National Marine Fisheries Service has been researching this whale. Since 1975, aerial surveys have been made and ice-based counting stations used to obtain data on the distribution, migration, and abundance of bowhead whales, as part of the Outer Continental Shelf Environmental Assessment Program being conducted in Alaska waters. As with all species, aerial surveys provide information on the distribution of whales, as well as visual estimates of their numbers, and photographs verify both the species and numbers of animals involved. The ice-based stations for the program are established on shore-fast ice at the edge of open leads where a twenty-four-hour watch is maintained —ice conditions permitting—and the number of bowhead whales sighted is recorded. The information now available provides us with some understanding of the natural history of this cetacean.

The bowhead whale inhabits arctic and sub-arctic waters in four principal areas: (1) from Spitsbergen westward to east Greenland; (2) in Davis Strait, Baffin Bay, Hudson Bay, and adjacent waters; (3) in the Bering, Chukchi, Beaufort, and east Siberian seas; and (4) in the Okhotsk Sea. It is one of the few marine mammals that spends all or most of its life in or near the loose edge of the ice pack, migrating north as the ice recedes in the spring and south as it extends in the winter. In spring, the bowheads migrate in the vicinity of Saint Lawrence Island and past the Chukchi Peninsula, through Bering Strait, along the northwest Alaska coast, then through the Beaufort Sea to the Amundsen Gulf. Some bowheads may also migrate through the Bering Strait and along the Siberian coast. In autumn, the whales move westward along the north coast of Alaska to the vicinity of Wrangel Island, where they turn south along the coast of the Soviet Union to the Bering Sea. During its spring migration, the bowhead is usually seen singly or in pairs, often in the company of belugas (*Delphinapterus leucas*). During the autumn migration, these animals are frequently seen in groups that may contain up to fifty members.

The bowhead is a large, robust whale whose profile at the surface typically consists of two distinct features: the low-triangular shape of the head, and the long, low-curving back that begins just behind the head and extends toward the tail. Younger animals, particularly females, are often rotund and their profiles may lack the distinctive dip between the head and back that is characteristic of older animals.

The bowhead's ponderous head forms more than one third the entire length of its body. Paired blowholes are located at the peak of the head. The eyes, slightly larger than those of cattle, are located low on the sides of the head near the end corners of the mouth. There are no external ears but only tiny openings that are located slightly above and behind the eyes.

The huge mouth is edged with transverse plates of baleen that extend downward and outward from their origin in the highly arched upper jaw. The total number of these black- or gray-colored baleen plates can vary considerably but averages about six hundred (three hundred on each side). These plates grow to a maximum length of fifteen feet in large adults, although most average ten to twelve feet. Plates near the middle of each row (or side) of baleen are the longest; they gradually decrease in length down to a few inches toward each end of the row. The interior edges of the baleen have hairlike fringes, which are used to strain plankton from the water.

The bowhead is black or dark gray, usually marked with white or cream on the chin and frequently on the underside, especially on the throat and around the genital and umbilical areas. A few small, white spots are sometimes scattered about the body. Piebald bowheads have been seen, as has one bowhead with a white tail; on rare occasions, albino adults or calves also have been sighted. When the animal breaches or is viewed overhead from aircraft, the white chin is distinctive. When the bowhead dives, it arches the rear portion of its back slightly above the surface and frequently raises its tail flukes into the air. The flukes are large and have reportedly reached a total span of twenty-six feet. Its flippers, however, are short and stubby.

The bowhead is a slow-moving, timid animal that retreats under the ice when alarmed. When undisturbed during migration, it travels on a fairly straight course at about two to six miles per hour. Its maximum speed—as when it is being chased—has been reported by Scoresby, a nineteenth-century whaler and author, to be about eight or nine miles per hour. When approached by whaleboats, it is reportedly capable of swimming in reverse for a short distance or sinking with such

A bowhead, taken from the icy waters of northwest Alaska, shows the high-arching jaw from which this whale's common name is derived. (Don Patten)

An adult bowhead and young travel in the vicinity of Point Barrow, Alaska, during spring migration. Little is known of the reproductive cycle of this rare species. The bowhead's distinctive white chin is visible in both of these animals. (Bruce Krogman)

rapidity as to leave a large momentary depression in the water.

Breathing behavior is apparently influenced by the whale's activity and individual physical characteristics. Generally, the bowhead surfaces to breathe from a few seconds to perhaps one or two minutes, blowing four to nine (sometimes up to twelve) times, and then submerges for five to ten (sometimes as long as fifteen to twenty) minutes. The calf must breathe more frequently, and spends about one half of its time at the surface. Wounded whales remain underwater for longer periods; the maximum underwater time was reported by Charles Scammon, a nineteenth-century whaler, to be eighty minutes. After the whale has sounded, it usually swims for about a mile in a straight line at depths of twenty-five to fifty feet before resurfacing. Eskimos and early whalers have reported that bowheads seem to follow an invisible route through the sea, even appearing at the surface to breathe in precisely the same places at which preceding individuals have surfaced.

The blow or spout of the bowhead whale is double and V-shaped, with the two jets diverging at an angle of thirty-five to forty-five degrees. The blow reaches a height of about twelve to fifteen feet and, when visible, has a mushroom shape. Atmospheric conditions affect the distance at which the blow can be seen. When breathing, the animal emits a loud sound, which can be heard for a mile or more, and exhales air that has an unpleasant odor. Sleeping whales breathe quietly, do not blow, and maintain equilibrium by means of their flippers. They may lie immobile at the surface for periods of as long as thirty minutes.

Sleeping whales can react violently when disturbed. One commercial whaler on two different occasions harpooned a sleeping whale after approaching it cautiously. Both times the animals reacted immediately and furiously in their flight to escape the hunters. Eskimo whalers have also reported the dangers involved in striking sleeping whales.

The maximum depth to which the bowhead can submerge is not well documented. Scoresby reported that a wounded bowhead broke its jaw by striking the bottom at a depth of 800 fathoms (4,800 feet). Others have stated that the bowhead can dive from a few hundred to more than 1,000 feet. These figures are based on the amount of line pulled out of whaleboats by harpooned whales but, because the trailing line arcs through the water, it is difficult, by such methods, to determine actual depths to which the whales dive. However, because these whales surface to breathe at frequent intervals, choose to follow the coast during much of their migration, and appear to frequent relatively shallow areas during the summer, they apparently prefer to inhabit shallow water.

The bowhead is fairly sensitive to touch, and a bird can startle it when landing on its back. It is also sensitive to sound and is easily frightened, retreating under the ice when alarmed. Early commercial whalers stated that these animals perceived the slightest noise within a radius of one mile, and that they reacted even when another whale had been harpooned twenty-one miles away. The whalers also reported that, although these whales reacted weakly to shouts, careless oar movements, or slight noises on the whaleboat or ship, such disturbances were sufficient to frighten them away. Even today, native whalers observe certain precautions when stalking bowheads: they steer the boat smoothly, do not let the paddles hit the boat or make splashes, and remain as quiet as possible, refraining from making unnecessary movements. Commands are usually given by hand signals or in hushed tones.

The visual acuity of the bowhead has not been scientifically evaluated. Because its eyes are located on the sides of its enormous head, the animal cannot see directly ahead or behind. For this reason, whalers approach bowheads from either the front or the rear if possible. Early commercial whalers had great respect for the bowhead's vision, as do the Eskimo whalers today. Natives have traditionally worn white parkas to reduce their visibility to the bowheads while hunting them; the hunters also cover their boats or umiaks with sealskins that are bleached almost white (following a whaling culture practice). When watching on the ice for passing whales, the hunters are careful to maintain low profiles with a minimum of movement so they do not frighten the animals.

Many cetaceans are vocal, and bowheads apparently are no exception. H. L. Aldrich, an early whaler and author, described what he called "singing" by this whale and wrote that whaleship masters also spoke of this phenomenon. Aldrich himself did not believe in this vocalization until he observed captains respond to "singing" when whales were not visible in the area, and in a short time, pursue and capture the animals. Aldrich wrote, "With bowhead whales the cry is something like the hoo—oo—oo of the hoot-owl, although longer drawn out, and more of a humming sound than a hoot. Beginning on F, the tone may rise to G, A, B, and sometimes to C, before slanting back to F again." Aldrich also stated that bowhead "singing" is almost never heard in the Arctic and inferred that it is a sort of call, or signal, among migrating whales.

The bowhead has several specialized features for life in arctic waters. The baleen-straining apparatus of its cavernous mouth efficiently filters abundant zooplankton from the water. An extremely thick, ten- to twenty-inch layer of blubber, which primarily provides the animal with a reserve of food, also provides insulation (far in excess of that needed) against the cold of ice-filled seas. The absence of a dorsal fin is advantageous for movement among the ice floes, and the massive head may be an adaptation for breaking through ice when necessary to breathe air. Reliable observers report that this whale can break through ice that is one to two feet thick. The blowholes are located at the apex of the promontory on the head, an area so distinctive that some early whalers applied the nickname of "Steepletop" to this whale. This feature may also be an adaptation to an ice-covered habitat, for it may permit surfacing for air in small openings that are large enough to admit this protuberance but not the entire head. It has also been suggested that air pockets may exist beneath the irregular ice, and that the whale breathes air there by inserting the breathing protuberance. Furthermore, this promontory is covered with a thick pad of connective tissue that appears to be a protective adaptation for its assumed ice-breaking role.

Although these whales are well adapted to life among ice floes, they are not completely free from danger within the ice fields, for entrapment in shifting ice fields can kill them. Whale carcasses without wounds have been found frozen in the ice, and Soviet Eskimos have been reported to search regu-

larly for such animals. Although the phenomenon of entrapped whales is rare, it occurs often enough to have become a part of the hunting technique employed by the Eskimos. Strandings of bowheads along arctic beaches also are infrequent. Because they usually float when dead, those that die of natural causes or as the result of injuries probably become frozen in the ice; after the flesh of the carcasses has been eaten by predators, the bones eventually sink.

The only known predators of bowheads are man and the killer whale (*Orcinus orca*). Most killer whale attacks have been by groups of between three and ten killer whales. In attacks on bowheads and other cetaceans, killer whales have frequently been seen concentrating on the tongues of their prey. In the western Arctic, these bowhead predators have been reported as far north as Barrow in the Chukchi Sea.

Bowheads are relatively free of the callosities or clusters of barnacles and "whale lice" that are found in abundance on its close relative, the right whale. Ectoparasites are limited to "whale lice" of the genus *Cyamus*. Soviet zoologist A. G. Tomilin has written, "The severe conditions of the Arctic protect bowhead whales from barnacle ectoparasites which thrive on the warm-loving black right whale [*Balaena glacialis*]. Low water temperature evidently prevents the barnacle from assimilating lime, necessary for building a calcareous shell." Only a few endoparasites have been reported, and were found in tissues of the intestines, liver, esophagus, penis, and the blubber. The absence of significant infestation by parasites may be due to the specialized diet of the bowhead, and the fact that it occupies a habitat that presents little opportunity for contact with other cetaceans that might transmit such organisms.

The diet of one of the largest whales in the world consists, paradoxically, of some of the smallest organisms in the oceans—small crustaceans that exist in tremendous numbers in arctic waters. Although the stomach contents of only a few bowheads have been examined, it has been found that shrimplike euphausiids, copepods, pteropods, and amphipods are its principal sources of food. These organisms are collectively known by whalers as "brit" (copepods) or "krill" (euphausiids), the vernacular Norwegian name. These and other small zooplankton that congregate in broad patches scattered throughout the polar waters are sometimes so abundant that they appear to discolor the water.

During feeding, the bowhead swims forward with its mouth open, sieving the abundant organisms through its baleen plates while the filtered water passes out the sides of its mouth. When the mouth is opened, the plates slide forward and spring to a vertical position forming a large seining basket for trapping food. When its mouth is full, the whale closes its lower jaw and raises its massive tongue to displace the water out through the baleen plates. The plates are flexible, and, when the mouth closes, they bend and fold backward into a groove between the tongue and the bone of the lower jaw. This diminishes the size of the mouth cavity and water flows from the mouth. At this point, the long, slender, flexible ends of the baleen are kept from being forced outward because the lower lip firmly rises several feet above the jawbone. After the water is displaced from the mouth, the whale swallows the retained food. It is generally believed that the bowhead does not feed on fish, although small fish occasionally may be ingested. It cannot swallow large fish because the throat passage is only a few inches in diameter.

If bowheads feed as other baleen whales do, then they feast during the summer when food is abundant and feed to little or no extent during the remainder of the year when food is scarce. This assumption is substantiated in part by the absence of food in the stomachs of migrating whales that have been taken by the natives.

When the bowhead was whaled commercially, it was too difficult to weigh such a huge animal, so specific information about its weight and quantity of food consumption is lacking. However, because the black right whale (*Balaena glacialis*) has been carefully weighed aboard factory ships, and because the right whale and bowhead have similar body proportions, the weight and food consumption of the bowhead can be extrapolated from information about the right whale. The weight of a right whale over forty-six feet long is estimated to be about one ton for each foot of length; for an animal less than forty-six feet, the length/weight ratio is approximately one-half ton per foot. Thus, a fifty-foot bowhead would weigh about fifty tons. D. E. Sergeant, a Canadian scientist, has concluded that the daily food demand for a baleen whale is four percent of its body weight. On this basis, the daily intake of food for bowheads fifty feet long can be estimated to be 4,000 pounds.

The bowhead's maximum length is not well documented. Most recorded information is suspect because it rarely describes how the measurements were obtained. Whales captured at sea were hastily flensed in the water alongside the ships to speed production and to minimize valuable time lost because of bad weather—a common occurrence in the Arctic. For this reason, carcasses were seldom measured, except those of unusually large whales that attracted attention. Total lengths were usually determined by visually comparing the length of the carcass with the length of the ship, which was known. Occasionally, the size was simply recorded as so many feet broad and so many feet in circumference; these measurements could be readily estimated by tools used to flense the animal. Because the blubber was removed from the carcass in a slight spiral, a fairly accurate estimate of the circumference also could easily be made. Accurate measurements of large whales cut up on shore or on ice have seldom been obtained because of the lack of equipment to pull the carcass from the water and because the ice was sometimes not strong enough to support the weight of the animal. In these situations, large animals were simply cut up in the water and reduced to portions that could be efficiently handled. Of the bowheads that were taken by commercial whalers and measured scientifically, most did not exceed sixty feet. Scoresby stated that of the 322 whales he took, the largest was fifty-eight feet long. There are reports in early literature of some bowheads reaching a length of seventy feet or longer.

Information on the bowhead's growth is scarce, but the available data provide us with a general pattern. At birth, the calves are between ten and fifteen feet long, as measured by the early whalers. These lengths agree with that of a newborn calf taken at Barrow on 20 May 1954, which was estimated by the Eskimos to be ten to twelve feet long and one to two weeks old. Two calves taken in autumn were determined to be eighteen feet long and about six months old. Many of the whales taken by Eskimo whalers in spring range in length from twenty-two to twenty-six feet and are believed to be yearlings—perhaps twelve months of age. After the first year of growth, the body length of an immature gray whale (*Eschrichtius robustus*) increases about ten percent yearly. Assuming a similar growth rate for the bowhead, an immature individual (less than four years of age) may range from twenty-six to thirty-two feet or more in body length.

Physical maturity, attained when fusions of the thoracic vertebral epiphyses with the centra are complete, occurs for males when they are forty-six to fifty feet long; females are slightly longer than that when mature. Some variation can be expected, however, in the length at which individuals attain physical maturity. More data are needed to establish with certainty this aspect of growth.

The bowhead reaches sexual maturity at a length of thirty-eight feet for the male and forty feet for the female, both sexes at age four years, according to Floyd Durham. Because most of the whales taken by the Eskimos are immature, it is difficult to obtain data about sexual maturity and reproduction.

The mating season is not well defined. Early observers reported the occurrence of reproductive behavior from January through late summer. Recent observations indicate that mating probably occurs during the spring migration and in summer, with the most mating probably occurring during April and May.

The gestation and calving periods also are not well defined, because scientific information about bowhead fetuses and newborn calves is rare. Recent reports suggest that most calving probably occurs during April and May, and that the gestation period is about twelve months. Mating and calving seasons can be expected to occur over some range in time and, therefore, probably overlap.

Because two calves with a female are rarely seen, it is believed that they produce a single young no more often than every two or even three years. We do not know how long the lactation period is or how long calves remain with their mothers. According to Scammon, the female nurses her calf near the surface. Adult females accompanied by calves have been seen between March and October. The fact that lactating females have not been taken by whalers in autumn indicates early weaning, perhaps at age five or six months. A small calf taken at Barrow in October was believed by Durham to have been weaned. From skull measurements, he estimated that the calf was about six months old and eighteen feet long.

Average and maximum life-spans of bowhead whales are unknown. During the era of commercial whaling, old harpoons were sometimes found embedded in the bodies of captured whales, indicating that bowheads can survive abortive hunting attempts. Early whalers reported that marks of ownership were stamped on the harpoons, thus providing information about the age and movements of bowheads. The validity of such reports is questionable, however. Whaling equipment from vessels removed from service was often purchased by other whalers, who may or may not have removed the original marks before using the equipment or trading it to the Eskimos. In one instance, an old harpoon bore marks indicating that the whale had been struck forty years before; another allegedly had been carried by a whale for twenty-four years. A few incidents have also occurred wherein discovery of old harpoons bearing identifying marks suggested that the whales had made the passage between the Atlantic and Pacific Arctic.

What of the future for the bowhead whale? The Eskimos have continued their harvest of bowheads for subsistence since the termination of commercial whaling for this species. Although these people normally do not keep records of whales they have taken, statistics from various sources indicate a harvest of about ten animals annually for the twenty-five years between 1945 and 1969. From 1970 to the present, however, the harvest has averaged twenty-nine whales annually. The increase is significant and causes concern for the continued survival of this endangered species.

This concern caused the International Whaling Commission, at its June 1977 meeting in Australia, to remove the exemption that had allowed Eskimo subsistence hunting and to declare an immediate moratorium on bowhead whaling. The United States chose not to object to the ban because it has been the leader in whale conservation for many years at the IWC. Instead, the United States developed a comprehensive scientific research and conservation program for the bowhead in order to provide for a controlled subsistence harvest by the Eskimos—a program that would preserve the central elements of their culture and protect the bowhead population.

At a special IWC meeting held in Tokyo, Japan, in December 1977, the United States therefore urged that the Eskimos be permitted to resume a limited, controlled hunt restricted to fifteen whales killed or thirty struck, whichever comes first. In addition, the Alaska Eskimo Whaling Commission, created in August 1977 by Eskimo whaling captains to represent their interest in bowhead whales, sent a delegation to the Tokyo meeting to plead for a continued subsistence hunt considered vital to Eskimo culture and economy. Ultimately the IWC decided to allow a quota for 1978 of twelve whales landed or eighteen struck, whichever comes first. Although the Eskimos are able to continue their traditional centuries-old hunt for another year, the IWC warned that if it appears that the endangered bowhead population does not receive sufficient protection, the ban will be reimposed.

It is clear that a crisis exists with respect to the continued existence of a remarkable but endangered whale and of an aboriginal whaling culture that is rooted in the past. Presumably, the question is not which one will survive, but rather how the continued existence of both can be ensured. Cooperative action by all interested parties can provide a timely solution before another victim of civilization is recorded in the history books.

Sperm Whales

by Dale W. Rice

If there were not already such an animal, one might say it was impossible. The giant sperm whale *(Physeter macrocephalus)*—with its huge, disproportionate head and corrugated body—is one of the most unlikely looking creatures on our planet. As one of the deepest diving cetaceans, it spends much of its time in an environment less known and less accessible to man than outer space. It is included in the family Physeteridae, along with its diminutive cousins, the pygmy and dwarf sperm whales, about which little is known.

Largest of the toothed whales, the male giant sperm whale may attain a length of sixty feet, although animals longer than fifty feet are scarce. The female is considerably smaller, rarely exceeding about thirty-seven feet. One fifty-nine-foot male was known to weigh fifty-eight tons.

The giant sperm whale is easily recognized by its huge head, which accounts for one fourth to one third of its total length, hence its Latin species name *macrocephalus*. Much of the head's bulk is taken up by a barrel-shaped organ, which whalers call the "case." It contains spermaceti, a clear liquid oil that, when cooled, hardens to a white paraffin-like consistency. A single, S-shaped blowhole is located on the left side at the front of the head. The long, narrow, rod-shaped lower jaw bears a row of about twenty-five teeth on each side. A few rudimentary teeth are usually present in the upper jaw, but they rarely show through the gums. The sperm whale's dorsal fin is rounded or obtuse. The tail stock, behind the dorsal fin, has a slightly scalloped dorsal ridge and a deep, rounded ventral keel. The surface of the body is irregularly corrugated, giving the animal a somewhat shriveled appearance.

Giant sperm whales live in all oceans of the world, from the equator to the edges of the north and south polar pack ice. Females usually remain in temperate and tropical waters between forty-five degrees north latitude and forty-five degrees south latitude. Although widely distributed, sperm whales tend to be most abundant in certain areas, which were known as "grounds" to the nineteenth-century American whalers. C. H. Townsend, former director of the New York

Off California, a bull sperm whale surfaces and blows. An off-center blowhole, barrel-shaped head, corrugated body, and low-triangular dorsal fin are distinctive characteristics of this species. (Dale W. Rice)

Aquarium, examined the logbooks of 1,665 voyages of nineteenth-century American whaling vessels and plotted by month the positions where 36,908 sperm whales were killed. His colored charts graphically show the seasonal migrations of the sperm whales. They shift northward during the boreal summer and southward during the austral summer.

Giant sperm whales are noted for their ability to make prolonged deep dives. Although females and young males tend to surface after fifteen to forty-five minutes, large bulls frequently stay down for over an hour. Carcasses of sperm whales have been found entangled in submarine cables lying on the bottom in water as deep as 3,720 feet. During the International Indian Ocean Whale Marking Cruise aboard the catcher boat *Pieter Molenaar*, we tracked sperm whales with sonar and found that their usual diving depth was around 1,600 feet. However, the sonar operator told me that he once tracked a large male at a depth of 6,000 feet. By listening to the clicks of sperm whales through an array of directional hydrophones, biologists have located them as deep as 8,200 feet. Off Durban, South Africa, two large, bull sperm whales were shot—after an eighty-minute dive—in water that was 10,476 feet deep. They had fresh, bottom-inhabiting sharks in their stomachs. It seems likely that the depth to which a sperm whale can dive is limited only by the length of time it takes it to get down and back.

Squid, particularly the larger species, are the main component of the giant sperm whale's diet. The stomachs of sperm whales taken off California and British Columbia contain mostly the large squid *Moroteuthis robustus*. I have measured squid specimens that were up to four feet five inches from the tip of the tail to the anterior margin of the mantle and eleven feet four inches to the tip of the tentacles. A thirty-six-foot giant squid (*Architeuthis* sp.) was found in the stomach of one sperm whale killed off the Azores. Small species of squid are also eaten, especially by the females and young males. In addition, sperm whales eat octopuses and deep-water fishes; off the California coast, these include rough-scaled rattails, sablefish, brown cat sharks, longnose skates, lingcod, hake, rockfish, and king-of-the-salmon.

There is no light at the depths at which sperm whales often seek their food. How do they find their way, and locate and capture their food in total darkness? Like the smaller odontocetes studied in oceanariums, sperm whales undoubtedly have a highly developed system of echolocation (sonar). They almost constantly utter clicking sounds that can be detected for miles with a hydrophone. These clicks are repeated at an average rate of about six times per second. Recordings of the clicks on an oscilloscope show that each click is composed of one to nine discrete pulses of sound, each lasting less than two thousandths of a second. This production of multipulse clicks is called "burst-pulsing." The burst-pulse technique is also frequently used in man-made sonar for distinguishing echoes in a

While arching its back to dive, the sperm whale shows its triangular dorsal fin and the series of notches on the dorsal ridge of the tail. (Dale W. Rice)

high-noise field. Sperm whale clicks also form a "signature"—that is, each whale utters clicks with its own characteristic frequency spectrum and spacing of pulses. Perhaps this individual difference permits a sperm whale to distinguish the echoes of its own clicks from those of other whales.

Another intriguing feature of the sperm whale's voice is what has been termed a "coda." Codas are stereotyped repetitive sequences of three to forty or more clicks. Each whale has a coda with a rhythm that differs from that of any other whale in the neighborhood. A sperm whale utters its coda only when it meets other sperm whales underwater. Presumably, the codas enable the whales to identify each other individually.

The sperm whale's skull has a large crest at the rear; the entire skull thus resembles a Roman chariot facing backward. The case, mentioned earlier, occupies much of this dorsal concavity. In theory, the bony crest acts as a parabolic sound reflector and the case, which is covered with strong tendons, acts as a variable-focus acoustic lens and permits the whale to beam the sound waves selectively.

Giant sperm whales are fairly long-lived, sociable animals. They are sexually mature at eight or nine years, and may live to age sixty or more. The females (including those that are pregnant and those with nursing calves) and the juvenile whales of both sexes congregate in "nursery" or "maternity" schools. These groups may vary in size from about ten to several hundred whales. The larger congregations consist of separate pods of about ten to twenty whales each and are scattered over several square miles. The maternity schools are sometimes called "harem" schools, but this is a misnomer because there may be either no adult male with them or there may be several. When the males reach puberty, they usually leave the maternity schools and form small bachelor schools. The old bulls lead a solitary life, except during the mating

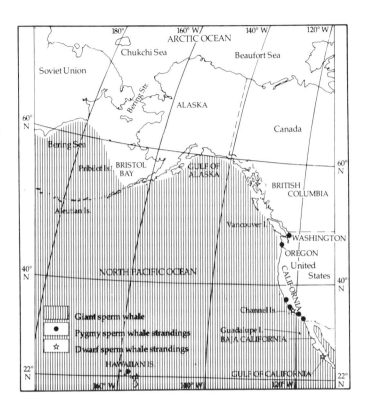

Sperm whale distribution

season.

In temperate latitudes, the female sperm whale usually comes into heat in spring or early summer. The mating season off California occurs from April through August. There is no data on the breeding season of those sperm whales living near the equator. After a gestation period of fifteen months, the female gives birth to a single calf, which is about thirteen feet long. To nurse her calf, the mother lies on her side at the surface; the calf, lying parallel to its mother, takes her teat sideways in the angle of its jaw. The milk—which is rich in fat and protein, and low in milk sugar—is pumped into the calf's mouth by means of a muscle layer covering the mammary glands. For about two years the calf continues to nurse, although it may begin to take solid food some months before being weaned. After her calf is weaned, the female does not come into heat again for a time varying from several months to over a year. Thus she can bear only one calf every four to five years.

Ambergris, at one time highly prized as a base for perfume, is a concretion that rarely forms in the intestines of sperm whales. It usually forms in lumps that look somewhat like large potatoes; masses weighing several hundred pounds have been found. People frequently bring me lumps of foul-smelling flotsam that they have picked off the beach, hoping that it is ambergris. It never is. Fresh ambergris has a characteristic, indescribable odor—neither pleasant nor unpleasant. Old ambergris has a musty smell reminiscent of a damp basement. Smooth and dark brown outside, ambergris lumps are firm and frangible, and pale yellow to gray inside. Horny, parrotlike beaks of squids are usually imbedded in them. The lumps are most simply identified by piercing them with a hot needle. If it is ambergris, it will melt into a chocolate-colored liquid and leave a tacky coating on the needle. Although largely supplanted by synthetics in the perfume industry, ambergris is still worth several dollars an ounce.

Sperm whale hunting began in 1712 in New England. During the following century and a half, the American high seas, open-boat, sperm whale fishery increased and prospered. By the early 1800s, voyages that often lasted five years were carrying American whalers to every part of the globe. This fishery reached its zenith in the mid-nineteenth century when over seven hundred whaling vessels were registered in American ports. Smaller numbers were registered in British and other foreign ports. During this period, over one hundred thousand barrels of sperm oil were imported into American ports each year, an amount representing an annual kill of about five thousand sperm whales throughout the world. The kill apparently had little effect on sperm whale populations. For economic

reasons, the fishery drastically declined toward the close of the nineteenth century, and petroleum (discovered in 1859) rapidly supplanted sperm oil as a lubricant and as lamp fuel.

In the 1860s, with the invention of the modern harpoon gun in Norway, a new age of whaling dawned. Whalers were now able to chase and kill the powerful, swift rorquals—particularly the blue and fin whales. Steam- or diesel-powered catcher boats, operating in conjunction with floating factory ships or processing stations on shore, were far more efficient than the old style open boats and hand harpoons. Although the modern fishery was based on rorquals and other baleen (whalebone) whales, a few sperm whales were also taken incidentally. Before World War II, the annual world catch of sperm whales rarely exceeded two or three thousand.

The population of adult sperm whales in 1946 is calculated to have been over one million worldwide, half of which lived in the North Pacific. Allowing for immature animals, the total at that time exceeded two million worldwide, with roughly a million in the North Pacific.

By the 1950s, the modern whaling industry had grown so large and efficient that it seriously reduced the baleen whale stocks on which it depended. Meanwhile, new uses had been discovered for sperm oil (such as in cosmetics, soap, and machine oil). As demand for the oil increased, sperm whale killing was greatly intensified until the world catch reached a peak of 29,255 in 1964. Catches in the North Pacific continued to climb until 1968, when 16,357 were killed there. Although catches have since declined, in part because of limits imposed by the International Whaling Commission, the sperm whale remains the most important species to the whaling industry. Over the past few years, the world catch has been stable at around 20,000 annually, of which about 7,000 are taken from the North Pacific. Soviet and Japanese pelagic whaling account for the bulk of this catch. The remainder is taken by shore stations in Japan, Australia, Peru, Brazil, Iceland, Spain, Madeira, and the Azores.

Most sperm whale stocks are still at or above the level that provides the maximum sustainable yield. The present world population is estimated at about 800,000 adults (or roughly 1.5 million total, including young animals), of which 380,000 adults (or about 740,000 total) are in the North Pacific.

In marked contrast to our extensive knowledge of the giant sperm whale, we know practically nothing of the lives of the pygmy and dwarf sperm whales. They are peculiar little whales, and are classified in a separate genus called *Kogia*, a latinization of the word "codger."

The pygmy sperm whale (*Kogia breviceps*) measures only nine to eleven feet in length; there is little difference between the lengths of male and female. Its head is relatively much shorter than that of its giant cousin, and the crescent-shaped blowhole is located on top of the head, as in most toothed whales. The mouth is set far back, giving the head a sharklike look—an appearance heightened by a pair of whitish "gill" markings on the otherwise dark gray body. There are twelve to sixteen pairs of sharp, hooked teeth in the lower jaw, and none in the upper jaw. The small, sickle-shaped dorsal fin is set far back on its body.

Pygmy sperm whales have been found stranded on tropical and warm temperate shores all around the globe. In the eastern North Pacific, the northernmost strandings occurred at Grayland and Whidbey Island in Washington State. In the eastern United States, they are one of the most frequently stranded cetaceans, yet they are almost never identified at sea. Those few observers who have seen them alive report that pygmy sperm whales are slow moving and lethargic, and are usually seen basking at the surface. They are either solitary or form small pods of up to seven individuals.

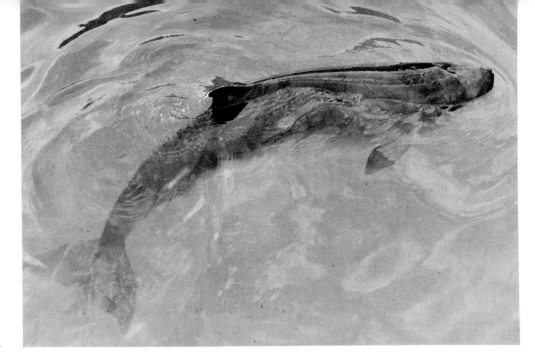

The stomachs of stranded pygmy sperm whales have revealed mostly squid and cuttlefish; crabs, shrimps, and fish have also been found. Almost nothing has been learned of reproduction in this whale except that the female may become pregnant before weaning her previous calf.

Pygmy sperm whales are rarely killed in the dolphin fisheries in Japan, the Lesser Antilles, and the Lesser Sunda Islands of Indonesia.

The dwarf sperm whale (*Kogia simus*) was, until recently, usually confused with the pygmy species. It differs in being even smaller—seven to nine feet when adult—and in having a much larger dorsal fin located mid-length on the body. The lower jaw has only eight to eleven pairs of teeth, but the upper jaw also has one to three pairs.

The geographical distribution of this species appears to be similar to that of the pygmy sperm whale. In the eastern North Pacific, dwarf sperm whales have been found stranded only at San Luis Obispo, California; Cabo San Lazaro, Baja California; and in Hawaii.

The rare pygmy sperm whale has a hooked dorsal fin and a much smaller head than its giant relative. (H. E. Winn)

Beaked Whales

by Dale W. Rice

The deep-diving beaked whales are the most elusive of all cetaceans. They are rarely seen alive. What little we know of their natural history has been pieced together, primarily from examining occasional carcasses cast on beaches. Yet among the cetaceans, the beaked whale family (Ziphiidae) ranks second only to the dolphin family in diversity and number of species. The eighteen species presently known range throughout the deep oceans of the world.

The rarity of beaked whales may be more apparent than real. They are inconspicuous at sea because they do not produce an obvious "blow." Nor do they congregate in large schools or ride the bow wave of vessels. However, in good weather conditions, experienced observers may sight them with unexpected frequency. During a seventy-day whale research cruise in the Indian Ocean in the southern summer of 1973–1974, we spotted pods of beaked whales—including at least four species—on twenty-eight occasions. Many were sighted by keeping a sharp watch *astern* of the vessel. Although this elusiveness may simply be due to their usually long dive times, it is also possible that, deep down, these whales hear the approaching vessel and wait until it has passed before surfacing. After a pod of beaked whales has sounded, you must stop the vessel and wait thirty or forty-five minutes or more if you want another look at them. Norwegian whalers claim that the North Atlantic bottlenose whale—the best known of the beaked whale family—can remain down for as long as two hours.

Beaked whales are "small" whales, ranging in length from twelve to forty feet. They have a rather small dorsal fin far aft and, unlike all other cetaceans, lack a median notch on the trailing edge of the flukes. Most distinctive are the long jaws, which are more or less prolonged into a narrow beak. Although the head shape varies, this characteristic beak is present in all species, as are a pair of deep grooves on the throat.

Beaked whales have no teeth in the upper jaw and only one or two pairs in the lower jaw. (In females, these teeth usually do not erupt through the gums.) Only the rare *Tasmacetus shepherdi* of the

A goosebeak whale breaches off Isla San Martin, Baja California. The size and position of the dorsal fin are characteristic of the beaked whales. (Stephen Leatherwood)

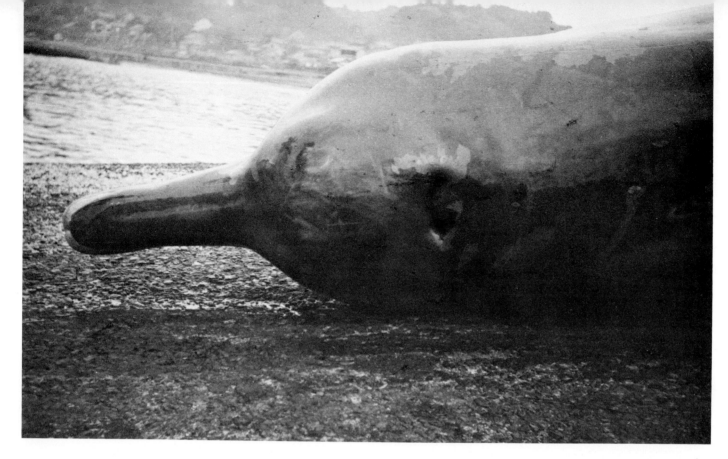

This dorsal view of the head of a giant bottlenose whale shows the derivation of its common name. (W. J. Houck)

Southern Ocean is an exception. Unknown as a species until 1937, this whale has a full complement of teeth in both upper and lower jaws.

Six species of beaked whales, belonging to three of the six known genera, are found in the North Pacific.

The giant bottlenose whale (*Berardius bairdii*) is the largest member of the family, rivaling some of the "great" whales in size. The adult female measures thirty-four to forty-two feet in length; the male is slightly smaller at thirty-three to thirty-nine feet. This whale and the North Atlantic bottlenose whale (*Hyperoodon ampullatus*) are the only two beaked whales that are hunted commercially.

Although this species is often listed in books as "Baird's beaked whale," the whalers who worked out of Richmond, California, and Coal Harbour,

British Columbia—the only English-speaking people familiar with this whale in its living state—always called it the "bottlenose whale." In Japan it is called *tsuchi-kujira*—*tsuchi* meaning a cylindrical wooden hammer with the handle centered in one end, and *kujira* meaning "whale." Both English and Japanese names allude to the shape of the animal's head, which bears a prominent, rather long, narrow beak that is well demarcated from a bulging forehead. There are two pairs of large teeth at the end of the lower jaw. The jaw is so undershot that the front pair of teeth protrudes beyond the tip of the upper jaw when the mouth is closed. The body is uniformly slate gray, often appearing dark brown when the whale is alive, with a few irregular white blotches on the belly. The skin is always extensively scarred with long scratches, many in parallel pairs.

These are quite likely made by the teeth of other members of their own species.

The giant bottlenose whale is unique to the North Pacific, ranging north into the Bering Sea as far as Saint Matthew Island and the Pribilof Islands, where individuals have been found stranded. I have seen these whales as far south as San Clemente Island off southern California. In the western Pacific, they are regularly seen as far south as Chiba Prefecture on the east side of Honshu, and Myazu Bay, Kyoto Prefecture, on the Sea of Japan side. Japanese whale-scouting vessels have also sighted them all across the North Pacific, south as far as twenty-five to thirty degrees north latitude in the central portion.

On the few occasions when I have observed giant bottlenose whales, they have been in tight pods of three to seventeen. The largest pod was particularly memorable. I was aboard the whale catcher *Allen Cody* west of Point Reyes, California, when we sighted the whales blowing leisurely at the surface. As we approached them, the skipper cut the engines, and we literally nosed into the midst of the unperturbed whales. Several times, one of them raised half its body obliquely above the water and then fell back. After a few minutes, the school sounded simultaneously and was not seen again.

Whalers in California and British Columbia rarely killed bottlenose whales because larger species were usually available. From 1956 through 1971, only fifteen of these animals were brought into the two California whaling stations. At Coal Harbour, British Columbia, twenty-four were caught between 1948 and 1967. Strangely, all but three were males.

Japan has the only regular fishery for *tsuchi-kujira*. At least since the year 1612, these whales have been hunted off the coast of Chiba Prefecture, where their dried meat is particularly relished. Since 1965, the catch has ranged from thirteen to

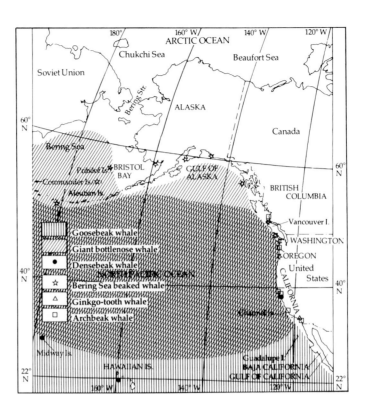

Beaked whale distribution. Almost all appearances of the four latter species here are strandings.

thirty-nine per year, with an average of twenty-six. According to Japanese whalers, the giant bottlenose whales, when struck by a harpoon, dive straight down—sometimes as deep as eight thousand feet.

Recent studies of animals landed at Japanese whaling stations have revealed that giant bottlenose whales attain sexual maturity at an age of eight to ten years, and may live to age seventy. The peak of their mating season is October and November, and they give birth mainly in March and April after a seventeen-month gestation period—the longest reported for any cetacean.

The stomachs of bottlenose whales that I examined at the California whaling stations contained mostly medium-size squids. Other items were also present, including rays, deepwater fish, octopuses, and crustaceans.

Because the two front teeth of the adult male bottlenose are always exposed to seawater and never come in contact with the upper jaw, they form an ideal site for the attachment of many stalked barnacles (*Conchoderma auritum*), which require a hard substrate. Around the barnacles and on the whale's skin, there are always many cyamids or "whale lice." There are two kinds, both of which are new species not yet scientifically described. The common one is closely related to *Cyamus catodontis* of sperm whales; the other belongs to the genus *Platycyamus*, hitherto known only from the North Atlantic bottlenose whale.

The goosebeak whale (*Ziphius cavirostris*) is the most widespread and frequently sighted of the beaked whales. In books, it is often called "Cuvier's beaked whale" in honor of the famous French naturalist who first described it in 1823. A few goosebeak whales are taken in the small whale fishery in Japan, where the whale is called *akabo-kujira* or "baby-face whale."

The adult female goosebeak whale is nineteen to twenty-three feet long; the male averages a slightly shorter length—eighteen to twenty-two feet. The adults can be recognized by a snow-white head and nape (apparently best developed in old males) and a short beak that blends into a sloping forehead. A single pair of teeth protrudes at the tip of the lower jaw. The rest of the body, which is often heavily scarred, is tan or light brown; when seen at a distance in bright sunlight, these whales often appear reddish.

Goosebeak whales have been found in all oceans of the world except in arctic and antarctic waters. In the Pacific, they range north to southeastern Alaska, the Aleutian Islands, and the Commander Islands. Along the west coast of North America, forty strandings of goosebeak whales were reported through 1968—far more than for any other species of beaked whale.

White-headed adults (old males?) are some-times solitary, but most goosebeak whales I have seen were in small pods of two to seven individuals. Nothing more can be said of their social behavior, and virtually nothing is known of their breeding cycle. And, although remains of medium-size squid have been found in the stomachs of stranded animals, nothing else is known about their eating habits.

The beaked whales of the genus *Mesoplodon* are so rarely seen that they have not acquired vernacular names; however, English book names have been coined for them. In the course of whale research cruises in the eastern North Pacific—totaling some five hundred days at sea during the past twenty years—I have never identified a *Mesoplodon*. In other parts of the world, however, I have seen at least three species on several occasions. They were usually in pods of two to six animals. One species, the scamperdown whale (*Mesoplodon grayi*) of the Southern Hemisphere, has the peculiar habit of sticking its long, needlelike, white snout out of the water as it breaks the surface to blow.

The eleven *Mesoplodon* species currently recognized range in all the world's oceans, except in polar seas. In general, they are rather small (twelve to eighteen feet) and have long, narrow beaks that are flattened from side to side. Most remarkable are the weird modifications of their single pair of teeth. In some species, these teeth are small and are located at the tip of the lower jaw. In others (including all four North Pacific species), they are large, laterally compressed, and located farther back in the jaw. Some modifications are even more odd. In the straptooth whale (*M. layardii*) of the Southern Ocean, for instance, the teeth curve around the upper jaw, thus preventing the mouth from being widely opened.

The only *Mesoplodon* species for which we have even rudimentary life history data is the North Sea beaked whale (*M. bidens*). Mating and birth usually take place in late winter and spring, and gestation

This goosebeak whale stranded near the mouth of the Mad River in northern California. Its white head is typical of adults of this species. The streaks on the body apparently were made by the teeth of other members of its species and the white spots are probably scars resulting from the bites of parasitic lampreys. (W. J. Houck)

lasts about one year. The calf is six to seven feet long at birth, and is weaned in about a year when it is some ten feet long.

The four species of *Mesoplodon* that have been found in the North Pacific cannot, as far as is now known, be distinguished in the field, except for the adult male densebeak whale. Identification requires examination of their skulls.

The densebeak whale *(Mesoplodon densirostris)* has an extraordinary appearance; in the adult male, the teeth are at the summit of vertical expansions of the jawbones and protrude above the forehead, somewhat like a pair of horns. Densebeak whales range throughout tropical and temperate seas around the world. I once saw one group of ten or twelve in the Hawaiian Islands. They blew leisurely at the surface for several minutes, and then dived. We waited forty-five minutes for them to come up, but we never saw them again. Besides Hawaiian waters, where they are frequently observed, the only other North Pacific records are strandings on the Midway Islands and near Pescadero Point,

A densebeak whale stranded on Midway Island shows the peculiar head shape of this species. (Courtesy of Ken Balcomb)

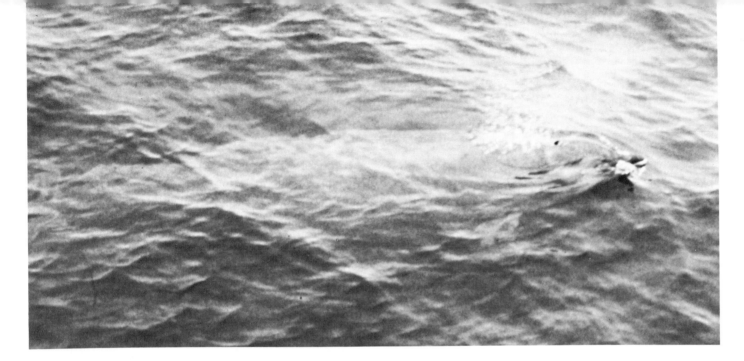

California.

The Bering Sea beaked whale (*Mesoplodon stejnegeri*), which has been known since 1885, is the most frequently encountered species. It ranges in subarctic waters north to the Pribilof Islands and Bristol Bay, and as far south as Yaquina Bay, Oregon, and the Sea of Japan.

The ginkgo-tooth whale (*Mesoplodon ginkgodens*) was first discovered in Japan in 1957. Several specimens were subsequently found around Taiwan. In 1963, a beaked whale that stranded in Sri Lanka (Ceylon) was described as another new species, but it was later identified as a ginkgo-tooth whale. In 1965, the skull of a beaked whale that had stranded at Delmar, California some eleven years before was reexamined and found to be a ginkgo-tooth whale. It is the only record of this species from the west coast of the United States. The teeth of this whale are shaped like the leaves of the ginkgo tree.

The archbeak whale (*Mesoplodon carlhubbsi*) was not recognized as a distinct species until 1963. Its scientific name honors Carl Hubbs, the renowned marine biologist of the Scripps Institution of Oceanography, who found the type specimen (the specimen on which the original scientific description was based) stranded at La Jolla, California, in 1945. The earliest known specimen was a skull found in 1944 on the ocean beach near Gray's Harbor, Washington. This species has since been found as far north as Long Beach on Vancouver Island, British Columbia, and also in Japan. It seems to range in more southerly, temperate waters than its relative, the Bering Sea beaked whale.

The six species listed above may not be the final tally of North Pacific beaked whales. In December 1975, on a beach in southern California, biologists found the carcasses of a *Mesoplodon* cow and calf that do not fit the description of any known species. It appears that, despite the efforts of curious cetologists, the lives of the beaked whales will long remain secrets of the dark deep.

This photo, taken off California's Catalina Island, is one of the few ever taken in the wild of a beaked whale of the genus Mesoplodon, possibly M. carlhubbsi, an archbeak whale. This animal was one of two that approached a research vessel and stayed with it for over half an hour. A hydrophone was used to record, for the first time, vocalizations of a beaked whale. (Don Ljungblad)

Porpoises and Dolphins

by Stephen Leatherwood and Randall R. Reeves

When we see porpoises moving so freely in their three-dimensional watery world, it is sometimes difficult to remember that they are mammals, as we are. Like all members of the order Cetacea, porpoises are more efficient, hydrodynamically, than anything man has yet invented, and are known to be equipped with a sophisticated sonar system for locating food, obstacles, and each other in the darkness of oceans, bays, and rivers. Some dive repeatedly to great depths without suffering from "the bends." All are remarkably adapted to live in the ocean and to exploit various portions of the ocean environment.

Porpoises occupy almost all oceans and major seas, as well as large river systems and even an inland lake on the Asian mainland. Their distribution, like that of other animals, is clearly not random. However, because of the limits of our present knowledge about the porpoises, we can make only educated guesses about what makes them choose one area over another. Topography of the ocean bottom is as varied as that of the more familiar exposed continents and islands. There are highly pro-

ductive coastal shelves, and beyond them deep abysses marked by fissures, trenches, sandy plains, volcanic mountains reaching near or above the water surface, and full-blown mountain chains of incredible height and extent. Above these is a fluid mass, set into complicated motion by the rotation of the earth and the movement of winds, always modified by the structure of the bottom and the continents.

Like the land, the oceans have rich pasturelands that are separated by areas of lower productivity. The horizontal and vertical distribution of "lower" forms of life—mainly plankton, fish, and squid—must in part determine the movements of porpoises and other top predators. Population concentrations of these top predators shift in response to diurnal, seasonal, and longer-term relocation of prey species. The behavioral patterns of a given porpoise species—its capabilities and strategies (for example, diving depths, food species, and feeding periods)—correspond to the particular "niche" it has specialized to occupy.

In many ways, the structures of communities in

The striking common dolphins are perhaps the most abundant dolphin in the southern areas covered by this book, from central California to the tip of Baja California. Herds, often containing more than a thousand animals, may be spotted from a considerable distance as they leap and gambol. When stressed, herds bunch tightly together like the group in this photo. (Stephen Leatherwood)

these oceanic pasturelands are analogous to veld communities on the plains and savannas of Africa. Historically, the veld supported huge communities of herbivores—impala, gazelle, giraffe, wildebeest, zebra—which made mass migrations from pasture to pasture, each group feeding on different portions of the available vegetation. These herbivores supported a complex gathering of carnivores, scavengers, and parasites. Although the boundaries of an oceanic "veld" are more dynamic and fluid than those of the veld, ocean communities exhibit the same basic principles of specialized exploitation and sharing of resources. In this simple analogy, phytoplankton (mostly diatoms) represents the ocean "graze"; fish, squid, and zooplankton (for example, copepods) the "grazers"; porpoises, the carnivorous predators; sharks, the scavengers; remora and a variety of barnacles, worms, and so on, the parasites. With this general concept as a framework, relationships of dolphins to one another and to their environments are discussed more easily.

Rather than grouping the animals treated in this chapter on the basis of their taxonomic relationships, we have chosen to treat them as integral elements of the ocean environment and to classify them according to habitat preferences, working seaward from the coast. In keeping within the scope of this book, we concentrate on only eight species known to live in the Pacific north of 22 degrees north latitude and east of 180 degrees west longitude. Our references to the creatures discussed here as "porpoises" and "dolphins" are mostly arbitrary and have no particular biological meaning. The distinction between the two terms is primarily etymological and not scientific. (The argument revolves around the origins of the two words and the manner in which they have been applied to the animals.)

The familiar bottlenose dolphin (*Tursiops truncatus*) is an obvious candidate with which to begin our discussion. Its smiling countenance and playful

Dolphins are generally born tailfirst so the precocious youngster's blowhole is late emerging into the world. (United Press International)

disposition have charmed moviegoers, television audiences, and aquarium visitors. Studies of its brain and behavior have led to speculation about cetacean intelligence and the prospects of interspecies communication. Much of our general understanding of dolphin biology and behavior also comes from observations of captive bottlenose dolphins, yet there are still many gaps in our knowledge of even this familiar species.

Bottlenose dolphins are found in coastal temperate and tropical waters throughout the world. In the eastern North Pacific, they are currently distributed from at least Point Conception, California, southward. Historically, there have been records of them as far north as Monterey, California.

Most researchers agree that there are two forms of bottlenose dolphins, one inshore and one offshore, though there is little agreement about exactly how these two forms can be differentiated. According to the best current information, the two forms in the eastern Pacific apparently can be separated with certainty only on the basis of differences in skull characteristics; there is, to date, no reliable way of distinguishing between them in the field. (Differentiation of the stocks is currently under study.)

Both inshore and offshore bottlenose dolphins apparently reach lengths of from ten to thirteen feet and weights of over six hundred pounds. If they follow the patterns of their Atlantic counterparts, females in the eastern North Pacific reach sexual maturity between five and twelve years of age, and males between ten and twelve. Each second or third year during their reproductively active years, females bear a single calf, which is born after a gestation period of twelve months. A calf may nurse for a year or more; it is gradually weaned during that period by increasing the percentage of fish and squid in its diet. During early stages of development, the calf is generally closely tended by its mother, who is often helped by other adult mem-

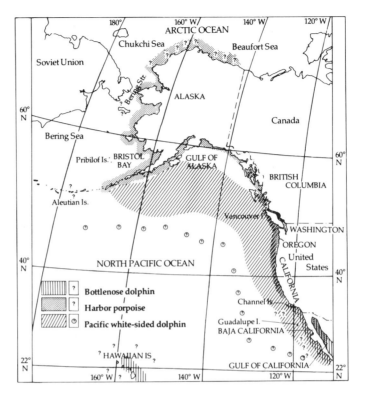

Bottlenose dolphin, harbor porpoise, and Pacific white-sided dolphin distribution. Ranges indicated on the maps in this chapter represent known and postulated limits of distribution for the species. Maps, as static entities, cannot fairly represent distribution of highly mobile animal species.

bers of the herd. Similar patterns are likely for other dolphin species.

The inshore *Tursiops* form frequents harbors, bays, lagoons, estuaries, and other shallow coastal regions from the southern border of Los Angeles County south to the tip of Baja California, and thence into the Gulf of California. It is usually encountered in groups of fifteen or fewer, which often patrol just beyond the surf line. It sometimes is seen body-surfing on the waves, dramatically rolling out seconds before the waves crash against the sand or rocks. Repeated observations of distinctively scarred or deformed individuals suggest that inshore bottlenose dolphins of the eastern Pacific, like those of the Gulf and Atlantic coasts of Florida, have limited home ranges along overlapping stretches of the coast.

This coastal *Tursiops* does not seem to mind living cheek by jowl with man; in fact, it sometimes seems to relish it. It readily approaches boats to hitch rides on bow waves or stern wakes, and it is attracted to a wide variety of fishing activities—feeding behind shrimp boats, and near drift, gill, and trammel nets. Fishermen in some areas consider it a nuisance because it competes with them for hooked or netted fish. Catholic in its tastes, the coastal dolphin takes a wide variety of fish and invertebrates, such as squid, clams, and crabs.

The apparent ease with which bottlenose dolphins adapt to the presence of man is deceptive. Heavy pollution can impair their health; accidental entanglement in gill nets can kill them; decimation of their food supply by nearshore commercial fisheries can stress "resident" groups; and concen-

trated boat traffic can injure individual animals or interrupt important activities.

The inshore form is successfully adapted to shallow, turbid, coastal waters. These areas are often noisy (adaption to noise is especially critical for animals whose acoustical sense is most important), heavily polluted, and contaminated with larger concentrations of disease-causing agents than are found in the open ocean environment. These factors combine to make this dolphin highly successful in captivity, where it may encounter similar conditions. The ease with which bottlenose dolphins become conditioned to captivity has led scientists to view them as the "white rats" of marine mammal research—the cetaceans most likely to become domesticated.

The offshore ecotype of bottlenose dolphins in

Bottlenose dolphin females reach sexual maturity between five and twelve years of age and bear a single calf each second or third year during their reproductively active years. (Stephen Leatherwood)

the eastern Pacific occurs slightly farther from the mainland—around the islands off California and Baja California at least as far north as Point Conception, and out in the open water at least to the 100 fathom curve. At least some of these animals also appear to have limited home ranges that are associated with particular islands. Herds of five hundred have been reported, although groups of twenty-five to fifty are far more common. Like bottlenose dolphins in other ocean areas, they are often observed in the company of pilot whales, an association from which one or both species may derive some advantage. The offshore bottlenose dolphin's diet consists primarily of squid, the pilot whale's preferred food. As such, the diet of the offshore ecotype appears more restrictive than that of the inshore type.

Bottlenose dolphins also associate with migrating gray whales, whose pressure waves apparently offer sensations similar to those provided by bow waves of vessels or the faces of fast-moving ground swells. It is conceivable that dolphins learned to "bow ride" long before humans ventured onto the sea, and that they ride bow waves of vessels because the sensation is similar to riding whales' wakes. Nearly all pelagic porpoises have been seen frolicking in the pressure waves of the large baleen whales—gray, humpback, blue, fin, and right—with up to four different kinds of dolphins hitching rides simultaneously. David K. Caldwell of the University of Florida Communication Sciences Laboratory has noted that frequent reports of right whales in Florida being attacked by sharks have actually proved to be mistaken accounts of bottlenose dolphins cavorting around them. Such behavior may be functional at times, facilitating a dolphin's movement from one point to another; but the inescapable impression is that surfing, bow riding, and coasting on ground swells are acts of play—sheer fun and entertainment.

Such lighthearted characterization does not

The diminutive harbor porpoise is generally regarded as being shy and fragile in the wild. This individual seems out of character with its lively behavior and acrobatics. (Courtesy of Copenhagen Zoo)

seem to apply as readily to the other nearshore porpoise of the eastern North Pacific, the harbor porpoise (*Phocoena phocoena*). North of Point Conception (approximately thirty-four degrees north latitude) and beyond the distribution of inshore bottlenose dolphins, harbor porpoises are found in some of the same habitats. Wary and discrete, the harbor porpoise rarely rewards onlookers with the kind of antics we have learned to expect from its more playful brethren. Rather than approaching vessels full of high-spirited curiosity, the harbor porpoise either goes about its inscrutable business, indifferent to the human presence, or flees quietly—almost secretively—revealing little more than an occasional glimpse of its triangular dorsal fin. In Alaska, for example, harbor porpoises are sometimes attracted to a stationary vessel with an idling engine, but they generally "run" when it tries to approach them. Even in areas where it is fairly common, the harbor porpoise is rarely observed, and when it is, the observer is often left wondering whether he in fact saw anything at all.

In spite of its shy disposition, the harbor porpoise is confined primarily to nearshore waters shallower than ten fathoms, where it must cope with an ever increasing level of human activity. Some evidence indicates that its numbers have declined markedly in San Francisco Bay and Puget Sound in Washington State. Although no one knows the reason for this, the evidence is alarming because we do know that the Baltic Sea population has almost disappeared in recent years as indices of human activity for that enclosed region (for example, intensity of fishing and pollution) have soared.

The distribution of the harbor porpoise is less well documented than that of the bottlenose dolphins. Very few harbor porpoises have been recorded south of Point Conception; strandings have been reported for Santa Barbara and Los Angeles. They are fairly common from Morro Bay, California, northward; notable concentrations occur around the coasts of the Gulf of Alaska, and they are also found along at least the eastern Aleutian chain and in the eastern Bering Sea. They have been known to wander as far north as Point Barrow, Alaska, sometimes extending as far eastward as the northwest Canadian coast in summer. In winter, they are found in Prince William Sound, Alaska, in perhaps greater concentration than anywhere else in the Pacific. The dramatic mass movements described for northeast Atlantic populations have not been observed in the eastern North Pacific, where these porpoises are seldom seen in groups of more than fifty. Nevertheless, clear seasonal shifts in abundance suggest migrations of some sort.

Although harbor porpoises were once a significant source of food for natives on the Pacific coast of North America, the animals now are not killed for food, except to a limited extent in southeastern Canada and northern Maine. Currently, the most serious direct threat to this species may be the many gill nets and fish traps that encumber much of its habitat. A worrisome level of incidental entanglement and entrapment is documented for

northwest Atlantic inshore fisheries, and the same problem exists on an unknown scale in the eastern North Pacific. Harbor porpoises have been taken in Washington waters by otter trawls, gill and tangle nets, purse seines, and salmon traps. They are frequently taken today by spring gill-netters in the Copper River delta of south central Alaska.

Rarely growing to more than six feet in length, this blunt-snouted porpoise is the smallest oceanic cetacean. Its coloration is nondescript—basically light ventrally and dark dorsally. A subtle stripe from the corner of the mouth to the flipper and a small triangular dorsal fin are the most notable external features. Little is known about the reproductive cycle of the harbor porpoise, but there is reason to think that the interval between calves for a given female is substantially more than one year. The harbor porpoise calf is reportedly longer relative to the mother's length than calves of any other cetacean species. This larger size is an important adaptation for a species living in cold water because the lower the ratio between an animal's body surface area and its volume, the less rapidly it loses heat. The harbor porpoise eats small fish and squid; in eastern North Pacific waters, it takes primarily fish of the herring family (Clupeidae).

A close relative of the harbor porpoise, known as the vaquita or cochito (*Phocoena sinus*), became known to science in the 1950s. Although it is almost identical to the harbor porpoise, its range appears to be restricted to the coastal waters of the upper Gulf of California. Virtually nothing is known about its life history because only a few specimens have been examined. The morphological differences between it and the harbor porpoise are slight, and it is probably safe to assume that many aspects of its biology are identical to those of the harbor porpoise.

Until recently, the vaquita was an unintended victim of the intensive Mexican fishery for totoaba, a large relative of the white sea bass. The gill-netters killed only a few porpoises in the last years of the fishery, which was officially closed in early 1975 because of the drastic depletion of the totoaba. The present condition of the vaquita is undetermined, but it is very likely in a vulnerable state and in need of immediate protection and study.

In general, as we leave the habitats of coastal *Tursiops* and *Phocoena* and move offshore, we begin to encounter larger herds of several species. And often, particularly seasonally, these species combine to form complex feeding aggregations in areas of high productivity. Distinctions among the species based simply on distances of their habitats from the mainland begin to break down and "habitat" differences become more difficult to ascertain.

Pacific white-sided dolphins (*Lagenorhynchus obliquidens*) sometimes come very close to shore—in Monterey Bay, Vizcaino Bay, and along the open coast of southern California—and less frequently enter Magdalena Bay and Puget Sound. In these areas, they are often seen just after dawn or just before dusk, feeding under a canopy of jawing birds. Their usual prey are anchovies, hake, and squid, although they take many other fish and red crabs (off Baja California) as well. The known range of this dolphin extends from Amchitka Island in the Aleutians throughout the Gulf of Alaska, and southward to at least the tip of Baja California. Records from the northern Gulf of Alaska are seasonal and appear to be associated with periods of more moderate water temperatures. The white-sided dolphin inhabits the coastal heads of deep canyons, and ranges seaward at least to the edge of the continental shelf.

Among the most gregarious of eastern Pacific delphinids, the white-sided dolphin occurs in herds of up to several thousand, though groups of less than two hundred are more usual. It is not uncommon to find them in the company of such other species as the common dolphin, Risso's dolphin, and the right whale dolphin. "Lags," a familiar

The Pacific white-sided dolphin, sometimes called the "hook-finned porpoise" because of its distinctive black and white dorsal fin, is among the most acrobatic of dolphins and porpoises, sometimes even accomplishing complete somersaults in the wild. (Ken Balcomb)

common name for white-sided dolphins, are found in small numbers from Monterey south to Gordo Banks, Baja California, in all seasons, but the year-round stock, including apparent "residents" around Cedros/Natividad Islands and several of California's Channel Islands, are augmented by a winter (October through February) influx of animals from the north that move southward and inshore as the water cools. In unseasonably warm years, it has been noted that populations south of Monterey remain small, suggesting that the normal shift does not always occur. By the end of May, the herds in southern California are diminished considerably as many of the animals have headed offshore to the north and west, remaining close to the 500 fathom curve.

Small numbers of lags have been successfully

maintained in aquariums; one individual survived just over ten years in captivity. The white-sided dolphin's handsome black, white, and gray markings include distinctive "gray suspenders" along the back and a two-tone dorsal fin. The female apparently calves in summer after a gestation period of unknown length. Unlike the harbor porpoise, the white-sided dolphin, which can be as long as seven feet, is an aerial acrobat and often leaps clear of the water, then splashes onto its side or back. It is the only dolphin in the eastern North Pacific that is known to accomplish a complete somersault as part of its natural, wild repertoire. Its tall, sickle-shaped dorsal fin slicing through the water can cause a splash that resembles the "rooster tail" of spray created by the lightning-fast Dall's porpoise. The froth that is worked up by a large herd of lags can be mistaken for the commotion that invariably announces the presence of a large aggregation of common dolphins.

The common dolphin (*Delphinus delphis*) is a cosmopolitan, pelagic genus. It is the common dolphin of literature and probably the most familiar small cetacean to ancient and modern mariners. Its coloration is striking and vivid—black, brownish black, gray, white, and ocher. An unmistakable, horizontal, hourglass pattern is formed on each flank, which explains other common names, hourglass dolphin and saddle-backed dolphin. Tuna fishermen refer to it also as the white-bellied porpoise. It has a long beak, like a bottlenose, though it is much slimmer and grows to be 7.5 feet long. (In the eastern North Pacific, several racially different stocks are recognized, which differ in length of beak, total size, and coloration.) Breeding is seasonal in the North Pacific with calving peaks in spring and fall. The female reaches sexual maturity between three and five years, after which she may bear a single calf every two to three years. Gestation is from ten to thirteen months.

Intensive radiotelemetry studies, primarily by

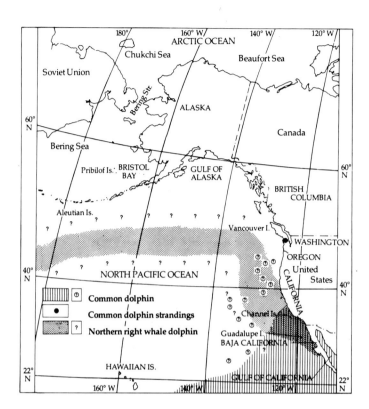

Common and northern right whale dolphin distribution

W. E. Evans of Hubbs–Sea World Research Institute in San Diego, California, have revealed more about *Delphinus* movements and behavior than is known about any other wild dolphin in the eastern North Pacific. The common dolphin is found in predictable locations—along such significant features of bottom relief as canyons, escarpments, and sea mounts, where currents are interrupted and the resultant upwelling supports a high level of productivity. It appears to be primarily a nocturnal feeder, and dives to depths greater than eight hundred feet, where it preys on organisms associated with the "deep scattering layer" (DSL). Its varied diet includes hake, anchovies, myctophids (lantern fish), and squid. The huge herds of hundreds or thousands of dolphins subdivide at night into smaller feeding groups. As dawn breaks and the DSL descends, the dolphins regroup to form large, resting herds. In the late afternoon, they scatter once again and resume feeding.

Common dolphins are probably not present in large numbers north of southern California, although they have been found stranded and dead as far north as British Columbia. As with lags, there seem to be "resident" stocks around the Channel Islands and some Baja California island groups. Huge herds are visible at a great distance as the animals leap and frolic. They will charge toward a boat from miles away and play at the bow for hours. Again like their white-sided cousins, common dolphins porpoise gracefully, leap clear to land on their backs or sides, or slap the water with their chins, as well as their tails, sometimes apparently as a signal to regroup.

One of us (Leatherwood) was aboard a research vessel off Baja California that had *Delphinus* riding its bow. After a few moments, white-sided dolphins began to filter in, displacing the common dolphins to deeper positions and eventually forcing them away altogether. Later, a group of large coastal *Tursiops* joined the party, intimidating the smaller lags into less desirable bow-riding tiers and then forcing them to leave. During a second sweep through the area by the boat, the pattern was repeated. Both *Lagenorhynchus* and *Delphinus* have been observed riding bow waves peaceably with *Lissodelphis*, a species with which both appear to associate frequently. *Tursiops* are found near feeding aggregations of the three other species, but they do not seem to intermix with them. Theories of dominance and mutual acceptance among dolphins remain imponderable and the meaning of such anecdotal accounts obscure.

The sixth species inhabiting the area covered by this book is the northern right whale dolphin (*Lissodelphis borealis*), a species limited to the North Pacific. Although its range overlaps that of the previous two species, it apparently extends into waters

farther offshore. It is most commonly seen with white-sided dolphins, and the north-south limits and movements of the two species are similar. The right whale dolphin moves north to the Washington coast (to at least lat 50° N) and offshore in summer, and south to Baja California (to lat 30° N) and inshore in winter. It is, like the white-sided dolphin, less abundant in mild winters south of Point Conception.

The right whale dolphin is the only dolphin in the eastern North Pacific that has no dorsal fin, and it is this characteristic that gives it its common name because the bulky right whale lacks the same appendage. Reaching lengths of about 10 feet (males) and 8.5 feet (females), the right whale dolphin is probably the most slender and streamlined of the small cetaceans. Its narrow tail stock and rel-

Northern right whale dolphins, easily identified by their tuxedoed appearance and finless back, often flee boats or other disturbances, working the sea surface into a froth. (Ken Balcomb)

The chunky, black and white Dall's porpoise is easy to identify. It is an active bow rider that can reach speeds of thirty miles per hour or more in bursts, often throwing off a rooster tail of spray as it surfaces to breathe. (Charles Jurasz)

atively small flukes add to its eellike appearance. It is a sleek, powerful animal—an impressive combination of raw strength and smooth grace. An all-black exterior is interrupted only by a white, hourglass pattern on the belly; the extent of this white area apparently varies between sexes. The newborn calf is cream-colored to grayish with only a muted color pattern; it apparently acquires the striking black and white "tuxedoed" look of an adult early in its first year.

Like white-sided and common dolphins, this species is often found in great herds of more than a thousand animals. Unlike the other two dolphins, however, it often shuns human contact and "runs" from boats. Two escape modes have been identified. One is subtle: The dolphin barely breaks the surface to blow. Its lack of a dorsal fin makes this

maneuver effective in all but the glassiest sea states. Otherwise, when a vessel persists in following the "sneaking" right whale dolphin, it will usually break into a series of low-angle leaps, which is a much less subtle escape behavior. A large herd will, in this manner, work the sea into a frothy turmoil. Although they do occasionally bow ride, they seem more inclined to do so when in the company of another species.

The right whale dolphin preys on squid and a variety of DSL organisms. It is suspected of being a late evening, nighttime, or early morning feeder. Beyond this, very little is known of its biology.

The seventh species is a stocky, aggressive creature called the Dall's porpoise (*Phocoenoides dalli*), named after the great American zoologist William Dall. It has a reputation for being the swiftest cetacean, reaching speeds of up to thirty knots in short bursts. Its swimming style is distinctive. When it rises aggressively to breathe, it slices along the surface, causing a "rooster tail" of spray that almost obscures the animal's strikingly marked body. (Curiously enough, recent observations in Prince William Sound and throughout the Gulf of Alaska indicate that the "rooster tail" is not characteristic of the Dall's porpoise population there.) This seven-foot porpoise—like its smaller near-relative, the harbor porpoise—seldom clears the water. Although it does ride bow waves, the Dall's porpoise is much more particular than most other species about which bow it chooses to ride. While it may approach a vessel moving at less than ten miles per hour, it is not likely to stay for long in such slow company.

The Dall's porpoise is a cold-water animal whose range extends south into southern California, and even to Ballenas Bay in Baja California, during winter and spring (October through June), and north from northern California to Alaska throughout the year. Their normal distribution appears to extend to the Pribilof Islands, and in summer they may reach as far north as Bering Strait. While groups of two to fifteen are usual in the lower half of their range, aggregations of up to two hundred have been seen in Alaska; in outer Bristol Bay and throughout the southern Bering Sea, they are abundant. Dall's porpoises are commonly found in the company of harbor porpoises in the deep fjords along the south coast of Alaska and in Prince William Sound, but they also extend far offshore, apparently continuously across the convergent currents of the North Pacific to Japan. They have been observed inside the Queen Charlotte Islands and in Puget Sound, but south of there they occur farther offshore (usually beyond the 100 fathom curve), except where deep canyons approach shore.

Little is known about the reproductive behavior of the Dall's porpoise. Two calving periods, one in

winter (February through March) and another in summer (July through August), have been reported for portions of the eastern North Pacific. However, most recent evidence suggests parturition, at least in the eastern Pacific, takes place throughout the year. Some segregation of the population in Monterey Bay seems to occur, with juveniles found close to the beach and larger adults well offshore. The species apparently depends to some degree on the DSL, and feeds at night on hake, lantern fish, and squid.

Of the species covered in this chapter, the Dall's porpoise may present the most serious conservation problem. In addition to large numbers taken intentionally for food off Hokkaido and Honshu, Japan, more than ten thousand are killed and discarded annually by the Japanese salmon fisheries, which use drift gill nets. Although most of this incidental mortality occurs in the western half of the North Pacific, some occurs in United States waters of the eastern North Pacific. The relationships among stocks of Dall's porpoises are unknown, although three separate stock units have been postulated in the western North Pacific.

The last species to be discussed fully here is included because of its common name—Risso's dolphin *(Grampus griseus)*. Risso's dolphin, also known as gray grampus, has sometimes been classed in a family of its own rather than among the Delphinidae or the Phocoenidae. Superficially it bears a closer resemblance to the pilot whale than to most of the dolphins or porpoises. In this regard, however, it is interesting that some evidence exists for interbreeding in the northeast Atlantic between the bottlenose dolphin and Risso's dolphin in the wild.

In the Western Hemisphere, the cosmopolitan grampus has hardly been studied. Because of sighting and stranding reports, it is known to occur as far north as southern British Columbia and south to Chile. It is primarily a pelagic species, occurring consistently farther offshore (beyond the 100 fathom curve), in general, than all the species treated above. Even over broad, sandy, abyssal plains, Risso's dolphins can be seen loafing at the surface, arranged in a manner reminiscent of stacked cordwood. At other times, they are scattered over a wide area and make prolonged dives into the azure depths.

For all we know, these thirteen-foot creatures are exclusively squid eaters, and their habitation of the pelagic zone probably reflects that food preference. Their sporadic inshore appearance in southern California seems to have occurred in warmwater years, when pelagic squid have been available in large quantities over the continental shelf. In 1966, when Dr. Robert Orr of the California Academy of Sciences (in San Francisco) summarized records of this species on the west coast, he knew of only several jaws collected in the nineteenth century and a specimen killed at San Mateo, California, in June 1963. Apparently he was unaware of correspondence from zoologist Charles Gilbert to F. W. True of the United States National Museum in which Gilbert claimed that around 1890, grampus were "abundant near Monterey Bay." A recent compilation of unpublished stranding and sighting records indicates that in recent decades, Risso's dolphins have extended their range north as they apparently did near the turn of the century, perhaps in response to long-term warming of the waters. They occur as far north as northern Vancouver Island (lat 50° N), with more northerly records made primarily in summer and fall. Observers have often found Risso's dolphins in the company of white-sided dolphins, right whale dolphins, and pilot whales. Both of us have seen grampus in inshore waters of southern California in recent years, primarily in late winter and early spring.

A newborn grampus has gray to gray brown coloration, but as it grows older it becomes covered with white scratches, which are usually ascribed to

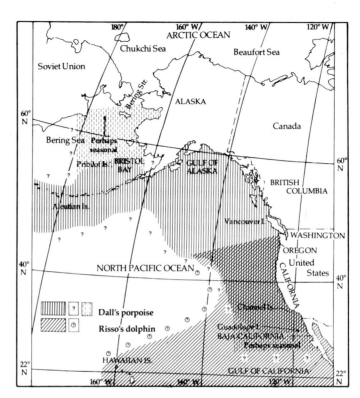

Dall's porpoise and Risso's dolphin distribution

the teeth of companions or the beaks of the squid on which the grampus preys. Old animals are almost completely white; reports of "white dolphins" usually refer to this species. The Risso's dolphin does not occur in great herds, as the common dolphin and white-sided dolphin do; groups of fifty or fewer are the rule.

While frolicsome at times, Risso's dolphins do not generally ride bow waves, at least not in the eastern North Pacific. In some places, however, they apparently do. For instance, around the turn of the century, the legendary Pelorus Jack, a Risso's dolphin, greeted boats entering Admiralty Bay in New Zealand for twenty-four years by racing to their bows and leading them into the harbor.

Although these eight species are the only dolphins common to eastern North Pacific waters

above twenty-two degrees north latitude, a variety of others have been seen alive or reported stranded north of that arbitrary boundary. It is important to remember that boundaries between ocean areas, even those with major differences, are not static. Over periods of many years, cetacean species appear to show a healthy disrespect for our simplistic zoogeographic classifications of them and will often show up outside the "limits" of the zones to which we imagine them confined. To further complicate an understanding of natural distribution, cetaceans often strand on the world's beaches for a variety of still incompletely understood reasons. Reports of strandings or the discovery of a skull on a beach do not necessarily say very much about the normal distribution or abundance of a species. Individuals that are sick, senile, or disoriented often wander outside

the normal limits of their range; also, carcasses can drift for many miles before they are found and reported. Finally, species for which a few incidental records are available in areas intensively studied (mostly near shore and near population centers) may be abundant in less frequently visited areas. Because of these difficulties, we mention at least four other dolphin species that occasionally appear off the west coast of North America.

A few striped dolphins (*Stenella coeruleoalba*) have been found stranded in British Columbia, Washington, Oregon, and southern California; live striped dolphins have been seen off southern California and 1,000 miles due west of Los Angeles. But because the species is seldom seen alive north of southern Baja California (above lat 22° N), these records either represent extralimital straying or

Risso's dolphins are perhaps the most pelagic of the "dolphins" in the eastern North Pacific. Deep divers that feed on squid, they generally inhabit broad expanses of open water apparently unacceptable to most porpoise species. (Larry Hobbs)

suggest an offshore distribution. The handsome striped dolphin is similar in appearance to the common dolphin, but can be distinguished by its greater size (it is up to nine feet long) and striking, black slash marks (one from the eye to the flipper, one from the eye to the anus, and one from the dorsal fin forward onto the side). The species increases in abundance from the tip of Baja California southward, especially in offshore waters.

The spotted dolphin (*S. attenuata*) and the spinner dolphin (*S. longirostris*) are tropical species that comprise the bulk of the incidental catch in the yellowfin tuna purse seine fishery. Both species occasionally venture into the Gulf of California (at least to lat 25° N). On the Pacific coast, spotters and spinners occur infrequently as far north as northern Baja California (lat 30° N) and southern Baja California (lat 25° N) respectively, primarily off the continental shelf, but areas of consistent concentrations lie south of Baja California (lat 22° N).

A weathered skull of a rough-toothed dolphin (*Steno bredanensis*) found on the beach in Marin County, California, in 1946, and a live stranding of three rough-toothed dolphins at the same location in 1975 were probably extralimital strays, because the remaining four records of the species in the eastern Pacific are from off the Central American coast (south of lat 15° N).

Superficially, porpoises appear to have a low-stress existence. Their only known natural predators are killer whales and large sharks. In the eastern North Pacific, evidence suggests that killer whales rely much more heavily on large fish for food than on marine mammals and that only adult males seem consistently inclined to attack fellow cetaceans. Curiously, Pacific white-sided dolphins and Dall's porpoises have been seen riding the pressure waves of traveling pods of killer whales, sometimes for long periods, after which they swim away unmolested. The relationship, then, between the supreme predator of the sea and its vulnerable,

smaller cousins is not automatically antagonistic.

As for sharks, it is certainly true that individual porpoises of many species have been found to have recent or long-healed scars from shark attacks, and it is not uncommon to find porpoise remains in shark stomachs. However, it is also true that sharks and porpoises live peaceably together some of the time. For instance, when squid are spawning around the Channel Islands off southern California, cetaceans and sharks are there together, sharing this abundant resource. Coastal bottlenose dolphins also are occasionally seen feeding, undisturbed, among sharks. Sharks are almost always present beneath large, moving herds of pelagic porpoises, and it seems reasonable to conclude that they move together as part of a community in which sharks prune the unhealthy or unwary porpoises from the populations, but otherwise share with the dolphins the other available resources.

In addition to predation, porpoises can be subjected to heavy parasite burdens, both externally (mainly barnacles) and internally (especially in the viscera and ear canals). Some of the parasites are

The handsome striped dolphin occurs only incidentally in the portions of the eastern North Pacific covered by this book. It resembles the common dolphin but is larger and has striking, black stripes on its back and sides, a feature that prompts the common name. (Courtesy of Stephen Leatherwood)

apparently nuisances and little more; others occasionally can become lethal. Porpoises also have their share of diseases—pneumonia, massive liver damage, congenital deformities, and viral infections.

Some "natural" forms of stress experienced by porpoises are tolerable. Man's activities threaten to undermine the balance that has been struck among marine organisms and also threaten to reduce dramatically the number and variety of creatures living in the sea. The inadvertent, yet systematic, yearly destruction of many tens of thousands of porpoises by tuna seiners and gill-netters does untold damage to stocks, the vital parameters of which (for example, abundance, productivity, genetic boundaries, and tolerance of harassment) are poorly understood. Direct removals by coastal fishermen, for food or to reduce competition in widespread areas, cannot be benefitting marine mammals. Finally, the most insidious threat may be our contamination of the environment, whereby we either poison life at a lower level in the porpoise's food chain or directly alter the porpoise's own re-

productive potential.

Any landlubber who has been to sea must appreciate the value of company in the lonely expanses of blue and green; an ocean world without dolphins and porpoises would be lonely indeed. Nothing lifts the spirits, nothing entertains, nothing *responds* like a tribe of bow-riding porpoises. They seek us out, neither from need (for what interest does a porpoise have in a scrap of fish tossed from some poor human's boat deck?) nor from mere curiosity (for a boat hull is a boat hull is . . .), but from a sense of pure fun. Herman Melville said that if you cannot appreciate the antics of a school of wild porpoises, then "the spirit of godly gamesomeness is not in ye."

Dolphins and porpoises are integral parts of marine communities and are a visible sign of the health and vitality of the oceans. With care and concern, we can prevent the greed and shortsightedness of some of us from creating a barren world in which these marvelous animals have no place.

The rough-toothed dolphin is sometimes seen in the North Pacific, usually around the Hawaiian Islands. Its most distinguishing feature is its long and slender snout, often white along both sides. (Ken Balcomb)

Pilot Whale

by Stephen B. Reilly

The pilot whale (*Globicephala macrorhynchus*)—with a variety of common names, an unsettled taxonomic status, and many gaps of information in its life history—is a creature of confused identity. (The confusion is ours, of course.) Some of its characteristics, however, are undisputed: it is among the most affable and intelligent of the cetaceans. In captivity, it has proved itself at least as intelligent as the well-known bottlenose dolphin. In the wild, the gregarious pilot whale is usually found in groups whose social structure seems to be highly organized.

Pilot whales are known by many names, including "potheads," which refers to their bulbous, blunt heads, and "blackfish," which reflects their dark appearance. In the eastern Atlantic, they associate with schools of herring, and, because fishermen there came to believe that the whales were "calling" them to fish, the whales became known as "caa'ing" whales. The name "pilot whale" is said to have a similar origin—a popular belief that the whales would "pilot" fishermen to their catch. Another theory relates to the social structure of these animals: a leader, or "pilot," is often at the head of their pods.

Pilot whales are, in effect, large dolphins. Although most scientists place them in the same family with the dolphins and porpoises (Delphinidae), a few consider them to be in a separate family (Globicephalidae). Taxonomists do not agree about correct classification of groups or about distinctions among the various pilot whale forms. Nevertheless, wherever they are found, pilot whales are similar. As a result of this basic similarity, some types of information obtained about pilot whales in one area may serve as a good indication for all.

Generally, pilot whales are found in the world's tropical and temperate ocean waters. They are more abundant where schooling squid, their preferred food, are found. In turn, pilot whales themselves are the prey of sharks, killer whales, and humans.

Potheads are black on the dorsal surface, except for a grayish, saddle-shaped area found in some forms behind the dorsal fin, and in some forms a slight blaze of varying intensity extending from the

A captive pilot whale displays the bulbous head from which its common name "pothead" is derived. (Courtesy of U.S. Naval Ocean Systems Center)

blowhole to the eye. In the water, the pilot whale is easily distinguished by a blunt, bulbous head and a long-based, recurved dorsal fin, which—in comparison with other cetaceans—is set far forward on the body. The ventral surface is usually marked by an anchor-shaped white patch under the chin, and a grayish area of varying extent and intensity on the belly. These features vary among regional forms and even within different pods in the same areas.

The long sickle shape of the pectoral fins is another distinguishing feature, more easily seen on beached or captive animals. The tail stock is laterally compressed and quite deep vertically. When the animal begins a long dive, this thickened tail stock is often exposed in a humplike roll followed by the dark flukes. Although the subadult male and female are usually indistinguishable on the basis of body shape, the adult male can be identified by the larger, more bulbous melon that protrudes noticeably over its upper jaw, the deeper keel of its tail stock, and its longer pectoral fins. The dorsal fin of the male of the North Pacific form appears to be longer and broader on the forward margin than that of the female and young. The male pilot whale in the North Pacific may grow to twenty-two feet in length, while the female is slightly smaller, reaching about eighteen feet. It is not until puberty that the male begins to grow faster and take on a mildly different form.

In the eastern North Pacific, the pilot whale can be confused with the false killer whale, which is also black, reaches comparable lengths, and is also sometimes called the "blackfish." However, the body of the false killer whale is considerably less robust, its head is smaller and gently tapering, and its dorsal fin is taller, more narrowly based, and set farther back on the body. False killer whales may sometimes ride the bow waves of boats—a skill that pilot whales are not known to practice.

Along the Pacific coast of North America, pilot whales are most abundant south of Point Concep-

tion (just northwest of Santa Barbara, California). From there north to the Gulf of Alaska, they are only rarely sighted; these infrequent movements north of Point Conception may be related to seasonal influxes of warmer temperate waters. Relationships of distribution, migration, and various oceanographic conditions are currently under study.

In the Atlantic, there are two well-defined species of pilot whales, distinguished by differences in distribution, skeletal and external morphology, and coloration. *Globicephala melaena* is called the long-finned pilot whale because its pectoral flippers reach at least one fifth of its body length in adulthood. The other Atlantic species, *G. macrorhynchus*, is called the short-finned pilot whale because the pectoral fins of adult animals are up to one sixth of the total body length. Some overlap does occur in these characteristics.

Unfortunately, our knowledge of pilot whales in the Pacific is less complete. There are at least two, possibly three, distinct forms present. One type, *G. melaena*, the long-finned variety, ranges north from the Antarctic convergence along the west coast of South America to Peru, in the cold Humboldt Current. Subfossil material discovered in Japan indicates that *G. melaena* was present in the North Pacific as recently as the tenth century.

Some controversy currently surrounds the eastern North Pacific form. *G. macrorhynchus*, the short-finned pilot whale, is variously described as being tropical (as this species is also in the Atlantic and Indian oceans) and as occurring from about Guatemala north to the Gulf of Alaska. Some investigators consider the eastern North Pacific form to be the same species as the pilot whale of the tropical Pacific (*G. macrorhynchus*), while a few regard it as a separate species entirely, most often called *G. scammonii*. The basis of this problem is as old as the study of biology: Just exactly what defines a species? Unfortunately, not all biologists accept the same set of criteria. The identity of the North

A captive pilot whale is accompanied here by a false killer whale (in the background). Although these species are sometimes confused with each other, close scrutiny shows that the pilot whale is larger, with a more bulbous head and a dorsal fin more widely based and set farther forward. (Courtesy of U.S. Naval Ocean Systems Center)

Pacific pilot whales is a case in point.

In 1971 the Dutch cetologist P. J. H. van Bree compared skull measurements of a number of proposed species of pilot whales, and, finding no significant differences, concluded that all tropical and temperate North Pacific pilot whales are of the same species: *G. macrorhynchus*. While acknowledging the similarity of skull characteristics, other scientists point out the larger overall size of the North Pacific form, its temperate distribution, larger melon, and flipper length intermediate between that defined for the short-finned and long-finned species. Because of these apparent differences, some biologists continue to recognize *G. scammonii* as a separate species. The problem is compounded by the fact that both of these "types," *G. macrorhynchus* and *G. scammonii*, seem to occur together along Baja California and off southern California, as well as near Japan. Without detailed studies of considerably more specimens, the controversy will probably not be resolved.

Squid is the pilot whales' major food item, although when squid are not available, some fish are consumed. In southern California, the seasonal distribution and abundance of pilot whales coincides strikingly with the occurrence of spawning squid.

A current theory holds that, in the toothed whales that consume primarily squid, there is an evolutionary trend toward reduction in size and number of teeth. While the predominantly fish-eating spotted dolphin has a total of 150 to 160 teeth, and the white-sided dolphin has 100 to 110, the squid-eating pilot whale has 40 to 48. Other squid eaters, such as the grampus and the beaked whales, have 4 to 12 and 0 to 4 respectively. This theory argues further that teeth are not necessary to capture densely schooling squid; teeth may even interfere with the process of engulfing large numbers of the prey.

Like other cetaceans, pilot whales generally swallow their food whole, without chewing it, and

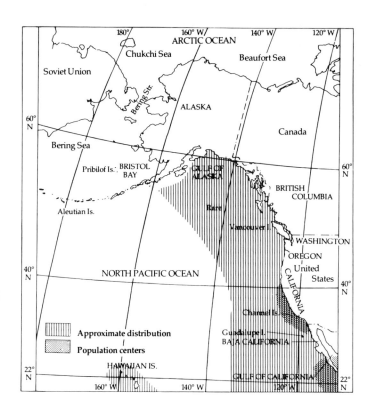

Pilot whale distribution

probably ingest using strong suction. Their small, conical, uniform teeth are designed only for grasping. The multichambered stomach, with a large chamber for storing vast quantities, is well adapted for periods of "gourmandizing."

In captivity, pilot whales consume four to five percent of their body weight per day, or up to thirty pounds for an average-size adult. From observations of stomach dimensions and digestion rates, a similar feeding rate has been calculated for wild stocks off Newfoundland.

The life history of the Pacific pilot whale is largely unknown. Fortunately, the closely related long-finned pilot whale of Newfoundland waters has been studied in detail by cetologist D. E. Sergeant of the Canadian Department of Fisheries and Environment. He found that most births take place during a six-month period, with a peak in August. Although females are probably able to conceive during any season, males showed peak sexual activity from April to September. Gestation lasts fifteen to sixteen months, and the young are suckled for up to twenty-two months. The entire cycle lasts an average of three years and four months.

Usually only one calf is born at a time, with slightly more males than females produced. By the late juvenile stage, the sex ratio is almost equal, while later as adults, fewer males than females are in the population. At birth, pilot whales measure just under six feet. Females become mature when about twelve feet long and six to seven years of age. Males are sexually mature when about fifteen to sixteen feet long, and around twelve years of age. Females were found to bear up to nine calves in their estimated forty-year lifetime. Males were estimated to live up to fifty years.

In the summer herds investigated at Newfoundland, over twice as many adult females as males were present, indicating either a higher mortality rate for males or sexual segregation on a geographic basis. This, along with observations of pilot whale pods at sea, is suggestive of the existence of polygyny in their social structure. One or a few males control a harem, at least for part of the year. Limited observations suggest that adult males separate from females and juveniles in winter months.

Adult male pilot whales are often heavily scarred, presumably from battles with one another. During these bouts, the whales bite, butt with their melons, and slap with their flukes. A dominance hierarchy may perhaps be attributed to them. In fact, there are indications of a complex, organized social structure among pilot whales.

In the eastern Pacific, three types of herds have been identified: traveling/hunting groups, feeding groups, and resting or "loafing" groups. The traveling/hunting groups seem to be the most organized. Their precise movements and cohesive structure indicate not only leadership and tight organization but also rapid communication. Such pods are not composed of evenly spaced individuals throughout but instead consist of a number of smaller subgroups. In southern California waters, these subgroups may represent age and sex groupings—adult males together, females and young together, and occasionally only juveniles together. In other areas, haremlike subgroups have been seen, composed of a few adult males and many adult females and juveniles.

In contrast to the highly organized traveling/hunting pods, the feeding groups are loosely structured, with members seemingly more concerned with capturing prey than associating with their fellow whales.

"Loafing" groups, usually of twelve to thirty or more, spend time floating almost without motion at the surface, close to or actually touching adjacent whales. Some mating activity has been seen in these pods, and nursing is most frequent at this time. Adult males slowly patrol the perimeter of these groups.

Generally, pilot whale pods are composed of anywhere from a few to as many as three hundred or more individuals. In southern California's temperate waters, the average winter pod is somewhat larger than the average summer pod. There are also indications that pilot whales are relatively more abundant inshore in winter months. Both the larger group size and greater overall numbers likely reflect responses to the abundance of spawning squid. When the squid abundance declines in summer, some whales depart, probably for deeper waters, while others remain. A few, identifiable by scars and unusual coloration, have been seen around California's Channel Islands throughout the year.

Strong bonds between individuals are well documented for both wild and captive pilot whales. Both scientific and popular literature include accounts of harpooned or netted pilot whales being attended by other whales that "stand by" or actually attempt to help the injured victim. In one case, a Marineland of the Pacific collecting vessel netted a young adult female, which struggled on a line for over five hours before being contained in a large rubber raft. Not only five or six other pilot whales but also several Pacific white-sided dolphins (a species often seen with eastern Pacific pilot whales) remained near the netted animal during the capture. The pilot whales swam just ahead of the tethered female, sounding in unison with her.

Both the long nursing period (nearly two years) and naturalists' accounts of females supporting injured or even dead calves demonstrate the intensity of the mother-young bond.

Due to its relatively large size, tight organization, and sensitive sonar, a pod of pilot whales is an efficient hunting unit. Bottlenose dolphins, white-sided dolphins, common dolphins, and sometimes other cetaceans regularly associate themselves with Pacific pilot whales, perhaps—at least in the temperate waters of the Pacific—in order to take advantage of this foraging efficiency.

Possibly the most perplexing behavior pattern of pilot whales and several other species is their tendency toward mass strandings, in which most whales usually die. Recent mass pilot whale strandings along the Pacific coast have occurred at Mazatlan and La Paz, Mexico, and on San Clemente Island off the coast of southern California, where twenty-eight animals swam ashore. So far, none of the many theories proposed to explain mass strandings has gained general acceptance. The popular concept of suicide seems unlikely, given our present knowledge about these and other cetaceans. The most prevalent theories among cetologists include the following. First, a combination of bottom or environmental conditions render the animals' sonar ineffective. This may be at least part of the explanation, as mass strandings occur in similar habitats, such as gently sloping beaches with sandy or muddy bottoms. Second, heavy parasite infestations in the heads of the whales render the sonar ineffective. Third, the pod leader for some reason loses his sonar (from parasites?) or for any other reason swims onto a beach. The strong social bond disposes the rest of the pod to follow. Fourth, the whales are fleeing from killer whales or other danger. This last theory is less frequently considered.

Like all cetaceans, pilot whales have efficient sonar on which they rely heavily for both navigation and prey location. Captive pilot whales have demonstrated that they can retrieve objects and swim efficiently about in a tank with their eyes covered. Vision in these animals also appears to be very good, although no experimental evidence is available on this point.

Pilot whales communicate by a variety of dolphinlike vocalizations. Some researchers have concluded that these vocalizations are limited to a few signals, such as a signature whistle and a sound for danger. Others argue that these sounds may constitute an actual language. If there is a complex language, it is currently beyond our capacity to recognize and understand it.

Pilot whale skin is quite sensitive and easily abraded. Sensitivity to physical contact may be important for communication. This is true not only for mothers and young, and for pod companions in a loafing group, but also as part of the ritual behavior of a mating pair. Mating behavior can take on a seemingly brutal nature, involving forceful head butting, fluke slapping, and biting—much the same as fighting among adult males.

In captivity, pilot whales often respond favorably to touch, seeming to enjoy a brisk rubbing with a scrub brush. They are easily trained and seem to survive better than most cetaceans in captive surroundings. Like their relatives, they are not easily dominated and respond much better to positive rather than negative reinforcement.

Aside from the antics required for oceanarium performances, pilot whales have been trained for relatively complex maneuvers for a few research projects. In the United States Navy's "Project Deep Ops," a pilot whale was trained to work untethered in the open sea. There he learned to locate objects at depths of up to 1,650 feet by means of beepers placed on them. The animal carried a recovery device in his mouth and attached it to the located object, which was then raised by means of a gas generator and a lifting bag. Pilot whales trained in this manner possibly could be used to help recover expensive oceanographic instruments or to carry out similar work.

The earliest record of a pilot whale fishery dates from the sixteenth century at the Faroe Islands, where a small, fairly stable yearly catch of around fifteen hundred whales continues to this day. The whales are captured by a "drive fishery" method whereby entire herds are driven ashore by villagers in rowboats and skiffs. Probably the largest drive fishery for these whales took place in Newfoundland between the mid-1940s and the mid-1960s, with catches approaching ten thousand whales during peak years.

Aside from an undetermined number of harpoon catches by sperm whalers in the nineteenth and early twentieth centuries, there is no history of direct exploitation in the eastern Pacific. Some live captures have been made in this area for oceanariums and research facilities.

Coastal waters of the Orient and South America will likely be significant pilot whaling areas for the future. In these areas of rapid human population expansion, it seems unlikely that the small coastal-dwelling cetaceans will be overlooked as the demand for protein continues. At present, only rudimentary information is available about the pilot whale stocks near Japan; even less is known of those off South America. In order to avoid the overexploitation of some of these stocks, it is imperative that the population biology of pilot whales in these areas be studied. Perhaps, with the current upsurge in research on this and other marine mammals, we will gain better understanding of the numbers, lives, and ways of the pilot whale in the not too distant future.

Killer Whale

by Victor B. Scheffer

The killer whale—boldly marked in black and white, often seen in waters frequented by man, and now recruited as the star performer in oceanariums—is one of the most familiar marine mammals. It is also one of the most controversial. Mention the words "killer whale" and you are in for an argument. "Vicious—bloodthirsty—eats its own weight in fish every day"; or from the other side, "intelligent—unique—harmless—an asset to humankind."

The killer whale (*Orcinus orca*) cruises throughout North Pacific waters in all months of the year. It ranges, in fact, through all seas of the world to the very limits of polar fast ice. No one knows its total numbers.

The male killer whale attains a known length of thirty-two feet and an estimated weight of nine or ten tons, the female a known length of twenty-eight feet and an estimated weight of five or six tons. The large triangular dorsal fin of the male attains a height of 5.6 feet, and that of the female about 3 feet.

The killer whale's flipper or "hand" is broad and rounded, like a large table-tennis paddle. In the male, it may reach a length of 6.7 feet and a width of 4 feet, while the width of the tail flukes, tip to tip, may reach 9 feet.

Little is known of the breeding habits of the killer whale. From evidence of fetal development in females taken by Japanese and Soviet whalers, mating may occur throughout the year. A chance aerial photo by S. Takashima on 22 June 1957 showed two whales in copulation near the surface of the sea, belly-to-belly. It is also known that the penis is completely retractile and, on a 22-foot male, measured 3.5 feet in length.

Nothing is known of the gestation period, though by comparison with another delphinid of a similar size—the pilot whale—it may last from thirteen to sixteen months. The killer whale calf is about eight feet long at birth and weighs an estimated four hundred pounds. (The Japanese have recorded a nine-foot fetus and a nine-foot newborn calf.) It nurses from its mother's two mammary teats, which are hidden in slits far back of the navel on her streamlined body.

This adult female killer whale has been dubbed "L-7" by scientists who have identified her since 1972 from her distinctive dorsal fin. She is a member of L pod, a group of fifty killer whales that spends time along the west coast of Vancouver Island and sometimes visits the inside waters of British Columbia and Washington State. (Michael Bigg)

The killer whale is highly social, habitually traveling in packs of from two to forty individuals. Family "togetherness" is a way of life, although females and young may stay slightly apart from the bachelors and bulls. In Washington State's Puget Sound, the social instinct of the killer once was exploited for capturing purposes. A hunter would fire a sixteen-inch harpoon into the back of the largest male, presumably the group leader or "pod bull." By following the brightly colored float that trailed from the harpoon, the hunter could follow the group for days or weeks. Fortunately, the humane methods clause of the United States Marine Mammal Protection Act of 1972 has put a stop to that kind of cruelty.

Killer whales will attempt to help one another when the need arises. David K. and Melba C. Caldwell of the University of Florida Communication Sciences Laboratory have summarized care-giving behavior in these animals. They describe a mortally wounded mother that stood by her dead calf and circled the body for an hour until she herself died; she never attacked the collector's boat. Another female lingered three days near Hat Island in Puget Sound after her calf was killed.

In a further instance (near Bellingham, Washington), a crew from Marineland of the Pacific (at Palos Verdes, California) reported that a lasso caught in the ship's propeller during the capture of a large female. "As she struggled in the water, she emitted a high-pitched, penetrating vocalization. After 20 minutes the high dorsal fin of a male killer whale appeared and the animal zeroed in on the female as if by radar . . . The two animals together charged toward the boat at high speed, veering only when they had approached to within five to eight feet . . . then together charged the boat again. This time they struck the boat." The crew killed both whales to save the boat.

The captain of a British Columbia ferry has told a remarkable story about care-giving, which oc-

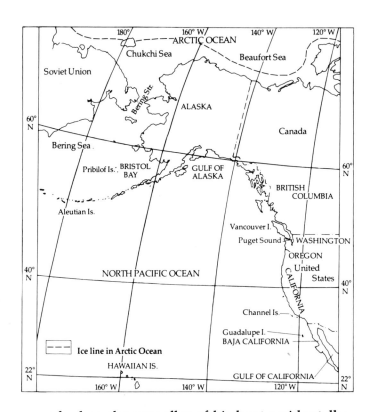

The killer whale is found in all oceans, particularly in cooler regions and coastal waters. It does not go north of the ice line in the Arctic Ocean.

curred when the propeller of his boat accidentally slashed a young killer whale. The captain turned about and saw a male and female supporting a bleeding calf. *Fifteen days later*, two whales supporting a third one—presumably the same group— were seen at the same place.

There is fragmentary information about the diving ability of the killer whale. One individual was found tangled in a submarine cable off Vancouver Island, British Columbia, at a depth of 3,378 feet! Another, chased by hunters in Puget Sound and burdened with a harpoon, line, and floats, remained underwater for twenty-one minutes.

Like all cetaceans, the killer whale is ultrasensitive to sound, which is its main source of information about the liquid world in which it lives. Ian MacAskie, a British Columbia biologist, writes that he was on one of three small patrol vessels in British Columbia, drifting quietly. When the vessels simultaneously started their engines, five killer whales popped to the surface—heads up, close ranked, poised for a second like dancers in a ballet.

The Royal Canadian Navy first recorded killer whale sounds underwater at the Queen Charlotte Islands in British Columbia in 1956. William E. Schevill and William A. Watkins of Woods Hole Oceanographic Institution in Massachusetts studied the voice of the first captive killer whale, Moby Doll, and reported that all the sounds were clicks. When rapidly repeated, the clicks resembled a scream. These strident screams are evidently used for communication and the separate clicks are used for echolocation. Biologists have used recorded killer whale screams to drive away beluga whales and fur seals from schools of valuable fish.

Some zoologists believe that echolocation failure may cause killer whales to run aground in shallow water. Among the many stranding records is the mass death of twenty killers on a New Zealand beach in 1955. Although onlookers tried to save some animals by heading them out to sea, the animals turned back and died with their companions.

The question is often asked, "Will killer whales attack people or boats?" I have never heard of a killer whale in captivity making a feeding attack on a pool companion, be it person or dolphin. This is not to say that a killer provoked by its trainer will not butt him or gently nip him. There are, however, some actual records—though they are extremely rare and unsatisfactory—of killer whale "attacks." In 1972, an eighteen-year-old surfer was attacked near Monterey, California, by an animal with a "glossy black head," which he later identified from pictures of various marine animals as a killer whale. About one hundred stitches were required to close three cuts on the young man's leg. "When the beast grabbed me," he reported, "I hit it on the head with my fist but got separated from the [surf] board. I thought for sure it would come after me again, but I was able to catch a wave and body surf to the beach." I wonder though: In his panic, could he have been sure of the animal's identity? Might it have been a shark?

The story of H. G. Ponting, photographer for the Scott party to the South Pole in 1911, has often been told. He was standing on Ross Sea ice and training his camera on a group of killer whales. "I had got to within six feet of the edge of the ice— which was about a yard thick—when, to my consternation, it suddenly heaved up under my feet and split into fragments around me; whilst the eight whales, lined up side by side and almost touching each other burst from under the ice and 'spouted.'" Did the killers take him for a seal, to be thrown into the sea where they could grab him?

The racing yacht *Guia III* was rammed and sunk by a whale, supposedly a killer, off the Cape Verde Islands, Portugal, in 1976. Four or five other whales circled the vessel as it sank. The attack took place at midnight, however, and the animals' identity must remain doubtful.

The most plausible attack is that recorded by Dougal Robertson in his book *Survive the Savage Sea*. In 1972, his forty-three-foot schooner, *Lucette*, was rammed and sunk in about a minute by one or more killer whales in a group of twenty. The passengers drifted toward the Galápagos Islands in survival crafts for thirty-seven days before they were saved. Although the sinking of the *Lucette* was exciting, it was of little biological value. Assuming that the attackers were killer whales (they were not seen by Robertson himself), the pod bull may have seen the vessel as a rival, or the vessel may have sailed between a mother and her calf. Or . . . ? We shall never know.

The name "killer" originated from the fact that this whale takes warm-blooded prey. Its enthusiasm for satisfying its appetite comes from a survival instinct similar to that of a hungry wolf in a flock of sheep—often miscalled the "joy of killing."

Of the few marine mammals that eat warm-blooded prey, the killer whale is the largest and swiftest, having a top speed of about thirty land miles per hour. John H. Prescott, former curator of Marineland of the Pacific, once saw a male killer leap clear of the water—holding an adult sea lion crosswise in his jaws!

Killer whale teeth are stout, deeply rooted, and conical, numbering about forty-six to fifty. Evidently they take quite a beating because in old whales they are often worn down to the gums, or even to a depth where the pulp cavity is exposed to infection. Growth layers in the roots of the teeth indicate that some individuals live to an age of at least twenty-five years.

How often the killer whale feeds is uncertain. In the Vancouver Public Aquarium in British Columbia, Moby Doll (actually a male) fasted fifty-four days before he took food; then he ate one hundred to two hundred pounds of fish daily, or four to eight percent of his body weight, until he died a month later. In captivity, he was offered a choice of food and took, in order of preference: salmon, lingcod, Pacific cod, certain rockfishes, ratfish (after the spines had been removed), and other fish.

Japanese whaling captains, between 1948 and 1957, recorded the food contents of 364 killer whale stomachs. The remains were, in order of occurrence: fishes (cod, flatfishes, sardines, salmons, tuna, and others); squids and octopuses; striped dolphins and porpoises (Dall's and finless); whales (beaked, sei, and pilot); and seals (harbor and ringed). Salmons were found in 1.6 percent of the stomachs. Soviet biologist E. I. Ivanova found "fish and squid," but no sea mammals, in ten stomachs of killer whales from the Kuril Islands. On the other hand, in 1968, United States National Marine Fisheries Service biologist Dale W. Rice reported mostly marine mammals were taken from the stomachs of ten killer whales in the eastern North Pacific.

Fish and squid are not, however, the food items that fill our literature with accounts of "savage" attacks. These stories deal with prey such as seabirds, seals, sea otters, porpoises, and whales. Killer whales undoubtedly attack their marine associates efficiently. The evidence comes from stomach examinations, eyewitness stories, and observations of parallel scars (spaced like killer whale teeth) on the backs of seals and whales.

The bloodiest stories are probably untrue or distorted. D. F. Eschricht, a Danish zoologist of the nineteenth century, found remains of thirteen harbor porpoises and fourteen harbor seals in one killer whale stomach! However, when we turn to the original 1862 account, we find that the remains were fragments of skin and bones representing animals eaten over an unknown period of time. Charles Bryant—a government agent in the Pribilof Islands, Alaska, in the 1870s—is supposed to have pulled eighteen and twenty-four fur seal pups from the stomachs of two killers, though that story actually originated among the harp seal fishermen of the North Atlantic and was probably embellished in the retelling.

We are just beginning to realize the value of the killer whale to education and research. About fifteen are now held in public aquariums in North America. After Kent Burgess at Sea World (in San Diego, California) had directed the training of Shamu, a female killer whale held there for seventeen months, he concluded that her species was no harder to care for than the smaller cetaceans he had often handled:

Within two months from the first training session, Shamu was performing before the public in a regular schedule of shows. The show was in the form of a skit about a whale and a doctor. Shamu went to the feeding platform for a 'physical examination,' during which she was required to show her reflexes by tail slapping. She then rolled over for her heartbeat to be checked. After this, she opened her mouth for an oral examination and had her teeth brushed; she then rinsed her mouth . . . After five months of training, the trainer was placing his head in Shamu's open mouth during the oral examination.

The killer is the largest whale to be held in captivity for any length of time. (However, baby gray whales have been held twice in California and small minke whales twice in Japan.) Being large and easy to handle, the killer has attracted physiologists who are intent on studying the blood circulation and blood chemistry, respiration, and sensory adaptations of a mammal that occupies a unique position on the "shrew-to-elephant curves" of animal science.

I once watched the operation known as "the letting down of Skana" at the Vancouver Public Aquarium in British Columbia. Periodically her pool is drained and she is examined by veterinarians, not only for her own good but for the benefit of other captive cetaceans. What is learned about her ailments and their successful treatment is helpful to other aquarium keepers.

Chimo, an all-white female killer whale captured alive near Vancouver Island in 1970 and held for nearly three years at Sealand of the Pacific (in Victoria, British Columbia), contributed to medical knowledge about a rare genetic condition known as the Chediak-Higashi syndrome. Found also in humans, mink, and mice, its victims are sensitive to bright light and are subject to recurrent infections as a result of blood-cell dysfunction. Veterinarians who studied Chimo gained understanding of her blood chemistry, which differed from that of nonalbinos. Because the C-H syndrome is inherited as a recessive trait, they also deduced that killer whales probably live in the same pods through several overlapping generations. This was later shown to be true by field studies conducted in Washington State and British Columbia.

The first killer whale captures—of Moby Doll in 1964 for the Vancouver Public Aquarium and Namu in 1965 for a privately owned Seattle aquarium—aroused great public enthusiasm for these intelligent sea mammals. However, as more killer whales were taken over the years, many people began to question the methods and ethics of killer whale hunting. During the 1970s, Americans and Canadians began to ask how marine mammals should be "used" for the benefit of humankind. Increasingly, citizens of British Columbia and Washington State—in whose waters these animals were caught—complained that local killer whale hunters were insensitive to public taste. For example, the bodies of four baby whales, trussed and weighted like Chicago gangsters, washed ashore in Penn Cove on Washington State's Whidbey Island in November 1970, at the scene of a previous hunt. Public reaction was predictably strong; it would have been weaker had the hunter not tried to conceal the accidental (not criminal) circumstances.

The ethics of killer whale hunting became a nationwide topic of discussion after a hunter cap-

Chimo, a rare albino killer whale, leaps for viewers at Sealand of the Pacific in Victoria, British Columbia. Her body shows the faint outlines of killer whale markings and the many scratches not usually visible against the black background of a normal killer whale. Although Chimo was impaired by faulty echolocation and a fatal genetic condition, she not only performed actively but also provided valuable data for medical science. (Delphine Haley)

tured six whales near Olympia, Washington, on the evening of 7 March 1976. He used two motorboats, a spotter airplane, and small explosive depth charges to frighten the animals into a net. In an atmosphere of strong public feeling, the State of Washington brought suit against the hunter and the aquarium corporation for which he was acting. Soon the federal government was drawn into the action. By then, three of the captives had escaped and one had been released because it was too large to keep. The corporation abruptly released the remaining two and agreed never again to hunt whales in Puget Sound.

Before they were released, the remaining two killer whales—an eighteen-foot male and a twenty-foot female—were radio-tagged by a University of Washington research team. On 27 April, the whales swam through the open doors of their pen and began to meander generally northward at the rate of about seventy-five miles per day. A tracking boat lost radio contact with them after nine days, though they were later seen in Pender Harbor and Jervis Inlet, both north of Vancouver, British Columbia.

In the early 1970s, while concern in the Pacific Northwest for the killer whales' welfare was growing, people began to ask, "How many whales are there? Do they travel between the United States and Canada? Will persistent hunting drive them into new travel routes where we won't be able to see and enjoy them?" The United States National Marine Fisheries Service in Washington State and the Canadian Department of Fisheries and Environment in British Columbia have cooperated to answer some of the questions. They began in 1971 with a one-day "census" based on whale sightings by seashore residents, boat operators, lighthouse personnel, and others.

The Canadians progressed to following and photographing the whales, later identifying individuals from their pictures on the basis of natural marks, such as size and shape of the dorsal fin, the

shape of the whitish saddle patch, and various nicks and scars. This was a particularly desirable method because it did not harm the subjects. The team, led by Michael A. Bigg, reported in 1976 that the enclosed waters from southern Puget Sound to northeast of Vancouver Island are the haunts of 210 whales in at least twenty pods or "permanent family units." Each pod averages about 10 animals. Some groups are resident, others transient; six pods periodically cross the international border.

In the United States, a team led by Kenneth Balcomb and Camille Goebel carried out a similar survey in 1976–1977. With the aid of seventeen thousand photographs, they concluded that four pods, which include about seventy animals, make up the resident population of Puget Sound, Georgia Strait, and the Strait of Juan de Fuca. Among

A female killer whale calf breaches off Nanaimo, British Columbia. In 1977 this animal was one of eighteen whales in J pod, a group that cruises the inside waters of British Columbia and Washington State. (Graeme Ellis)

them is the well-known "J Pod." Wandering continuously the year-round—day and night—at three to four knots, it is the most often seen group of whales in United States waters.

It has often been suggested that persistent hunting of killer whales in Puget Sound may have "spooked" those that used to visit there in prehunting years. Don Goldsberry, the principal hunter, thinks not. He points to the fact that Japanese hunters have pursued killer whales for many years in waters off Japan without reporting a drop in their numbers. On the other hand, Forrest G. Wood—curator of Marineland of the Pacific in the 1960s—made this observation about the collecting of porpoises:

In time it became apparent that netting bottlenose porpoises was getting more and more difficult. If the collec-

tors were after a group of animals that were feeding in the upper reaches of a tidal creek they often could no more than get the motor of the net-setting boat started before all of the porpoises were streaking out of the mouth of the creek. The only plausible explanation was that these animals had encountered the Marineland collecting crew on one or more previous occasions and had learned to recognize the sounds of their outboard motors. Eventually the collectors were going farther and farther afield to find porpoises. . . .

No doubt killer whales in the wild and in well-run aquariums will continue to arouse wonder and delight in the minds of all who see them. Since 1964, when the first killer whale was taken alive, we have learned a great deal about this species and, indeed, a great deal about our own attitudes toward all the sea mammals.

J pod—most famous and familiar of the killer whale groups in the Pacific Northwest—remains in Georgia Strait and Puget Sound instead of moving to the outer coasts, as other pods often do. This photo shows a large bull, two cows, a juvenile behind the bull, and a very young calf (closest to the camera). (Graeme Ellis)

False Killer Whale

by Victor B. Scheffer

The false killer whale (*Pseudorca crassidens*) was named long ago when naturalists used the word "false" to mean "resembling." Although this sleek animal superficially resembles the killer whale, it differs in size and shape. The false killer is shorter—males are up to eighteen feet long and females up to sixteen feet. Its flippers are narrower and more tapered, with a distinctive hump near the middle of the leading edge. The dorsal fin, which is so distinctive in the killer whale, is only up to sixteen inches high in the false killer, and is recurved or sickle-shaped. While the true killer is strikingly patterned in black and white, the false killer is black, often washed with gray on the underside.

Primarily tropical or subtropical, false killer whales are seldom found north of Baja California. They may, however, move seasonally in pelagic waters not often surveyed by scientists. Stephen Leatherwood, biologist of the United States Naval Ocean Systems Center (in San Diego, California), has compiled records of false killer whales from the west coast of the United States and Mexico. A false killer shot in 1937 near Olympia, Washington, is the only record north of southern California. Along Washington, Oregon, and most of California there is no record of these animals. A few false killer whale skulls found on San Nicolas Island in California's Channel Islands were interpreted by cetologist Edward Mitchell as evidence of a mass stranding. Elsewhere in this area there have been only two sightings and two collections.

Farther south, particularly in waters off the continental shelf, false killer whale records increase in frequency. Leatherwood has seen or been told of false killers at such widely scattered locations as near Sixtymile Bank, around Guadalupe Island, outside San Benitos Islands, west of Gordo Bank—about fifteen records in all. The false killer whale has also been sighted in the Gulf of California.

These animals are gregarious and have been known to run aground in groups of two hundred or more. Off southern California in 1959 and 1963, groups of about three hundred false killers, each occupying an area two miles long and a half mile wide, were seen. Each was composed of subgroups of from two to six animals. Some whales within the

A false killer whale shows its conical teeth—an efficient aid for catching fish and squid. (W. J. Houck)

1959 group were said to be "traveling so closely packed that they may actually have been touching each other." They often jumped completely out of the water. While traveling, they made a continuous squeaking noise, like "a rather drawn out high squeak of a constant pitch."

Similar sounds were heard on another occasion by two boaters who were passing near a group of false killers. From a distance of 150 to 200 yards, the sounds were described as "piercing, harsh, and quite consistent." An analysis of the voices of nineteen cetacean species by William E. Schevill and William A. Watkins of Woods Hole Oceanographic Institution in Massachusetts described the false killer's voice as a "nearly single-frequency squeal."

As for swimming speed, false killers can move along at twelve to fourteen knots, or fourteen to sixteen miles per hour. A Dutch captain, W. F. J. Mörzer Bruyns, has written that "when approaching a ship they jump with low fast curves, just clearing the water. They ride the bow wave of small boats, but are probably not fast enough to keep up with a big ship."

Little is known of the false killer's breeding behavior. A wide variation in size of fetuses taken from stranded females at the same time of year suggests that mating is not sharply seasonal.

Unlike most delphinids, the false killer characteristically shakes and dismembers its prey, a habit indicating that it feeds mainly on large organisms. It is known to take large pelagic fish and squid. Remains of three squid in the fifteen- to twenty-pound range were found in the stomach of one individual that became entangled in a tuna longline in the Gulf of Mexico. False killers in this area are a minor nuisance to fishermen because the whales occasionally steal fish from the lines. One stolen fish that fell from a whale's jaws was a sixteen-pound snapper (*Lutjanus*). The stomach of a harpooned false killer whale yielded the remains of three amberjacks (*Seriola lalandi*). False killers feed-

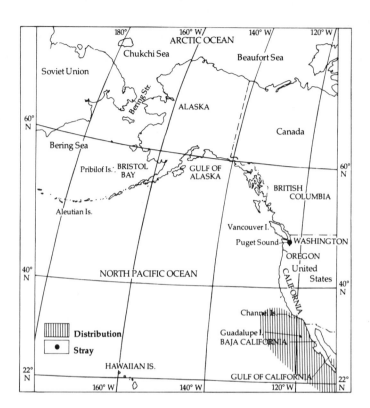

False killer whale distribution

ing in schools of bonito (*Saira lineolata*) off southern California have been seen chasing these big, powerful fish so intently that the whales' bodies would rise halfway out of the water. Among the Hawaiian Islands, false killers are occasionally seen capturing mahimahi (*Coryphaena*). One such fish seen in a whale's jaws was estimated to be an eighteen- to twenty-pounder. In captivity, a subadult female held for twenty-two months consumed a daily average of forty-five pounds of fish and squid, amounting to 4.6 percent of her body weight.

False killers are rarely displayed; only two were held in North American aquariums in 1976. I believe that the first to be taken alive was an eleven-foot female captured for Marineland of the Pacific in 1963. To the astonishment of her captors, she began to feed on her second day in the aquarium, while

The false killer whale is often confused with its relatives, the killer whale and pilot whale. It is differentiated from the killer whale by a solid black color, from the pilot whale by a generally more slender shape, and from both species by a more recurved dorsal fin. (Stephen Leatherwood)

on the third day she was taking mackerel from the keeper's hand! She proved to be amiable and she learned quickly, both through observation and through standard reinforcement training. She was soon "shaking hands," "dancing," "singing," and leaping on cue. She enjoyed rubbing her body against, or mouthing, other dolphins in her pool, although that trait is not unusual among captives. She was "courted" by a male pilot whale and permitted intromission. On one occasion she aided a postpartum dolphin (whose newborn infant had died at birth) by gently pulling the afterbirth from the birth canal, seemingly with the cooperation of the dolphin.

False killers have seldom been used in research. Scientists at Hawaii's Sea Life Park "bugged" a captive male by feeding him a harmless radio capsule concealed in a fish. For fifty-six hours, the capsule broadcast his body temperature; finally it showed up on the bottom of the tank, still announcing the ambient temperature. The whale's deep body temperature varied from 96.8 degrees Fahrenheit when he was resting to 99 degrees Fahrenheit when he was most active.

After studying the chromosomes of a false killer, University of California biologist Deborah A. Duffield concluded that the species is more closely related to other dolphins and porpoises than to its name-relative, the "true" killer whale.

Belukha Whale

by Francis H. Fay

The belukha (*Delphinapterus leucas*), resident of arctic and subarctic seas around the pole, is one of the most abundant whales of the North Pacific. It is, however, one of the least known to residents of the western United States and Canada because it does not normally venture south of Alaska. There, as in the rest of its circumpolar range, it resides mainly in areas of seasonal pack ice where its white body blends well with its surroundings.

This whale's common name is Russian and comes from the nominal form of the adjective *belii*, meaning "white." According to the preeminent Russian cetologist A. G. Tomilin, the names "belukha" and "beluga" are equally correct. Although the latter is more commonly used in North America, I prefer the former, because "beluga" is also the name for the fish from which the finest Russian and Middle Eastern caviar is obtained—the white sturgeon (*Acipenser huso*) of the Black and Caspian seas.

Although the world population of the belukha numbers at least one hundred thousand and may be even twice that number, these are only rough estimates because the animal seems to be continuously on the move. The belukha usually travels in small groups of two to ten individuals, with a large male leading each group. Herds of up to one hundred groups are not uncommon, and up to one thousand groups occasionally have been sighted during migrations. Their migration patterns and the seasonal range of particular herds, however, are largely unknown.

The belukha is a relatively small, though conspicuous, whale. The adult male tends to be somewhat larger than the female, averaging a length of eleven to fifteen feet and a weight of thirty-three hundred pounds; the female averages ten to thirteen feet and weighs about three thousand pounds. The largest male and female on record were twenty-two and twenty-one feet long respectively; each probably weighed about five thousand pounds.

As the name *Delphinapterus* (meaning "dolphin without a fin") indicates, these whales have no dorsal fin, though some have a low ridge on the back in the usual position of a fin. The body is robust

The large frontal bulge or "melon" of the belukha is thought to relate to the reception of underwater sounds. The melon is filled with clear oil and may be changed in shape by muscular control. (W. J. Houck)

and appears somewhat lumpy or muscular rather than smooth and streamlined. The head is relatively small and remarkably maneuverable, and has a short snout or "beak" and a large frontal bulge or "melon." Clear, fine oil fills this melon, the shape of which the whale apparently can change at will by muscular control. It is believed that this is done to facilitate reception of different kinds of underwater sounds, for the belukha has a particularly wide repertoire of calls and seems unusually sensitive to acoustical signals from any source.

The "language" of the belukha—or "sea-canary" as it has been called by mariners—is not yet understood, but it is clearly complex and important to the animal. A vocabulary of at least eleven different calls was recorded by W. E. Schevill and B. Lawrence (of Woods Hole Oceanographic Institution and Harvard University respectively) while monitoring the activities of these whales in the lower Saguenay River in Quebec. They described the calls as high-pitched, resonant whistles and squeals, ticks and clucks, mews, chirps, bell-like tones, sounds resembling an echo sounder, sharp reports and trills, and other sounds suggesting a crowd of children shouting in the distance. Presumably, these sounds are used mainly in communication among whales and perhaps for locating food in murky waters, where vision is of little use.

The belukha's food consists of about one hundred different kinds of marine animals, including various kinds of octopuses, squids, crabs, shrimps, clams, snails, sandworms, and a wide variety of fishes. Even miscellaneous debris—bark, plants, sand, stones, and paper—have been found in belukha stomachs. Because it is swallowed whole, the size of the food consumed is limited only by the capacity of the belukha's mouth and esophagus. Fish larger than about nine pounds are rarely eaten. One belukha was found choked to death by a twenty-pound cod that it had attempted to swallow! Fishes such as capelin, cod, herring,

smelt, and flounder make up the bulk of the diet in spring, summer, and fall; the little polar cod (*Boreogadus saida*) is believed to be the belukha's mainstay during the icebound winter. In some estuaries, young salmon making their way to the sea are particularly relished by this whale; biologists in Alaska have learned to discourage these depredations by broadcasting underwater the excited calls of the killer whale—number one natural enemy of the belukha.

The occasional presence of the pork worm or trichina (*Trichinella spiralis*) in the flesh of belukhas suggests that they may occasionally eat other mammals. Experiments in both Alaska and Siberia, however, have shown that marine mammals like the belukha also could acquire these parasites simply by eating the scavenging crustaceans that have fed on the carcass of an infected mammal, such as a polar bear. Arctic travelers and residents are cautioned, therefore, not to eat the raw or incompletely cooked flesh of the belukha because the parasitic infection (trichinosis) can cause serious illness and even death. Furthermore, in some areas, mercury levels in belukha flesh exceed government standards for human consumption.

The belukha's nearest relative, the narwhal, usually has only two teeth in the front of its mouth; one of these teeth becomes a magnificent tusk in the male. The belukha, on the other hand, may have as many as forty-four teeth (but usually has forty) evenly distributed in its upper and lower jaws. The first teeth emerge when the animal is about one year old (they are not preceded by an earlier set of "milk teeth," as occurs in most other mammals), and are gradually lost (without being replaced) through injury or infection. Adults often have only eight to ten teeth on each side of the upper and lower jaws, with the greater number usually in the upper jaw. These are simple, conical teeth, suitable for catching and holding prey, but of little use for chewing or cutting. Sharp-pointed in

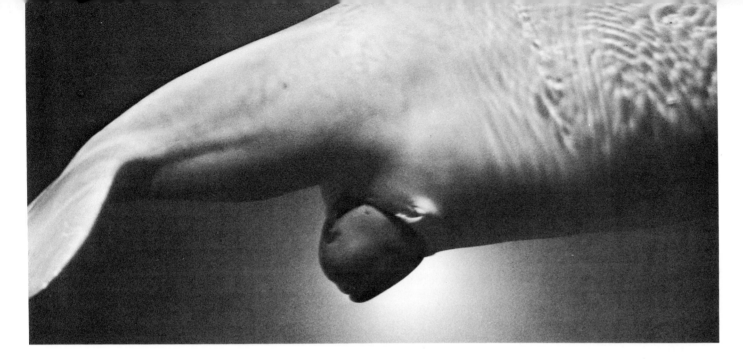

youth, they become rounded and flattened by wear in old age.

The belukha's stomach is said to be comprised of five compartments, though only the first two are strictly comparable in structure to the stomach of other mammals. The last three are enlargements of the upper end of the small intestine and may have an absorptive, rather than a digestive, function. The intestine beyond these compartments is rather slender but amounts to some seven to nine times the length of the animal.

Belukha females mature rapidly and may mate for the first time when about five years old, whereas the males may not participate in breeding until three or four years later. As young adults at the peak of their reproductive development, belukhas are capable of producing a calf every other year. Their rate of production declines as they grow older. (The oldest belukhas probably are about twenty-five to thirty years old.)

Birth of belukha calves takes place mainly in warm (fifty to sixty-eight degrees Fahrenheit) estuaries. The time of birth varies so widely in differ-

ent localities that belukhas were once thought to calve and mate at any time of year. Recent investigations by Russian and Canadian biologists, however, indicate that the five- to six-foot-long calves are usually born between May and July, and that mating occurs about ten months later. In a few localities, the calves may be born as early as March or as late as September. The gestation period is estimated to be about fourteen months, with one calf usually produced; rarely are twins or triplets born. Females with calves generally stay together in herds separate from the adult males.

Belukha calves may suckle for one to two years. Weaning is a gradual process. Because they are toothless for the first year, young belukhas are unable to capture large fishes and are restricted to feeding on shrimps, small fishes, and other small animals that they can capture easily.

At birth the calves are pale gray, becoming darker bluish or brownish gray by the time they are about a month old. With increasing age, they become progressively lighter; these color changes are useful in estimating the age of individuals in a

This male belukha, at the Vancouver Public Aquarium in British Columbia, was the first belukha to be born in captivity. Weighing 75 to 100 pounds at birth and measuring 4.5 feet, it swam unassisted to the bottom of the tank and then to the surface for its first breath of air. Unfortunately, it died of a severe bacterial infection about four months later. (Jeremy Fitz-Gibbon)

herd. Usually they are dark gray until they are about two years old, lighter gray for the next three or four years, and mostly white by the time they reach adulthood and full physical maturity at five to six years of age. However, even in adulthood they retain traces of their former dark color along the trailing edges of the foreflippers and flukes.

Belukhas abound along the western coast of Alaska south to Bristol Bay; a small population exists also in Cook Inlet, Alaska. A group of about twenty was sighted recently in Yakutat Bay about 300 miles east of the inlet. The most southerly record in northwestern North America is of one sighted in Puget Sound, Washington, in the spring of 1940.

The Cook Inlet and Bristol Bay herds seem to remain in those areas all year, while other herds apparently winter in the central Bering Sea, some moving up into the Yukon River delta and Norton Sound in spring, while others move on through Bering Strait to Kotzebue Sound and the Arctic Ocean. A large herd of about five thousand is known to calve at the mouth of the Mackenzie River, Northwest Territories, in June.

Although this whale will travel in the open sea, it generally remains in the shallow waters of the continental shelf where it feeds in 20 to 40 feet of water. Its greatest known diving depth is about 130 feet. When feeding on or near the bottom, the animal dives for not more than three to five minutes at a time, surfacing to breathe for only one or two seconds. When traveling at a steady two to five miles per hour in migration, the belukha usually submerges for only thirty to forty seconds, then surfaces to breathe for about one second, then submerges again, and so on. It can sustain a top speed of twelve to fourteen miles per hour for about ten to fifteen minutes when necessary, such as when it is frightened or is trying to escape from predators.

The belukha will enter fresh water if the food

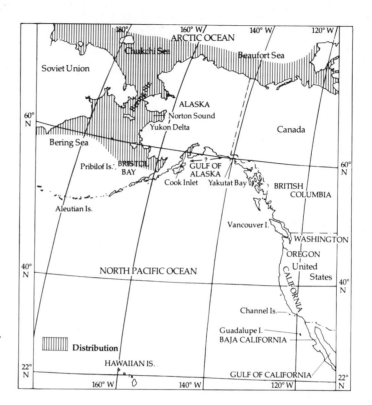

Belukha whale distribution

supply warrants it. A few have been seen nine hundred to twelve hundred miles up the Anadyr and Yukon rivers, which empty into the Bering Sea. Because these rivers are rather muddy, contact between group members or between the group and its food supply (usually small fishes such as smelt) presumably is maintained principally by acoustical means and perhaps also by taste. Russian biologists have noted that the mouth of the belukha and other toothed whales has unique sensory areas that may function as highly sensitive "taste buds" for detecting the presence of other animals. They also note that this group of whales has a pair of anal glands, much like the scent glands of many land mammals. Because whales cannot smell underwater (the nasal passages are used only for breathing air), it is conceivable that the scent glands and the taste re-

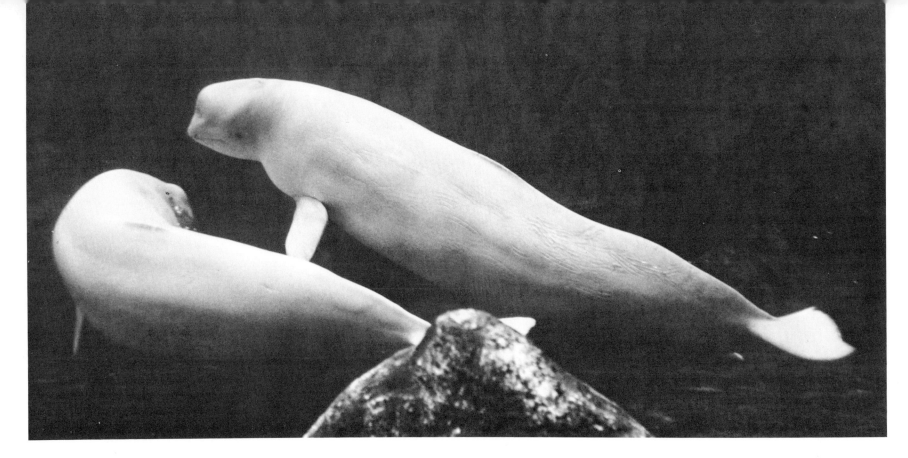

ceptors in the mouth function in a kind of chemical communication system that helps to maintain the integrity of the group or herd when in murky water. The effectiveness of their communications, acoustically and otherwise, is often apparent to hunters that capture belukhas with nets. When one animal locates a hole in the net, the entire group speedily escapes through it, even in muddy water.

In northwestern North America, belukhas have been taken for thousands of years by subsistence-hunting Eskimos, who drive the herds into shallow water where the animals can be easily speared or shot, and retrieved. Recent catches in western Alaska have amounted to less than three hundred animals per year. For the most part, the skin, blubber, and meat of these animals are used as food, and the long sinews in the back are used to make thread for sewing skin garments. Commercial hunting—principally with the aid of nets and weirs—is common in the Soviet Union and eastern Canada. The main products of this industry are leather that is used for work boots, shoelaces, harnesses, and drive belts for machinery, and meat that is used for animal foods. In the Soviet Union, oil from the belukha's melon has been used for making margarine, soap, and salves, and the intestines have been used for making high-grade sausage skins.

At the present time, the demand for belukha products remains small and relatively insignificant, but it probably will grow in the future. As the earth's expanding population exhausts nonrenewable resources, it will become more dependent on renewable animal and plant resources in order to sustain itself.

Two belukhas are highlighted in the New York Aquarium. In the wild, these whales blend into the icy background of their circumpolar range. (Ken Balcomb)

Narwhal

by Murray A. Newman

Because of its distinctive spiral tusk, the narwhal (*Monodon monoceros*) has achieved a unique place in history. This small arctic whale's long tooth, which can extend nine feet in the male, has been highly prized for centuries. The ancient Chinese used the tusks to decorate sword and dagger hilts. In the sixteenth century, tusks were bartered from the Greenlanders and sold for up to $5,000 each at European courts, where they were used as a powdered antidote for poison. Queen Elizabeth I is said to have considered a narwhal tusk one of her most valuable possessions, and Tsar Boris Godunov sent the Shah of Persia seven pieces of a tusk while negotiating an alliance against the Turks.

It was generally believed that the tusk came from the mythical unicorn—a strange, horselike animal with a horn growing out of its forehead. The narwhal itself was first associated with the tusk in 1648 when Tulpius examined a stranded specimen at the island of May (British Islands). In 1758 the great Swedish naturalist Linnaeus gave the animal the name *Monodon monoceros*, meaning "single

tooth, single horn." Its familiar name, "narwhal," is of Scandinavian origin—*nar* meaning "corpse"—and apparently refers to the grayish color of the skin.

The studies of Canadian scientist Arthur Mansfield in the early 1960s at Koluktoo Bay in northern Baffin Island established much basic information about narwhals. The adult female is known to reach a length of thirteen feet and a weight of 2,000 pounds; the male, on the other hand, measures up to fifteen feet in length and weighs up to 3,530 pounds. The young are colored a dark monotone, while adults become progressively lighter with age, developing numerous gray and dark brown spots. Hair germs are present in early fetal development, but there is no hair on the skin of juveniles or adults. The head is bluntly rounded, beakless, and relatively small. There is no dorsal fin—certainly an advantage to a species that swims around ice. Instead, there is a ridge about one inch high running along the back. The flippers are short, broad, and rounded at their tips.

The adult mouth is small and, except for the

Off Bylot Island in eastern arctic Canada, a group of narwhals, including two tusked males, are sighted from the air. Like other arctic marine mammals, narwhals are difficult to photograph in the wild. (R. Greendale)

male's tusk, toothless. Narwhal embryos, however, have two tooth buds on either side of the upper jaw, according to the Dutch cetologist E. J. Slijper, and behind them are four dental papillae, which may occasionally develop into small teeth completely covered by gum. In the male, and sometimes in the female, one of the two left tooth buds, an incisor, develops into a tusk that has no counterpart in other mammals. It is six to nine feet long, straight, spirals counterclockwise from the animal's point of view, and has tuskal pulp extending from its base in the skull to the very tip of the tusk.

Pierre Dow, a researcher at the Vancouver Public Aquarium in British Columbia, has intensively studied the tuskal pulp, describing it as a vascular organ that contains normal connective tissue in which most of the blood vessels are capillaries. The heavy bands of collagen fibers present are not normal for other mammals; they may relate to unusual structure and function. This tusk cavity remains open throughout the animal's life, with new growth from below continuously compensating for the wearing away of the crown. If the tusk breaks, infection is possible—potentially a serious threat to the animal. However, it is also possible that infection is avoided because of dentine deposits, which fill the broken end. This reparative function could explain descriptions by old whalers of narwhals with broken tusks exhibiting a "plug" in the broken end.

What then is the function of this complicated spiral tusk? Although most believe it is simply a secondary sex characteristic analogous to the beard of a man or the antlers of a deer, there are many other theories. Some believe it is used in spearing fish for food; others think it may be used in digging for food. Still others think it is used in fighting or in defense against enemies. (Some say that male narwhals are careful not to hurt their tusks when fighting, and turn their heads to one side to avoid breaking them.) One scientist maintains that the tusk is used in breaking ice frozen over the surface;

another says there is no evidence for this.

In the summer of 1825, the British whaling captain William Scoresby observed schools of fifteen to twenty males off Greenland. The animals raised their heads above the surface and touched each other with their tusks, as if fighting. Many followed the ship and played around the rudder. Other observers report that when narwhals sometimes become trapped in the ice, a group will remain together, keeping a breathing hole open. Their tusks have been seen jutting through these holes, giving rise to the theory that they are used for breaking the ice. At these times, the animals are vulnerable and the Eskimos may take large numbers of them. Narwhals have been encountered at the surface, apparently asleep, and have been seen resting their tusks obliquely above the surface of an ice floe.

Researchers and associates with the Vancouver Public Aquarium have suggested various functions for the tusk. John Ford believes that it may be an important determinant of social structure through visual or tactile signaling. He thinks it may also have effects on male vocalization. Along this line, Robin Best, another research associate, suggests

A male narwhal lies on the beach at Pond Inlet, Baffin Island. The narwhal's tusk, which spirals to the left, develops from the left canine tooth and may grow up to nine feet in length. (Murray A. Newman)

that the tusk may be used for "acoustic jousting"—sound may be channeled along the tusk, perhaps producing maximum sound intensity at the anterior end of the tooth in an acoustic wave guide. Pierre Dow thinks the tusk may function as a cooling mechanism to eliminate excessive heat generated by spurts of abnormal physical activity.

The most northerly of any cetacean species, the narwhal is found only in arctic waters. It lives within the drift ice and is seldom found farther south than seventy degrees north latitude. Although once numerous in its circumpolar distribution, it is now relatively rare in the Eurasian Arctic. In Siberian seas, it primarily occurs far from shore. The narwhal is rare or absent in the Beaufort Sea and in the western Canadian arctic where shallow shelves extend far offshore. This may be because it prefers deeper water, in contrast to its arctic relative, the beluga, which seems to prefer the shallow waters of river deltas. The narwhal also seems to be rare or nonexistent in Alaska waters; since 1928 there have been only six official reports of narwhals either alive, stranded, or known to have been in the area because of tusks found on the beach. North of Alaska, there are even fewer observations, mainly because of the insurmountable ice pack. In August 1950, three narwhals were reported near a Soviet drift-ice station about five hundred miles northwest of Point Barrow.

Most commonly found between Europe and America, narwhals exist in considerable numbers on both sides of Greenland and in the Canadian archipelago east of Boothia Peninsula. In summer, they move north along the east coast of Ellesmere Island with the drifting ice as far as Alexandra Fiord and into the inlets of northern and eastern Baffin Island, including Prince Regent Inlet, Navy Board Inlet, and Pond Inlet. At the south end of Baffin Island, they are seen at Clyde Inlet, and occasionally at Cumberland Sound, Frobisher Bay, and Cape Dorset. Late in autumn, the northern populations move out into open water in Baffin Bay and move south along the west coast of Greenland as far as Disko Bay. On Greenland's east side, they are common between Angmagssalik and Scoresby Sound.

In addition to Canada's largest populations in Lancaster Sound and northeastern Baffin Island, narwhals also occur in northern Hudson Bay at Repulse Bay and Southampton Island. Their winter range is largely unknown.

Between 21 June and 31 July 1976, scientists at Cape Hay on Bylot Island (northern Baffin Island area) counted 6,145 narwhals moving along the coast. From this, they estimated that there must have been 8,000 to 10,000 narwhals. For the most part, groups of males headed the migration. Mixed groups and young animals were most frequent in mid-July, and females with newborn calves occurred at the end of the migration. The peak of migration was 15 July when 1,842 narwhals were seen at a rate of 275 per hour between midnight and five in the morning. The usual group size was 3 to 8, but other groups were as large as 12 to 21.

Rolph Davis and his colleagues in an environmental research firm in Toronto, Ontario, have estimated that only forty percent of the Baffin Bay narwhals move along Bylot Island and that thirty percent pass along the Devon Island coast, and the other thirty percent move in mid-Lancaster Sound. From this they conclude that there must be at least twenty thousand and perhaps as many as thirty thousand animals in this northern population. This is up to two or three times the ten thousand estimated previously by Arthur Mansfield for Canada and northwestern Greenland.

Canadian author and explorer Fred Bruemmer has noted thousands of marine mammals inhabiting Inglefield Bay along the northwest coast of Greenland in the summertime. This bay, which is sixty miles long and twenty miles wide, apparently provides a refuge because of its extensive ice fields along the edge of the glaciers, as well as a rich source of food. He estimates that there are 2,000 narwhals there in the summer. It is likely that this represents an extension of the northern Canadian stock, perhaps part of the thirty percent alluded to by Davis and associates as moving along the coast of Devon Island.

In contrast to this northern Canadian population, the population seen at the north end of Hudson Bay each year consists of approximately only two hundred to three hundred animals. This is probably the group that has not only been seen in Repulse Bay but also at Cape Dorset, Coral Harbour, and Igloolik in Foxe Basin.

This small whale swims rapidly, dives deeply (a harpooned narwhal sounded to twelve hundred feet, according to Scoresby), and remains underwater for a considerable length of time. It also vocalizes, as do most other toothed whales. Researcher John Ford says that they generate clicks, squawks, and whistles, and are "extremely loquacious" underwater. Some whistles seem to be emitted at lower frequencies than those noted in other toothed whales, but the significance of this is not known.

Echolocation appears to play an important role in the narwhal's orientation, judging from the clicks. In other cetaceans, the repetition rates of clicks have been shown to be related to the "target range," or the distance from the echolocating animal to the object being investigated. At Koluktoo Bay, the clicks were concentrated at ranges corresponding to the depths of the bay (300 feet) at a repetition rate of six to seven clicks per second. In contrast, beluga whales in the shallow waters of the Mackenzie Delta have common target ranges of about 33 feet and click frequency of forty to sixty clicks per second. John Ford suggests that, at least in shallow water, much echolocating in both narwhals and belugas may be directed toward the ocean bottom.

The narwhal, like some other cetaceans, has specialized acoustic tissue at the point where the

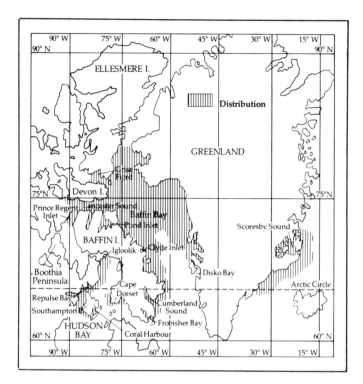

Narwhal distribution

jaw and the auditory bulla (ear bone) attach. Theoretically, the jaw receives sound waves from the environment and transmits them to the ear mechanism through this acoustic tissue.

Recent investigations in the Canadian Arctic by marine mammalogist Robin Best and Dean Fisher indicate that conception usually occurs about mid-April and births usually occur about mid-July. Assuming a gestation period of fifteen months and a lactation period of about twenty months—as in the beluga—calving would occur about once in three years.

Most of the young are born when the pregnant females are entering their traditional summer areas in deep bays and inlets. Usually only one calf is born at a time, although twins are known. At birth the narwhal measures approximately five feet in length and weighs around 180 pounds. The newborn calf appears to be adequately protected from thermal stress of cold water by a one-inch layer of blubber. (This is unlike the beluga calf, which is usually born in the comparatively warm environment of a river estuary.) In adulthood, the narwhal's body heat is retained in the frigid environment by an extraordinary coating of blubber, which constitutes thirty to thirty-five percent of its body weight. In one animal, I found it to be four inches thick at the thickest point.

The narwhal's main food has been described as cephalopod mollusks, probably the squid *Gonatus*, in Canadian waters. However, recent studies have shown that narwhals in the Pond Inlet area of northern Baffin Island feed mainly on arctic cod and fair quantities of pelagic shrimp. The summer movement in the Lancaster Sound area is interpreted by biologists David Sergeant and Keith Hay as a migration to feed on arctic cod exposed by the disintegrating ice fields. Greenland halibut have also been found in their stomachs. On Ellesmere Island in 1970, we observed a young male tethered alive at Grise Fiord readily taking fourhorn sculpins from the hand of his keeper. It is not known whether free narwhals feed on this species of fish. The small, toothless mouth of the narwhal, particularly when surmounted by the impediment of a long tusk in the male, looks like an inefficient device for catching fish. Perhaps male and female narwhals have somewhat different diets.

Natural enemies of the narwhal are the walrus, killer whale, polar bear, and Greenland shark, though it is doubtful if these animals are significant predators. The Greenland shark is sluggish in the intensely cold polar water, but a group of these sharks was sufficiently active to attack Arthur Mansfield's netted narwhals at Koluktoo Bay in the early 1960s. Walruses probably attack narwhals only in unusual circumstances. The killer whale is not adapted to life in drifting ice because of its high dorsal fin, and it may not attack narwhals very often, although it is known to attack belugas off Greenland. It is occasionally seen in the Pond Inlet area of Baffin Island. The polar bear attacks from the ice when the narwhal surfaces to breathe.

Without doubt, the greatest natural danger to the narwhal is its harsh and treacherous physical environment. In autumn or early winter when it must migrate offshore to find permanently open water, large groups are sometimes trapped in bays when they linger too long, and continuous ice barriers form around them. As the temperature falls, the ice barriers extend and the open water around the animals freezes, thus reducing the surface available to them. In Greenland, this phenomenon, called a *savssat*, is well known. Two *savssats* caused the destruction of over 1,000 narwhals in west Greenland during the exceptionally cold winter of 1914–1915.

The first Vancouver Public Aquarium expedition to the Arctic was a fact-finding mission to the Pond Inlet area in the summer of 1968. We were told by the Inuit that narwhals move into the inlet from Baffin Bay each summer as the ice begins to crack and open up, and that groups of narwhals appear in three main waves—the first in early August, the second in late August, and the third in mid-September.

While most of the 4.5-foot-thick ice breaks up in July and August, it continues to move back and forth with the tidal currents and remains a great problem to boats. The break up, however, enables narwhals to enter inlets and come close to shore. At Koluktoo Bay, the ice was completely gone and the water temperature was forty-two degrees Fahrenheit instead of the thirty-two degrees Fahrenheit at Pond Inlet. There were many narwhals there, as well as many ringed seals, arctic char, and small shrimplike crustaceans. It seemed that the whales, seals, and fish were all feeding on the crustaceans. The Inuit told us that the whales had entered the bay the day before our arrival and might remain there for three weeks or more.

The Inuit were interested in only the skins of the narwhals. Because it contains a high concentration of vitamin C, it is one of their favorite foods and an important dietary consideration. Living through the winters without fruit or vegetables, the Inuit would otherwise contract scurvy, a disease caused by vitamin C deficiency. The skin was removed in strips to which some blubber adhered. This was boiled in chunks and eaten with much salt and pepper. Called *muktuk*, it was soft, smelled quite good, and tasted like some other kind of seafood, perhaps lobster or steamed clams. It was very rich and none of us felt like eating much of it. The thick skin also can be made into durable leather.

Without question, man is the narwhal's chief predator, although the actual effect of hunting is still subject to controversy. These small arctic whales are potentially threatened by the modern guns and hunting techniques of northern people. Randall R. Reeves, a writer who recently visited Baffin Island, has pointed out that the high price for narwhal ivory—$35 per pound—is quite an incentive for hunting them. He claims that over four hundred were killed during the summer of 1974 near the small settlement of Arctic Bay on northern Baffin Island; even though a Canadian law was passed in 1971 that limited each Inuit hunter's take to five per year, this might be more killing than the population could sustain if each hunter were successful. Canadian biologists Arthur Mansfield, Tom G. Smith, and Brian Beck calculated that the kill could be as high as 1,100 per year in Greenland and Canadian waters, taking into account an estimated loss of fifty percent. This would exceed the narwhal's estimated annual population production of 900.

Hunting is now subject to settlement quotas, presently set at 335 for the Canadian Arctic (100 each for Arctic Bay and Pond Inlet), and scientists feel confident that this level of hunting does not seriously threaten the species. Nevertheless, the steady hunting pressure, together with the prospective industrialization of the eastern Arctic, pose a danger to this species. The somewhat separate, small population at the northern end of Hudson Bay is particularly endangered and, because of its small numbers, could easily be wiped out by some extraordinary event. More field information is needed on the narwhals of the latter region.

It would be of great value if the narwhal, which we now believe numbers more than twenty thousand in Canadian and Greenland waters, could be observed and studied in an aquarium. Under these circumstances we could greatly increase our understanding of its behavior and biology while at the same time maintain public interest in its conservation. Unfortunately, attempts to keep narwhals in captivity have not been successful. They are difficult to catch and hold under northern conditions, and the general logistics are costly and complicated. A reliable life support system must be provided from the moment of capture until they are released into their aquarium pool many days later. Although in nature they live in a relatively bacteria-free environment at near freezing temperatures, during transport they overheat and become exposed to bacteria and viruses toward which they may have little resistance. This situation continues in captivity, and residual parasites—which, under normal conditions, are not a serious health problem—proliferate in the captive animals. Special care has to be exercised to maintain the health of the aquarium narwhals. Added to all of these problems is the danger to the tusk of a male narwhal in a concrete pool. We know that captive walruses suffer from dental erosion and infection, and this could be a problem in narwhals.

Much has been learned about the narwhal in recent years. We hope we now know enough to maintain some of these fascinating animals in captivity in order to sustain a public will to protect them.

Plate 1

Minke whale
(Don Calkins)

Plate 3

Sperm whale and calf
(Dale W. Rice)

Opposite: Blue whale
(Ken Balcomb)

Giant bottlenose whale
(Ken Balcomb)

Plate 4

*Gray whale
(Ken Balcomb)*

*Right whale (Courtesy of
World Wildlife Fund)*

Humpback whale
(Allen A. Wolman)

Bowhead whale
(Bruce Krogman)

Plate 6

Killer whale
(Ken Balcomb)

Opposite: Spotted dolphins
(William High)

Dall's porpoise
(John Hall)

Spinner dolphin
(E. W. Shallenberger)

Plate 9

*Common dolphin
(Stephen Leatherwood)*

*Rough-toothed dolphin
(E. W. Shallenberger)*

Plate 11

Steller sea lion
(David E. Withrow)

Opposite: Walruses
(Kathy Frost)

Sea otter
(Gwen Jameson)

Plate 12

*Hawaiian monk seal
(Dale W. Rice)*

*Opposite:
California sea lions
(Karl W. Kenyon)*

*Guadalupe fur seal
(Luis A. Fleischer)*

Female ribbon seal
(Kathy Frost)

Ringed seal pup
(Lloyd Lowry)

Plate 15

Polar bear
(Jack W. Lentfer)

Female spotted seal
(John Hall)

Plate 16

*Pacific harbor seals
(Steven J. Jeffries)*

Pinnipeds
Seals, Sea Lions, Walrus

*P*innipeds—the seals, the sea lions, and the walrus—are those "feather footed" sea mammals that have successfully adapted to marine life, while at the same time retaining their ties to land. They all have large eyes, prominent snouts, and fusiform shapes. Most particularly, they are characterized by four swimming flippers ("Pinnipedia" means "feather-" or "fin-footed"), which, to varying degrees, permit them to enjoy life in both worlds.

The pinnipeds, like the cetaceans, were classified with the fish by early taxonomists because of their efficient marine adaptations. The head, smooth and rounded with little or no external ears, blends smoothly into a spindle-shaped trunk. The streamlined body tapers from the head to a small or vestigial tail between the hind legs. The body is further smoothed by a coat of thick subcutaneous blubber, which provides reserve energy, buoyancy, and insulation. The overall design is fluid and flexible—a combination of power and grace—to allow for absorbing the crushing impact of the Pacific surf, hauling out on ice or rock-bound coasts, and executing the agile maneuvers needed for catching prey at sea.

Less modified through evolution than the cetaceans, the pinnipeds have kept their hairy coats, perhaps as protection from sand or rocks when on land. They have also retained the hindlimbs, which, along with the forelimbs, evolved into swimming flippers. The three limb bones are short and strong, attached by many muscles and almost completely withdrawn into the body; only the flippers protrude. The digits are connected by a web of skin to provide increased surface area.

Although once known as a separate order (Pinnipedia), the pinnipeds are now considered members of the order Carnivora. Members of three taxonomic families are found in the eastern North Pacific and Arctic. The eared seals (Otariidae) include two fur seals (the northern fur seal and the Guadalupe fur seal) and two sea lions (the Steller sea lion and the California sea lion)—all identified by inch-long, furled external ears. The walrus, that unique arctic resident, has a taxonomic family (Odobenidae) of its own. Last and most numerous in species are the earless or true seals (Phocidae), which have smooth, round, and earless heads. They have adapted to various ecological niches within this region: four are ice-associated seals—the bearded, ribbon, ringed, and spotted seals; two are denizens of generally more temperate latitudes—the Pacific harbor seal and the northern elephant seal; and one is a subtropical species—the Hawaiian monk seal.

Paleontological evidence shows that the eared seals branched off from the same ancestral line that gave rise to the bears. This seal group originated in the North Pacific about twenty-two million years ago, during the early Miocene epoch, and spread from there to the Southern Hemisphere. One offshoot—the walrus group—spread from the Pacific to the Atlantic about seven or eight million years ago, in the late Miocene, and then became extinct in the North Pacific during the early Pliocene (about four to five million years ago). Only within the last million or so years has the walrus returned, via the Arctic Ocean, to the Pacific sector of the Arctic.

The earless or true seals are believed to have branched from a stock that gave rise to the weasel family, with the earliest true phocid known from the middle Miocene (about fourteen million years ago). These seals evolved for the most part in the North Atlantic, from which one subfamily spread south to the Antarctic. Among these were the elephant seal—which probably immigrated to the North Pacific from the south—and the Hawaiian monk seal—whose migration route to Hawaii is unknown but, according to one theory, may have occurred via the central American seaway. The other subfamily, including the ice seals and the harbor seal, is relatively new to the North Pacific and Arctic, having moved here via the Arctic Ocean during the mid- to late Pliocene about three million years ago.

Today, pinnipeds in eastern North Pacific and arctic waters come in a variety of sizes and shapes, from the largest—the 2-ton northern elephant seal—to the smallest—the 140-pound ringed seal. The overall spindlelike design varies from the sleek elegance of the California sea lion to the massive bulk of the walrus. In color, the assorted patterns range from rings, ribbons, or spots to solid tones of brown, tan, black, white, or gray, depending on species and age.

Pinniped habitats in this region are equally varied. The terrain on which they congregate includes the landfast and floe ice of the Arctic and the ragged cliffs of the Aleutian Islands, the boulder-strewn beaches of British Columbia and Oregon, the sloping sands of Hawaii, and the lava caves of Guadalupe Island off Mexico. On land they have only one requirement—relative isolation from man and other land predators.

At sea, pinnipeds may also occupy different marine zones. Some, such as the harbor seal, the walrus, and the ice seals, frequent relatively shallow waters near land or ice over the continental shelf; others, such as the elephant seal, may move off hundreds of miles from land during different seasons. Northern fur seals will swim out as far as the continental slope and—in the case of both the female and the young—will migrate many thousands of miles each year. No matter how far they roam at sea, however, pinnipeds must keep a terrestrial tie. For the pivotal points in their life cycles—mating and birth—they must return to land or ice.

The four otariids or eared seals—the two sea lions and two fur seals—are unique to the North Pacific. Although quickly identified by their external ears, other features set them apart. They have somewhat longer necks than their earless relatives, and they have completely bare flippers with small nails set back on the topsides. The most fundamental external difference, however, is in their means of locomotion. Eared seal forelimbs are supple and long, comprising as much as one third the body's length; they are tipped with broad flippers, made larger because of cartilage that extends beyond the five digits. The hindflippers can be turned forward under the body and used for four-footed movement on land. When swimming, propulsion is centered in the forequarters: the foreflippers are used as oars, while the hindflippers are held, soles together, as a rudder. On land the foreflippers support the eared seal's body; they extend sideways with a right angle bend at the wrist. All of the flippers are used alternately when walking. At a faster pace, the sea lion achieves a sort of swaying gallop by using its foreflippers together and bringing up the hindflippers together. Although such locomotion may seem awkward, eared seals are powerful swimmers and surprisingly agile on land: the Steller sea lion can haul its one-ton weight onto the steepest shores; the California sea lion has set a pinniped swimming speed record at twenty-five miles per hour; the northern fur seal has been known to swim at speeds of up to fifteen miles per hour when frightened. Before the rapid charge on land of either bull fur seal or sea lion, no human would hesitate for long.

Earless or true seals are more specialized than the fur seals or sea lions. Lacking external ears, they hear through small holes on either side of the head. Their flippers, furred and usually tipped with well-developed claws, are smaller than those of their eared relatives. The foreflippers are moved at the shoulder, being rigid at the elbow and wrist. The digits are mobile and used for grooming, clinging to surfaces, or hauling out on the ice. Only the sand-loving species, the elephant seal and the monk seal, lack this digital mobility.

Locomotion for this group is centered in the hindquarters. The earless seal's hindflippers cannot be turned far forward, thus land travel is more difficult. Over rocks, sand, or ice, they wriggle inchworm fashion, sometimes using their foreflippers to push themselves along. As awkward as this may

seem, some species have been known to cover more than one mile an hour on ice. When swimming, they use their hindflippers, along with lateral movements of the body. The foreflippers are held close to the body or used as rudders and stabilizers. Water is their true element: there they quickly recover the grace and agility of all pinnipeds, using fast turns and skillful tactics in pursuing prey.

The walrus, lone member of the family Odobenidae, combines features of both eared and earless seals. Its means of locomotion is a blend of

Two members of the eared seal family—the Steller sea lion and the California sea lion—display the short, furled ears that distinguish them, along with fur seals, as a family. The California sea lion in the background is a mature male, having a pronounced forehead or sagittal crest. The Steller sea lion in the foreground is a female, lighter in color and lacking the sagittal prominence. (Ken Balcomb)

both: at sea it paddles with the foreflippers in eared-seal fashion and uses the hindflippers in the lateral motions of the earless seals. On land it moves its hindflippers in the manner of eared seals, and has been known to travel up to twenty miles over snow when stormy weather dictates. Walrus flippers are smaller than those of the eared seals, although still quite well developed. The tail, which is small in the other two families, is vestigial in the walrus.

All pinnipeds have whiskers and the normal mammalian hairy covering, which is kept lubricated and waterproofed by the secretions of sebaceous glands. Although all have a coarse coat of guard hairs, only the fur seals possess a dense layer of underfur, which, in the northern fur seal, amounts to three hundred thousand hairs per square inch.

The underfur hairs trap small bubbles, keeping the skin dry, while the stiffer guard hairs protect the body from abrasion. Pinnipeds are born with a woolly coat called lanugo, which provides extra warmth and protection in the first weeks of life. The lanugo is white or gray in ice seal pups (earning them the name "white-coats") and jet black in the newborn monk and elephant seals. (In the harbor seal, the lanugo is shed before birth.) Molting for pinnipeds usually occurs after the breeding season. It is most spectacular in the elephant seal and monk seal as an epidermal molt, whereby the outer skin layer is shed along with the old pelage.

As carnivores, pinnipeds consume a variety of flesh, ranging from krill and other crustaceans to cephalopods or fish—and occasionally even a bird or another seal. They usually eat the common sea-

The smooth, rounded head of the earless seal family is visible in these two monk seals, mother and pup, swimming in the shallows of one of Hawaii's Leeward Islands. Small holes on either side of the head are all that remain visible of the external ears in these seals. (Karl W. Kenyon)

food of an area, swallowing moderate-sized species whole and headfirst to avoid being scratched by fins. Larger catches are shaken into bite-sized pieces. For such catholic tastes, pinniped teeth have evolved for grasping and tearing food rather than for chewing. The crowns of molars in some species have cutting edges for crushing and piercing crustaceans and mollusks. Eared seals have prominent canines, plus a pair of enlarged outermost incisors for seizing food or fighting, while earless seals have smaller and more uniform incisors in the upper and lower jaws. The most dramatic modification occurs in the walrus whose entire snout region houses the two rootless canine teeth that develop into three-foot tusks.

For unknown reasons, some pinnipeds seem to ingest stones deliberately. Pebbles and rocks as large as tennis balls have been found in their stomachs. Answers to this mystery range from the need to grind up food or stomach parasites, to a requirement for extra weight during times of fasting.

Like the cetaceans, pinnipeds are expert divers. More important than having large lungs for storing oxygen is the seal's efficient use of oxygen, by which it can stay submerged longer than terrestrial mammals without suffering brain damage or "the bends." Just before or during a dive, the seal exhales. When its breathing stops, the seal's heartbeat slows, thereby conserving oxygen. Adult seals can slow the heart rate from a normal speed of 55 to 120 beats per minute to 4 to 15 per minute. This phenomenon—called bradycardia—develops more rapidly and lasts longer as the seal grows older; it also develops more rapidly in smaller pinnipeds.

During the dive, the seal's peripheral blood vessels are constricted, and circulation is reserved for the vital heart and brain, thus reducing oxygen consumption by one third. Extra oxygen is stored in the more rigid parts of the lungs where nitrogen absorption is less possible, in the blood (which has a volume one and one-half times that found in a man of similar weight), and in the myoglobin of the muscles. An added benefit is the pinniped's high tolerance to carbon dioxide and lactic acid; this means that the urge to take new breaths of air—so familiar to humans—is minimized, and that pinniped muscles can continue to function without oxygen for a longer time than muscles of land mammals. On returning to the surface, the seal's heart regains its normal speed within five or ten minutes, and its blood is reoxygenated by the increased heart rate and a few deep breaths of air.

This efficient use of oxygen allows for deep and lengthy dives. The following maximum depths have been recorded for North Pacific and arctic pinnipeds: 623 feet—northern fur seal (5.6 minutes); 820 feet—trained California sea lion; 600 feet—Steller sea lion; 295 feet—walrus (10 minutes); 994 feet—northern elephant seal (40 minutes); 656 feet—Pacific harbor seal (28 minutes); 295 feet—ringed seal. The ability to remain underwater for long periods has also modified the pinniped's breathing rhythm at the surface. Seals may wait up to ten minutes before taking a breath, after which they take a series of fifteen or twenty short breaths—a pattern that varies considerably among individuals.

Usually in spring and summer, most pinnipeds congregate for pupping and breeding. The elephant seal and all male eared seals establish territories and maintain "harems" of females at this time. Harem bulls—those mature males capable of holding and defending a territory—arrive first. The cows arrive some two weeks later; they haul out on the territories of the bulls, who may attempt to prevent them from wandering into other territories. Within a week after the cows arrive on land, they give birth to a single pup, and after another week mating occurs. Between breeding and defending their territories during this two-month stay on land, the bulls are occupied full time; they do not go to sea to feed until the breeding season is over.

Walruses are also thought to be polygynous, although they do not maintain a strict harem system. The earless seals (aside from the elephant seal) are less ritualized than the other pinnipeds in their mating behavior. Most are thought to be promiscuous, with mating occurring two to four weeks after the birth of the pup. Some, however, form family groups of male, female, and pup at breeding time.

Delayed implantation—the process whereby embryonic development is postponed so that birth will occur at a more favorable time—is known to occur in the Steller sea lion and northern fur seal, and in the bearded, ringed, and harbor seals. With the exception of the walrus, it is believed to occur in all pinnipeds.

Female eared seals, the walrus, the bearded seal, and monk seal have four retractable mammary teats for nursing the young; other earless seals have two. The mother's rich milk, which is about forty-five percent fat, enables the pup to gain weight quickly. Nursing continues up to six months for most eared seals, the greatest duration being up to two years for some Steller sea lions. The walrus pup, another slow developer, nurses for almost two years, during which its tusks take shape. For the earless seals, the nursing interval is much shorter—between two and four weeks. Then the pups are on their own. Although precocial at birth and able to swim soon thereafter, most pinniped pups—except for brief practice sessions—wait a month or so before venturing into the sea.

Sight and hearing are the most highly developed of the pinniped senses. The eyeballs are large and well adapted for vision in both environments. Underwater the pupil expands to admit as much light as possible for sighting fast-moving prey; at the surface the pupil contracts to a vertical slit. The adjustment from dim depths to daylight is said to be rapid. To compensate for the refractive index in water, the lens is thickened to almost a spherical shape, and to intensify light at murky

depths, the retina is backed by a tapetum layer. There are no tear ducts; instead a protective oil is secreted over the cornea.

Pinnipeds hear above water in the manner of all mammals. They receive underwater sounds via the meatus, or tube to the inner ear. Studies show that harbor seals have good but limited directional hearing underwater; they react to signals up to 160 kilohertz. Their hearing in air, although good, is said to be about 12 kilohertz (15 to 20 kilohertz is the upper range for humans). Some scientists be-

The walrus, sole member of the family Odobenidae, displays its characteristic tusks and wartlike skin. This walrus bears the blanket of thickened skin on the neck and body front usually seen in old males. (Paul G. Hansen)

lieve that the identification by a female of her pup may be auditory when she is not close enough to smell her offspring. Some evidence of echolocation in the California sea lion and in some earless seal species has been found and, although insubstantial, might also explain the healthy condition of partially blind seals that are sometimes found.

Small olfactory lobes in the pinniped's brain indicate that the sense of smell is not strong, although it may be helpful in locating lost pups. Taste buds are present but may not play an important role because pinnipeds swallow food whole. As for touch, the sensitive moustachial whiskers of pinnipeds are useful when examining food and strange surfaces, particularly for the bottom-feeding walrus or bearded seal. Close body contact is apparently more common in some seal species than in others: elephant seals lie touching one another, as do California sea lions; monk seals tend to lie separated, as do the ice seals.

Age in pinnipeds is determined by counting the growth layers in the teeth. Using this method, the harbor seal is known to have reached the age of thirty-three years in captivity and thirty-one years in the wild; the northern fur seal, twenty-six in the wild. The greatest age reported for a pinniped is forty-three years for a ringed seal.

Throughout their lives, pinnipeds are plagued by parasites in the intestines, heart, lungs, and blood. Mites attack the nasal cavity and lice cling to the skin. Parasites in large numbers are fatal to seal pups—along with starvation, overcrowding, and bacterial infections.

Large predators, many of them sea mammals, kill their share of pinnipeds. Killer whales prey on northern fur seals, California sea lions, elephant seals, and harbor seals. Polar bears spend much of their time at leads in the ice, waiting for the ringed seal or the occasional bearded seal to make an appearance. Sometimes a rogue walrus will forsake its usual diet of clams to kill a ringed seal. In more tropical waters, tiger sharks are the deadly predators of Hawaiian monk seals.

Because of their tendency to congregate at predictable times and places, pinnipeds have been easy targets for humans seeking fur, oil, or ivory. Nineteenth-century sealing reduced the Guadalupe fur seal to the edge of extinction. Its comeback from a few known animals is a tribute to the pinniped's powers of survival. Human predation also reduced the northern elephant seal to 100 animals and cut the walrus population in half during a single decade after 1871. The northern fur seal, with a population of 4.5 million in 1870 and 200,000 in 1914, was saved from a worse fate by international agreement.

Today the Soviets continue to take seals and walruses in the Bering and Chukchi seas. In the United States and western Canada, the pinnipeds are enjoying relative peace and protection, with the exception of internationally regulated killing of northern fur seals each year and a harvest of ice seals and walruses by subsistence-hunting Eskimos. However, in spite of protective legislation, more subtle predators—in the form of chemical effluents, clam dredges, fishing nets, and offshore oil exploration—may threaten the pinnipeds.

A hardy and successful lot, the pinnipeds have adapted to some of the roughest terrain on earth. Theirs is a rigorous existence in an unforgiving environment, sometimes filled with strenuous migrations and hierarchal battles. With this way of life, survival does not come easy, but as a group the "feather-footed" ones have maintained very well.

D. H.

Northern Fur Seal

by Clifford H. Fiscus

The most truly oceanic of the North Pacific seals, the northern fur seal (*Callorhinus ursinus*) rarely comes ashore, except on its home islands during the breeding season. During the rest of the year, it ranges across the subarctic waters of the North Pacific Ocean and Bering and Okhotsk seas, and into the Sea of Japan. This mammal was first described by the German naturalist Georg Wilhelm Steller who, during Bering's voyage in 1741, appropriately called it the "sea bear."

The northern fur seal belongs to the family Otariidae (the eared seals) and is the only member of its genus, *Callorhinus*. Originally, the fur seals that bred on the Pribilof Islands, Commander Islands, Robben Island, and several of the Kuril Islands were believed to be three distinct species. In recent years, however, seals tagged as pups on their islands of birth have been known to intermingle on the breeding grounds and at sea in both the eastern and western North Pacific. For this reason, and because taxonomists cannot distinguish one from another, all northern fur seals are now considered one species.

Probably the most distinctive features of the northern fur seal are its thick, waterproof underfur and its unusually large flippers, which are—relative to its body size—almost twice the size of those of its sea lion relatives. The hair and fur fibers of its thick coat number about 370,000 per square inch. Its flippers play a thermoregulatory role of maintaining an even body temperature; its dense fur effectively insulates other parts of the body and prevents heat loss. The eyes of this mammal are large and its night vision is apparently good; its ears are tightly rolled cylinders, each having a wax-coated orifice, which prevents the entrance of water; and its nostrils close when it dives.

The northern fur seal is inquisitive and, when not alarmed, may swim quite close to boats, rearing out of the water to get a better look. When it rears up, it exposes its light-colored or gray throat. On land, it appears yellowish brown because of rookery filth stains, while at sea it usually appears black. When sleeping at sea, it lies on its back with hindflippers folded forward and held in place by a foreflipper. Old-time sealers described this as the

An adult bull northern fur seal stakes out its territory on the Pribilof Islands. For the next three or four months, he will stay here without entering the sea to eat, in order to defend his territorial boundaries and acquire a harem. (Karl W. Kenyon)

A northern fur seal floats at sea in a typical resting posture— on its back with its nose and three flippers above the surface. Old-time sealers called this the "jug handle" position. (Karl W. Kenyon)

"jug handle" position.

Adult females weigh from 65 to 110 pounds in springtime, when they are in prime condition and often pregnant. Adult males in prime condition on their breeding territories weigh between 300 and 615 pounds. Newborn pups weigh 10 and 12 pounds for females and males respectively. Of course, these are average weights: some seals weigh less; some, particularly older animals in prime condition, weigh more.

The maximum life-span of a fur seal probably does not exceed thirty years. A few seals tagged as pups have been recovered at twenty-one years of age. Counts of growth rings in their canine teeth indicate ages up to twenty-six years for females and up to seventeen years for males.

The northern fur seal population is approxi-mately 2 million, of which roughly 1.4 million in-habit the Pribilof Islands, United States, in the east-ern Bering Sea. Fur seal colonies are located elsewhere around the North Pacific rim and their estimated numbers are: Commander Islands, Soviet Union, western Bering Sea—265,000; Robben Is-land, Soviet Union, Okhotsk Sea—165,000; several of the Kuril Islands, Soviet Union, western North Pacific—33,000; and San Miguel Island, United States, eastern North Pacific—more than 2,000.

As mentioned earlier, fur seals range across the subarctic waters of the North Pacific. In the east, they are found south to about the latitude of the California-Mexico boundary, and in the west, they are found south to about the latitude of Tokyo, Ja-pan. Offshore, scattered seals are found in sub-arctic water, which extends south to about the

California-Oregon state line although it shifts northward seasonally.

At sea, the fur seal tends toward solitude, although pairs and groups of three are fairly common. The largest group seen in my fifteen years of ocean research numbered about 100 animals, which were feeding on a large school of anchovies. Fur seal density is extremely variable, numbering up to 70 or more per square nautical mile. One day in March 1972, 169 seals were seen from a vessel during a twelve-hour cruise off Grays Harbor, Washington. During twelve other days in that month, the number of seals sighted ranged from none to 44. Transects run off California and Washington have shown few fur seals within ten to fifteen nautical miles of shore. Most were located along the continental slope and in areas where the topography causes upwellings of nutrient-rich water and an abundance of prey species.

The Pribilofs, a group of remote and rocky islands in the Bering Sea, are the main breeding grounds for the northern fur seal. The maximum number congregate there between July and September. The older pregnant females arrive first, from mid-June on. As the season progresses, younger pregnant and nonpregnant females of all ages haul out on land. The peak of the pupping season occurs in early July. By early August, the nursing females have fanned out in the ocean on feeding forays to about 100 miles from land and, in some cases, as far as 260 miles, returning at regular intervals to nurse their pups.

The female fur seal has a bicornuate or double-horned uterus, which permits her to breed soon after parturition. Her new pregnancy occupies the uterine horn that lay dormant during the past year. Within a few hours or days after her arrival on the rookery, she gives birth to her pup; between five and ten days after the birth, she comes into estrus and mates, usually with the bull in whose territory she gave birth. The ovary associated with the

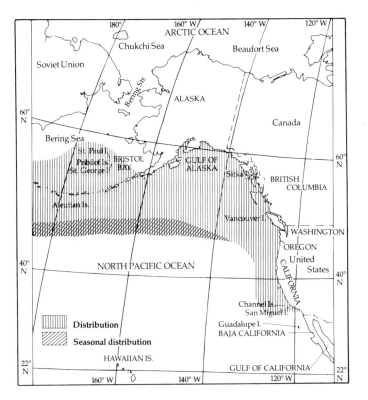

Northern fur seal distribution. Stragglers are found north to Bering Strait.

dormant uterine horn releases an egg about the time the female is bred. After its union with the sperm, the egg develops to the blastula stage, floats in the uterine horn as a "blastocyst" until late October or November, then implants itself on the uterine wall and resumes growth.

Most female fur seals mature sexually at the age of four or five years: over eighty percent of those between the ages of seven and sixteen are pregnant each year. Age extremes of three and twenty-three years have been observed among pregnant females. Twins are rare. Of three twin births on record, only one of each pair survived to weaning age (about four months). Males and females are born in nearly equal numbers.

As with females, the males arrive in descending order of age, the older animals first. Most of the territorial males, many of whom have been on the rookeries since early May, abandon their territories for other parts of the islands or the sea by mid-August. Some adult males have been sighted in the vicinity of the eastern Aleutian Islands by mid-August. Younger males, mostly from three to five years old, begin to haul out on areas adjacent to the rookeries in late June and continue to arrive through July and into September. Most of the new males appearing on land in August and September are two-year-olds. A few yearlings arrive in late September and October. Most remain at sea, however, and do not return to their island of birth until they are two years old. Some of the older seals may also remain at sea throughout the year.

In October, seals of all ages and both sexes begin to leave the islands, with the peak of the departure for most seals occurring in early November. Perhaps only a hundred or so—usually adult males—of the multitudes found on the Pribilof Islands in summer can still be seen there by December.

Most adult males winter in the northern North Pacific Ocean south of the Aleutian Islands, and eastward into the Gulf of Alaska, although a few probably remain in the Bering Sea throughout the winter. A very few may migrate south with the females and younger males.

By the time the pups leave the islands in early November, they have molted their black birthcoats in exchange for coats of silvery gray. They are now competent swimmers after spending many hours in the water since late August. They begin their migration alone, as do the other seals, appearing in the passes of the eastern Aleutian Islands between mid-November and early December. During some years, severe westerly storms may drive a few pups southeastward into Alaska's Bristol Bay.

Heading south, females and young males begin to appear in late November along the continental slope and shelf from Sitka, in southeast Alaska, to

Washington, and by early December as far south as San Francisco. They are sometimes found in considerable numbers off Washington in December, and from Sitka southward to the Channel Islands of southern California in January. Young males are never so abundant as females of the same age in the southern parts of the range. Pups of both sexes arrive off the coast from southeast Alaska to Washington in January; some move southward into California waters. They are found off California in the largest numbers from March through May but

Mother and pup northern fur seals assume the characteristic resting posture of fur seals on land. The foreflippers support the body, extending sideways with a right-angle bend at the wrist. (Karl W. Kenyon)

are never so abundant there as off the coasts of Washington, British Columbia, and southeast Alaska.

The northern fur seal is quite abundant well offshore of Washington from late November to June. It is occasionally sighted in the Strait of Juan de Fuca and a few straggle into Puget Sound almost every year. Beachcombers on the outer coast occasionally find dead fur seals among debris deposited on the beaches by winter storms. In 1959, a female came ashore on the Washington coast and gave birth to a pup, one of the few times that this behavior has been known to occur on other than an established breeding rookery. During recent excavations at Ozette Village, Cape Alava, Washington, Washington State University anthropologists have found that the fur seal was the most important marine mammal taken by the sea mammal hunters of Cape Alava over the last 2,000 years (up to 1900). Of the mammal remains found at the site, eighty percent were those of fur seals.

The northward migration of fur seals from California waters begins in March; however, a few may still be seen there in early June. The fur seals breeding on San Miguel Island probably stay off California throughout the year. Elsewhere, the migrating seals pass northward through Washington waters from March into June, coming through in waves similar to bird migrations. They may be abundant in one locality for a few days then only a scattered few are seen until the next wave passes through. The movement of schools of prey species also affects the migration patterns of fur seals and influences the length of time they may linger in an area.

Large numbers of seals of both sexes and all ages are found from April through mid-June in the Gulf of Alaska from the Fairweather Ground on the eastern side of the gulf to the Portlock and Albatross Bank grounds off Kodiak Island on the western side. Some evidence indicates that late migrating seals may travel directly across the eastern North Pacific Ocean toward passes of the Aleutian Islands from the vicinity of La Perouse Bank, off the Strait of Juan de Fuca, rather than follow the routes of earlier migrants along the great circle of the coastal shelf north and westward through the Gulf of Alaska. Thus, the annual migratory cycle is completed as the seals once more arrive on the Pribilof Islands.

Fur seals tend to congregate at sea in areas of an abundant food supply. They usually feed at night, probably because most prey species rise toward the surface after dark and are more readily available. Recent studies of fur seal diving behavior showed many shallow dives of up to 11 fathoms (66 feet) that lasted less than 1 minute, which may indicate travel or shallow feeding, and deeper dives of 11 to 76 fathoms (66 to 456 feet) that lasted 2 to 5 minutes, which probably indicate feeding activities. The deepest dive recorded was one of 104 fathoms (624 feet), which lasted 5.4 minutes.

Underwater, fur seals can swallow whole fish and squid about ten inches long or less. They bring larger prey to the surface where they break or tear it into smaller chunks by shaking.

About sixty species of fish and squid have been identified from the stomach contents of fur seals taken in this part of the world. Over the years, food species of major importance have been: off California—anchovy, hake, several species of squid, and saury; off Washington—anchovy, herring, hake, several species of squid, saury, rockfish, and salmon; and off Alaska in the North Pacific Ocean and Bering Sea—walleye pollock, capelin, sand lance, herring, several species of squid, and Atka mackerel.

Commercial exploitation of the Pribilof fur seals began with the discovery of their breeding islands in 1786–1787 by Russian fur hunter Gerasim Pribilof. During the period of Russian ownership (1786 to 1867), it was estimated that more than 2.5

million skins were taken. The population reached a dangerous low between 1806 and 1834. As a result, between 1835 and 1867 the harvest of male seals on land was restricted and the taking of females forbidden. The population increased as a result of these measures.

With the purchase of Alaska in 1867, the United States acquired the Pribilof Islands. In 1868–1869, sealing was unorganized; reports of the number of seals taken during these two years range from 225,901 to 329,000. In 1870, the first of two twenty-year leases of sealing privileges was awarded. Some 1,854,029 skins were shipped from the islands between 1870 and 1889; during the second lease period (1890 to 1909) 342,651 skins were taken. From 1869 to 1911, fur seals were taken, with few restrictions, throughout their range. Between 1889 and 1909—the heyday of pelagic sealing—over 600,000 seals were reportedly taken, most of which were females. All fur seal populations declined rapidly during this period. By 1909, only 200,000 to 300,000 seals remained on the Pribilof Islands.

Years of negotiation, beginning in the 1880s, finally produced the North Pacific Fur Seal Convention of December 1911. This convention prohibited pelagic sealing except by aboriginal people using primitive methods; it arranged for a sharing of skins taken on land by member countries—Great Britain (for Canada), Japan, the Soviet Union, and the United States. This convention was in effect until October 1940. The four nations negotiated a new treaty in 1957 entitled "Interim Convention on Conservation of North Pacific Fur Seals," which is still in effect.

On Saint Paul Island in the Pribilofs, bull northern fur seals struggle for the most desirable spots on the breeding ground. Most battles of this kind do not result in serious wounds because the bulls are well protected by their tough skin and thick, resilient coat of blubber beneath. (Karl W. Kenyon)

Since December 1908, the responsibility for research and management of fur seals associated with the Pribilof Islands has been assigned to a succession of federal agencies and is currently delegated to the United States National Marine Fisheries Service. The fur seal population is managed by a research and management team of scientists of this service. Regulation of the take ensures that only those seals not needed as replacements for the breeding stock are taken and that the harvest is carried out in the most humane way possible without undue stress to the animals. Because the fur seal is polygynous, many more males than females can be, and have been, harvested.

Only young males are presently harvested, although a few females may be accidentally taken each season. Through 1972 seals were harvested each year on both major islands of the Pribilof group; however, since 1973 no seals have been taken commercially on Saint George Island. Set aside as a research study area in 1973, Saint George Island is being used to compare the growth and behavior of an unharvested population with that of the harvested Saint Paul Island population.

Recent man-caused hazards to which the fur seal is exposed at sea include discarded, lost, or abandoned fishing nets and net fragments. The arrival of fur seals on their home islands with net fragments around their necks caused enough concern by the late 1960s to merit discussion at meetings of the North Pacific Fur Seal Commission. Fur seals, curious by nature, will investigate flotsam and jetsam at sea. They swim through and rest on floating kelp patches; when discarded fish netting is encountered, they treat it as they would kelp and consequently may become entangled. As a result, some die of starvation, and others return to land where they are sometimes rescued and cut free of the entwining gear. In 1974 and again in 1976, commission members were asked to inform their respective governments of the serious nature of the

problem and request that they take action leading to its elimination. In 1976, brochures and posters were circulated to the fishing industries of Japan, requesting them to refrain from discarding netting into the oceans. The United States and Canada are cooperating at present in a similar venture.

Oil is another hazard at sea and at the shorelines of rookeries. A recent study on the physiological impact of oil on pinnipeds revealed that small amounts of crude oil on the fur increased thermal conductance, resulting in increased heat loss and a consequent increase in metabolic rate to maintain body temperature. Oil encountered at sea in any amount will probably affect fur seals by rendering their dense underfur ineffective as an insulator.

When another bull or a human being trespasses on his chosen territory, the bull northern fur seal gives vent to a deep bellow. With thrashing flippers, he propels his 500 pounds of muscle and blubber over the boulders toward the intruder. (Karl W. Kenyon)

Guadalupe Fur Seal

by Luis A. Fleischer

A rugged island some 140 miles off Baja California is the principal stage for one of the most remarkable comebacks among the marine mammals. Guadalupe Island, a twenty-two-mile stretch of volcanic rock rising steeply out of the Pacific, today harbors on its east side the only breeding population of the Guadalupe fur seal (*Arctocephalus townsendi*). This remote habitat is the only site for survival of a species that was so severely reduced by sealers at the end of the nineteenth century that in 1892 there were thought to be only seven animals left.

Before the end of the eighteenth century, British and Yankee sealers as well as Aleuts brought from Alaska by the Russians began exploiting the Guadalupe fur seal on the islands off Mexico. The slaughter throughout this fur seal's original range was massive and unrelenting. For example, in only nineteen days during 1805, the crew of a British ship took 8,338 fur seals, almost surely of this species, at the San Benito Islands off Baja California.

Before exploitation, the Guadalupe fur seal's range extended from Revillagigedo Islands off the west coast of Mexico north to California's Channel Islands, its distribution overlapping that of the northern fur seal. Recent osteological evidence indicates that it may have been found as far north as the Farallon Islands off San Francisco; however, other studies propose that the fur seal of the Farallons may have been the northern fur seal.

Information on species' abundance before and during the large-scale sealing is scarce, in part because the locations of prolific rookeries were kept secret by early sealers. It is clear, however, that the early sealers were unaware that the fur seal they were harvesting was a different species than that found farther north. The population before near extermination was probably as high as twenty thousand on Guadalupe Island alone. By 1892, when Charles Haskins Townsend spent ten days exploring the rocky Guadalupe coastline, he found only seven fur seals. Ironically, he left the island with the first scientific specimens (four skulls) of the species only two years before it was believed to be nearly extinct.

A female fur seal and her pup cool themselves in the shallows of Guadalupe Island. This species, which survived the seal slaughters of the nineteenth century, was once believed to be extinct. The female here displays the distinctive collielike snout that aided in reidentifying this rare species. (Luis A. Fleischer)

In 1897, naturalist C. Hart Merriam published the description of the Guadalupe fur seal as a new species, and named it in honor of its collector, Charles H. Townsend. Merriam related it to the Southern Hemisphere fur seals, genus *Arctocephalus*, of which the Guadalupe species is the only one found north of the equator. For the next thirty years, the Guadalupe fur seal was to be known only by the characteristics of its skull.

The story of the Guadalupe fur seal's rediscovery is filled with suspense. In 1926, two fishermen noted a small group of fur seals on Guadalupe Island and reported their find to the San Diego Zoological Society, which engaged them to obtain a pair of specimens. To the joy of all, the two bull fur seals delivered in 1928 had the distinctive features of the Guadalupe species. A few days later, Charles Townsend pronounced the Guadalupe fur seal rediscovered. There were only a few unsubstantiated sightings in following years, however, with the last report of a living seal made in 1949 by George Bartholomew, a zoologist from the University of California at Los Angeles, who saw a solitary bull on San Nicolas, the most remote of the Channel Islands. When the same bull seal was not seen in following years, the situation appeared bleak once again.

Finally, during a 1954 expedition to Guadalupe, biologist Carl Hubbs (of the Scripps Institution of Oceanography in La Jolla, California) made a last effort on the final day of his trip. "Just before dark, after straining eyes had failed to locate any sign whatever of a fur seal," Hubbs saw one perched on a rock at the mouth of a cave. It emitted a roar unlike either an elephant seal or a sea lion. "Full of expectation," he wrote in an article for *Pacific Discovery* (1956), "we turned right into the surge, where in the early dusk I could plainly see the sharp, almost collie-like snout, coarse guard hairs overlying silky smooth fur, oversized flippers, and other characteristics of the Guadalupe fur seal."

There were at least fourteen still in existence.

Today, due to protection under Mexican law (Guadalupe Island is a marine mammal sanctuary) and the assurance of such international legislation as the United States Marine Mammal Protection Act and the United States Endangered Species Act, the Guadalupe population has escaped the threat of extinction. At present, there are slightly more than 1,000 Guadalupe fur seals along the east side of the island.

A member of the otariid or eared seal family, the Guadalupe shares certain characteristics— external ears, mobile hindflippers and foreflippers on land, and some social behaviors—with the sea lions. It is further distinguished as a fur seal, along with eight other worldwide species, by its thick underfur and large foreflippers. The flippers are bare except for hair at the wrist, and act as thermoregulators as well as propellers.

Undoubtedly, the most distinctive feature of the Guadalupe fur seal is its elongated snout with a pointed muzzle, which makes this animal one of the most "handsome" of marine mammals. Its large eyes, with corneas that compensate for the index of refraction, and expandable pupils, provide good vision for both land and water environments—the evolutionary compromise of all pinnipeds. Its ears, capable of limited movement, are scroll-shaped and have muscles to seal them tightly when submerged. The seal's overall color is dark brown, with lighter shading on the chest, especially in adult males. In the water it appears shiny dark brown, with golden color on the chest.

Sexual dimorphism occurs in this species, as in other eared seals. The male Guadalupe fur seal measures six feet four inches in length and the female four and one-half feet, with weights of approximately 350 and 100 pounds respectively.

The maximum life-span of the Guadalupe fur seal is between seventeen and twenty years. We calculated this estimate from photographs taken in

A bull fur seal rests on the lava boulders of Guadalupe Island. Thick underfur and large foreflippers distinguish this species as a fur seal. (Luis A. Fleischer)

A bull fur seal and two members of his harem, one with a nursing pup, occupy a sheltered lava cave on the east coast of Guadalupe Island. (Luis A. Fleischer)

1968 of an eight- or nine-year-old seal called "Lefty," which I saw again in 1976. "Lefty" also revealed a high homing tendency in this species because of his habit of returning to the same cave every breeding season.

Like other members of the genus *Arctocephalus*, the Guadalupe fur seal likes rocky habitats such as those along Guadalupe's east coast. This preference differs from that of other pinnipeds—such as the northern elephant seal, for example, which occupies sandy stretches along this coastline. For the Guadalupe fur seal, volcanic caves along the east side provide shelter from the prevailing winds, launching spots from which to take a swim when temperatures soar, and places to breed.

Reproductive behavior is similar to that of all polygynous pinnipeds, beginning with the attachment of males to a territory and the defense of their boundaries with complicated displays of aggression shown to any intruder—even the well-intentioned biologist. Unlike other seals, the Guadalupe bull fur seal will take an occasional swim, leaving the territory but patrolling it from the water.

The arrival of the pregnant females introduces a new element into the cycle, which is changed further with the appearance of the newborn pups. The pups, born in late June or July, are precocial and able to swim within a few hours. Like other seal pups, they will try to avoid contact with the sea for the first few days. The pups are sometimes the victims of the wind and waves on stormy nights. During my last visit to Guadalupe, I found a few dead pups drifting with the current.

There are no data on weaning time, but extended maternal care is assumed for this seal, based on the habits of other *Arctocephalus* species. Mating is presumed to occur about a week after the pup is born, with delayed implantation reserving the time of birth for the next season.

The Guadalupe fur seal's diet is still unknown. Because of its opportunistic feeding habits, a variety

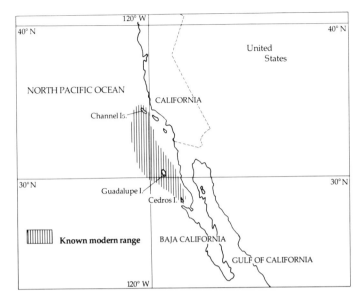

of rockfish common in this area is presumed to be a principal item.

No land predator exists for this seal. However, the precipitous coastal slopes of the island permit large marine predators, such as the great white shark, to come in close to shore and take this pinniped.

My field evidence indicates that the seal population on Guadalupe is growing slowly, expanding along the east side. Today, this fur seal is found north to the Channel Islands, with major concentrations on Guadalupe. Although some animals may have strayed as far north as the Channel Islands, there is no evidence that they breed anywhere but at Guadalupe Island. The southern limit of its range is Cedros Island off Baja California.

Obviously, there are many crucial questions to be resolved about the biology of this fur seal. Because it is again present in some numbers, we are fortunate to have the chance to fill in this scientific knowledge and—this time—to ensure its survival.

Guadalupe fur seal distribution. Guadalupe Island is presently the only breeding island.

Steller Sea Lion

by Roger L. Gentry and David E. Withrow

The chilly waters of the North Pacific are the province of the Steller sea lion (*Eumetopias jubatus*). Remote, windswept islands scattered from northern Japan to central California are the focal points to which the widely scattered adult sea lions are drawn each summer. These islands are also the dispersion points for thousands of young sea lions born into the complex but temporary societies formed there. This annual pattern has recurred since at least 1742 when the German naturalist Georg Wilhelm Steller first described it; its roots reach back to the first appearance of these animals in the fossil record, several million years ago.

Also known as the northern sea lion, the Steller is the largest of the eared seals. It generally resembles its southern relative, the California sea lion, except for its larger size and lighter color. Male Stellers often exceed ten feet in length and weigh over 2,200 pounds. The females are noticeably smaller, usually measuring seven feet in length and weighing 600 pounds. Male Stellers are tan or cork colored, with darker shading on the chest and abdomen; females when young are comparatively lighter, but their coats darken with age. The pups are silver black. Underwater, Steller sea lions appear white in color, whereas California sea lions are much darker.

The Steller sea lion breeds along the west coast of North America from San Miguel in California's Channel Islands northwest to the Gulf of Alaska, along the Alaska Peninsula, and throughout the Aleutian and Pribilof islands. Off Asia, it breeds in the Kuril Islands, Kamchatka, and on islands in the Okhotsk Sea. Some animals move as far north as Saint Lawrence Island in the Bering Sea during summer months.

Fewer adult males are seen along the California coast during the winter than in the summer, indicating that individuals migrate northward in winter and return in early summer. The adult and sub-adult males of the Aleutian rookeries move north in late summer and return when the ice forms. These sea lions have been observed hauling out occasionally on the ice. There is also seasonal movement throughout the Aleutian Islands.

The world population of the Steller sea lion is

A battle-scarred bull Steller sea lion defends his "harem" on Buldir Island in the Aleutians. (Karl W. Kenyon)

approximately 250,000. Current studies suggest that the Gulf of Alaska populations are stable; however, research indicates that populations in the eastern Aleutian Islands may be experiencing a drastic decline in breeding animals. The western Aleutian Islands have not been surveyed recently and their current status is unknown. The California population has undergone a steady decline since the 1920s, and a sharp decline since the late 1960s. The cause for this is still unknown; it may relate to new movements within the range, disease, or deaths from fishermen's nets or rifles.

In the past, the Aleutian natives relied heavily on the Steller sea lion. Sea lion skins were used for boat coverings, harnesses, waterproof clothing, and boots; the meat was consumed by humans as well as animals; the fat became fuel. Now largely replaced by synthetics, sea lion products are unnecessary, so few animals are taken by the Aleuts each year.

Steller sea lions are difficult to observe at sea, hence most of our information is collected when they haul out during the breeding season. The on-land phase of this yearly cycle is best known because the animals gather predictably at certain sites. Even though this phase is short, lasting less than three months, it is of great significance because all the reproductive functions take place on land.

When visiting a breeding island, or rookery, for the first time, several facts are immediately obvious. The males are perhaps three times larger than the females, and the females may outnumber the males by as many as ten to one. It also becomes apparent that the males are quite immobile, each remaining within an area of about 2,100 square feet, and are evenly spaced throughout the rookery. Females, on the other hand, may lie next to one another in dense clusters, or wander freely across the rookery.

The difference in size, numbers, and spacing between males and females is largely due to the behavior of males, whose threatening encounters

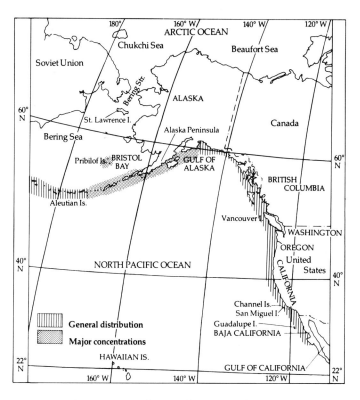

Steller sea lion distribution

are conspicuous on the rookery. Males attach themselves to a piece of terrain, stay within definable boundaries, and threaten any male that approaches. During the threats, both opponents hurl themselves on their bellies, face to face, only inches apart. They hiss and puff at each other, ending with a bout of rapid neck fencing and sometimes biting. A fight follows if either opponent passes beyond the boundaries of these mutual displays. Because of these threat displays, the males space themselves evenly, and the spacing determines the number of males on a restricted rookery. Competition for space in part accounts for the large size of the males.

Because males hold repeated threat displays, the display locations can be used to define each male's territorial borders. Most boundaries follow natural lines, such as faults or ridges in the rock, which give an uneven shape to each territory. The greater the separation between territories, the more stable the boundary. Males whose territories are well delineated geographically may successfully breed in the same location for four seasons with no change in boundaries.

Male Stellers not only stay geographically fixed at a rookery but also rarely, if ever, leave during the breeding season. Thus they may not feed for up to sixty days, their only water coming from body fat stores or filthy tidepools. This need for body fat also accounts for their large body size. During this period they may make more than four hundred threat displays, have a dozen fights, copulate with up to thirty females, and chase away many juvenile males. The reproductive season seems to impose almost unparalleled physiological stresses on male eared seals. Small wonder that few, if any, withstand these rigors for more than four years of life!

Although the females do not defend territories as the males do, their behavior is also divided into yearly phases. Most females arrive at the rookery only a few days before delivering a single pup.

Within two weeks they mate with a territorial male, usually only once, and then settle into a routine of feeding at sea and returning to suckle their young. Weaning usually occurs before the pup is one year old; however, there are several reports of females suckling yearlings.

While males defend discrete territories, the more gregarious females show a different social behavior. In all studies on this species, no lasting social organization, such as a dominance or leadership hierarchy, has been found among the females. Instead, they form loose assemblages in which the memberships are continually changing, and, except for an occasional threat or not-so-gentle nip, there is little aggression among them.

During the reproductive season, the behavior of females toward each other changes markedly. A day or two before giving birth, some females become aggressive and may force others away from them. Occasional fights erupt between two such females so that spacing increases among all individuals. But this effect is only temporary and never reaches the proportions of the male territorial sys-

On California's Año Nuevo Island, three male Steller sea lions fight over territory. The animal on the right is covered with blood. (Roger L. Gentry)

tem; females again tolerate each other only a few days after giving birth.

A superficial glance at a rookery sometimes reveals clusters of females associated with a male, with open spaces between adjacent clusters. In the past this arrangement has been interpreted as semipermanent "harems" over which the males are masters; the evolutionary consequences of this situation have been discussed by many authors. We now know through prolonged observation that these groupings do not last and that there are no bonds between males and females. The females naturally tend to group together; the spaces between clusters usually form when females avoid the territorial boundaries where male threat displays occur. Although males try to herd females away from territorial boundaries, they are usually unsuccessful and females cross them easily.

Females show no lasting attachments to specific males or to selected territories. A female may give birth in one territory, copulate in another, and reside in several others with her pup before the season ends. If a female leaves a territory and returns to it repeatedly, it is usually to rejoin a pup left there. Therefore, what has been termed a harem structure among eared seals is really a collection of animals using the same area, with males unsuccessfully blocking the movements of normally gregarious females.

The silver black pups, born in June and July, are quite precocial. They can walk and suckle within half an hour of birth, and if forced, can swim weakly within a few hours. David Withrow saw a newborn pup only a few hours old fall from his rock into the water. The little fellow swam for fifty minutes, clawing at the edge until he was able to find a ledge and pull himself to safety out of the water. Interestingly enough, the mother made only a weak attempt to rescue her pup, then focused attention on her still suckling yearling.

During the first two weeks of life, pups remain

Adult male and female Steller sea lions copulate. Sexual dimorphism is characteristic of these animals—males may be three times larger than females. (Roger L. Gentry)

with their mothers, suckling often and avoiding other pups and females. After about two weeks, when the mothers have copulated and have resumed their nightly feeding trips to sea, the pups voluntarily enter the water for the first time and begin to interact with one another. Each day the pups spend more time chasing and mock-fighting with their fellows. If a pup's mother dies, chances are the pup will also die, because fostering of young, although known to occur, is infrequent in this species. In fact, females bite and toss any pup but their own.

Weaned sea lions, including pups of the previous year, have a different yearly cycle than the adults. Most animals one and two years old do not return to the rookery. However, when the males are about three years old they return to the island and gather on separate nonbreeding or "bachelor" areas. There they spend many hours together chasing and mock-fighting or making occasional forays into the breeding areas where they are chased by resident males. They do this every year until they are large enough to compete for a territory among the females. Young females, on the other hand, may return to the rookery to breed in their third year, and return every year thereafter to bear a pup or copulate.

When the breeding aggregation breaks down in August, males leave the rookery immediately, and females follow within a few months. In California, a general northward migration leaves few Steller sea lions there in winter. In Alaska, a general southward migration brings animals into warmer water at winter's approach; however, in the eastern Aleutian Islands about eighty percent of the breeding population is still present on the islands at least through October. To date we do not know the length, duration, or path of migration for individual sea lions. We know some of the islands they use in the winter, but not their pattern of going to sea and returning.

An important event for the females, and for the whole species, occurs some three months after the breeding season ends. At that time the fertilized egg carried by the female attaches to the uterine wall and begins active growth. The cause of this "delayed implantation" is not known, but its effect is clear: it sets the date when all pups will be born in the next year, and thus determines when males

and females should gather at the rookeries.

Although the sea lion's hunting methods are unknown, examination of stomach contents and observation of its daily movements suggest that it feeds mostly at night. Most feeding occurs in less than six hundred feet of water, usually not more than fifteen miles from shore.

Both males and females appear to be opportunistic feeders, consuming flatfish, rockfish, or whatever fish is available in large numbers. In all studies to date, no commercially valuable fish, such as salmon, have been found as a major dietary item. The dependence of sea lions on these stocks may have been exaggerated because they are rarely seen feeding except when they occasionally molest fishing gear. The coexistence of sea lions and what are now considered commercially valuable fish has obviously lasted millions of years.

With the coming of spring, the great Steller sea lions approach a new reproductive season. They are drawn from their winter haunts toward their respective breeding areas. There, with a timing perfected through the ages, the social system entities emerge, mesh, and conceive the new lives for species survival.

A female Steller sea lion suckles both pup and yearling—an unusual sight. (Roger L. Gentry)

A Steller sea lion gives birth on Año Nuevo Island. (Roger L. Gentry)

California Sea Lion

by Bruce R. Mate

The California sea lion (*Zalophus californianus*) is probably best known for its performances in "trained seal" acts at zoos, circuses, and aquariums. External ears, a lack of dense underfur, and the ability to move on land using all four flippers distinguish this agile pinniped as a sea lion rather than a true seal, which is earless, or a fur seal, which has dense underfur.

Both the California and Steller sea lions haul out on eastern North Pacific shores. The California sea lion is smaller, darker, and more tropical in distribution than its northern counterpart, the Steller or northern sea lion, and its tapered head is more "doglike." Males may reach a total length of eight feet and weigh 800 pounds, while females are usually no longer than five feet and weigh no more than 250 pounds. Sea lion pups appear almost black in color, while adults vary from light chocolate brown when dry to black when wet. In Mexico, the female's color is much lighter, approaching the buff tan color of the northern sea lion. Although there are many apparent differences between the two species, early marine mammal authorities (including the well-known Charles Scammon) frequently did not discriminate adequately between them.

Three distinct populations of California sea lions exist, and each has been designated as a separate subspecies: *Zalophus californianus japonicus,* from the Sea of Japan, may now be extinct; *Z. c. wollebaeki,* from the Galápagos Islands, numbers between 20,000 and 50,000 individuals; and *Z. c. californianus,* which breeds along the west coast of North America from the southern tip of Baja, Mexico (lat 23° N), north to the Farallon Islands off San Francisco (lat 38° N), and throughout the Gulf of California, consists of 100,000 to 125,000 individuals. The latter population is the best known, and the most collected marine mammal species in aquariums, with 423 in captivity as of 1976. Because of its smaller size and appetite, and its more natural adaptation to warmer climates, it is preferred over the Steller in captivity.

California sea lions are powerful swimmers and efficient divers. They are capable of reaching speeds of up to fifteen or twenty miles per hour and, when pursued, "porpoise" on the surface. Some subadult

The slim, dark bodies of California sea lions are contrasted with a lone Steller sea lion (upper right). (Karl W. Kenyon)

and adult males migrate following the breeding season from Mexico and California north up into British Columbia, moving about one thousand miles in two months. Both sexes are thought to be capable of twenty-minute dives, although dives of two to five minutes duration are more frequent. This species can descend to at least 450 feet.

In the wild, California sea lions play by tossing kelp in the air or body surfing on swells near shore. They have also been observed leaping entirely out of the water. As pups, mock-fighting occurs. This jousting neck to neck and biting of flippers is similar to the territorial jousting of adult males.

Pupping and breeding usually occur on island-based rookeries during May and June. Males usually establish territories on sandy beaches along the water's edge. Females breed with a territorial male usually within ten days of giving birth to a single pup. After the breeding season, many of the adult and subadult males move north of the breeding range, some going as far as British Columbia, to spend the winter. (The females usually remain within the breeding range.) As the migratory male population moves northward, it becomes smaller as individuals drop out to spend the winter at various hauling areas. During this time, many male California sea lions haul out at locations used by the Steller sea lion during the breeding season. At some of these locations, the two species intermingle, while other locations may be used exclusively by one species or the other. In mixed groups, it is possible to detect the presence of California sea lions by their color, size, and distinctive doglike "bark," which is different from the lower pitched "roar" of the Steller sea lion.

The age of sea lions and many other mammals can be determined from the annual growth increments found in the teeth. In captivity California sea lions usually live twelve to fourteen years. One animal was known to live to age thirty-one—an

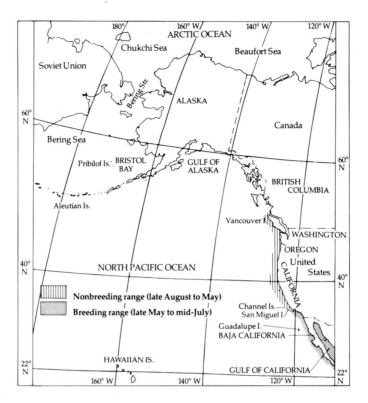

California sea lion distribution

unusual record. Such longevity may not occur in the wild. Most of the male sea lions found along the northwest Pacific coast during fall and winter are between four and fifteen years old. Animals younger than four apparently do not migrate that far north, and adult males over ten comprise only a small segment of the population.

At about age five, male California sea lions develop a distinctive sagittal crest, or "bump" on the top of the head, due to the growth of this portion of the skull. The crest becomes increasingly prominent during the animal's adult life—hence the sea lion's generic name, *Zalophus,* derived from the Greek intensive prefix *za* and *lophus,* meaning "crest." This crest is often more striking in older animals because the normally dark hair of the sea lion turns to light brown or tan in this area.

Except for the sagittal crest development, the age of California sea lions is often difficult to determine because of variability in growth rates among individuals. A four-year-old, for example, may be considerably smaller than some two-year-olds. Sea lions are therefore usually sorted into rather crude age class categories in most field studies: pups, yearlings, nonbreeders (subadult males and females together), adult females, and adult males. Females first breed around age four or five. Although males may be sexually mature at the same age, they usually are not able to defend breeding territories until they are older and larger, probably at age nine.

Commercial exploitation, particularly along southern California, was instrumental in reducing the populations of many pinnipeds and almost caused the extinction of some species. While California sea lion populations were not reduced to the same extreme as those of the northern elephant seal and the Guadalupe fur seal, many were taken once the more favored species were depleted. During this century, sea lions have been killed for dog food and taken alive for commercial entertainment in zoos, circuses, and aquariums. Today, it is illegal to kill or capture (except by special permit) any species of sea lion in the United States or Mexico.

No one knows how populations of California sea lions have changed since the white man began to influence their numbers. Although the total numbers of California sea lions were never accurately assessed during the nineteenth century, it is well known that thousands were killed during that time for their oil. It is safe to say that the species was reduced during the nineteenth century and has increased over the years to a population that now probably inhabits its entire preexploitation range. In fact, this sea lion's northern range has changed during this century. In the late 1930s, the Steller sea lion was the most abundant pinniped in the Channel Islands, numbering over two thousand; it is now present in that area only on San Miguel (the northernmost island) in low numbers. During that same period, the California sea lion population has grown to at least thirty-five thousand. Despite the larger physical size of Steller sea lions, it would appear that circumstances have changed to favor California sea lions. Both animals are opportunistic feeders, and come ashore on similar types of areas to breed and rest. California sea lions may "out compete" northern sea lions for some critical resource, such as food or space, that both species require.

Population size is influenced, of course, by birth and death rates. Over the last few years, there has been concern about whether the annual birth rate for both California and Steller sea lions has been decreasing. Without sufficient information about the past performance of these species, it is difficult now to say accurately whether such a phenomenon is occurring. However, high concentrations of chlorinated hydrocarbons, such as DDT, have been found in the tissues of most marine mammals as have pathogenic bacteria and viruses. Together, these are thought to reduce reproductive success by causing premature births (abortions) and increasing the mortality rate of newborn pups. Pup mortalities in this and many other species of pinnipeds may be largely related to weather conditions; a severe storm during the pupping season may be responsible for large numbers of pups being swept off the rookery and drowning or dying from exposure. Sharks and killer whales are natural predators of sea lions; sea lion remains are often found in their stomachs.

Various parasites have been found in the California sea lion, but not much is known about the effect of these organisms on their hosts. Diseases among marine mammals are not well known, although instances of infection are found in wild animals and illness in captive animals is common. Many problems of captive animals probably arise

Perhaps best known in captivity as "performing seals," California sea lions in the wild are naturally playful. Here they rest in the surf. (Karl W. Kenyon)

from diet and the increased exposure to exotic microorganisms not encountered in the wild.

During the fall of 1970, the occurrence of large numbers of sick California sea lions prompted an investigation by a number of agencies and academic-research institutions. The illness was diagnosed as leptospirosis, a disease that is caused by any one of several species of *Leptospira* (a spirochete bacteria) and is common to many wild and domestic terrestrial mammals. While this disease typically results in few deaths, some data suggested a rather high mortality rate. This may be typical for many species exposed to a new disease, although there is suspicion that this particular disease has been associated with sea lions for some time. Because there are no previous records of confirmed leptospirosis in California sea lions, it is difficult to conclude whether this or other natural diseases may be the effective regulators of their population numbers. During the fall of 1947, many sick and dead sea lions were found on California beaches. Although the tentative diagnosis was streptococcal pneumonia, it may have been leptospirosis.

The incidence of leptospirosis during 1970 was the first widespread disease ever observed under natural circumstances in any marine mammal. The disease is spread via the urine, allowing an infected animal on the hauling grounds to expose large numbers of healthy sea lions to the organism. The Steller sea lion's anatomy and physiology are very similar to that of the California sea lion. Although these two species seasonally cohabit many hauling areas, Steller sea lions have not shown any symptoms of leptospirosis. One explanation of this phenomenon may be that the environment of the winter hauling areas is too harsh for survival of the bacteria, hence it cannot spread to other individuals. Or, the bacteria may be species-specific and unable to infect the Steller sea lion, even under optimal conditions. California sea lions may have been exposed to *Leptospira* bacteria during their breeding season in the more temperate surroundings of southern California and Mexico. Follow-up studies indicate that this disease was still present at low incidence levels in 1976.

While there have been dramatic changes in the breeding range and the apparent abundance of these animals in the last fifty years, man has played a role in limiting the distribution of sea lions. Although occasionally found seventy-five miles offshore, sea lions are more conventionally considered nearshore animals. Historically, coastal states have frequently viewed these animals as competitors for fish. As a result, bounties, open seasons, or state hunters frequently have been used in certain areas to reduce seal and sea lion numbers. River systems were particularly well guarded, especially where fishing for anadromous fish occurred.

The United States Marine Mammal Protection Act of 1972 forbids the harassment or killing of any marine mammal. As a result of reduced harassment by man, plus the pinnipeds' opportunistic feeding habits and quick learning ability, both seals and sea lions are again using upriver areas. Kitchen middens up several rivers indicate that pinnipeds were probably utilized by Indians in these areas before the white man arrived.

In the face of reduced fishery resources—due in part to overfishing, the destruction of fish spawning habitat from poor forest practices, hydroelectric power dams, and pollution—social and political pressures are mounting to have the effect of marine mammals as competitors determined or reduce their numbers. While commercial conflicts (such as California sea lions taking fish off of ocean trollers' hooks) have been documented in some areas, it is the sport fishermen who are now concerned about the appearance of California sea lions in rivers. Whether the sea lions take "too many" fish or not, fishermen report that the mere presence of a sea lion inhibits the fish from biting.

A recent observation on the Columbia River in Washington State demonstrates the sea lion's upriver range and foraging ability. During April 1977 a California sea lion was seen immediately above Bonneville Dam, some 146 miles from the ocean. No one knows whether this animal went upstream through the locks or up the fish ladder at the dam. State officials and the public watched as this animal ate the fish coming up the fish ladder. As people tried to decide how to cope with this new phenomenon, the animal hopped onto a barge headed through the locks and disappeared downriver. In light of such occurrences, it will be interesting to see how man and sea lion try to cope with one another over the next few years.

Walrus

by Karl W. Kenyon

The walrus (*Odobenus rosmarus*) shares certain characteristics with both the otariids (eared seals) and the phocids (earless seals). Other physical attributes, however, are unique to this pinniped—its skin, methods of sleeping at sea and feeding, and its distinctive tusks. Thus the walrus is placed in a taxonomic family (Odobenidae) all its own.

Superficially the walrus resembles the phocids in that it lacks external ears. It also shares some basic structural characteristics with the otariids, such as the ability to rotate the hindflippers forward, enabling it to walk on a solid surface. In contrast to its pinniped relatives, however, the molting of its short, rusty brown fur is so extreme that the male walrus becomes hairless, its "warty" skin exposed to the elements. In the water, this skin appears whitish in color, but when the animal rests in warm sunlight, blood circulation increases and the skin turns quite pink. Also unique to the walrus are the paired air sacs in its neck; these can be inflated to hold the head above water when the animal sleeps at sea.

Most distinctive of the walrus's adaptations are its heavy canine teeth or tusks, which, in the male, may be up to 39.5 inches long and weigh as much as twelve pounds. The female's tusks are slimmer and lighter. The tusks aid the walrus in hauling out on the ice packs where it sleeps, molts, and gives birth to its young. Blunt, peglike cheek teeth or postcanines are also present in the walrus's mouth. Examinations of the dentine layers of these teeth indicate that its life expectancy is between twenty and thirty years.

The walrus gathers food from the sea bottom, usually at depths of 120 to 200 feet. Some writers have presumed that it uses its tusks like a grub hoe to dig clams. To biologists this seems unlikely. Because the tusks show wear primarily on the frontal surface, it seems probable that the walrus glides along the bottom, using its tusks like sled runners, while its heavy whisker pads search in the mud for clams. The whiskers of wild walruses are worn off short, while in captivity (where food is furnished) they may grow long. This observation supports the conclusion that the muscular whisker pads are actively used during feeding.

Adult male walruses—one with a missing tusk—sun on Round Island, part of Alaska's Walrus Islands State Game Sanctuary. (Karl W. Kenyon)

The walrus's feeding technique is peculiar: its highly vaulted mouth, a unique structural feature, works with the tongue to produce suction, much like a vacuum cleaner. Equipped in this manner, it apparently separates clam meat from the shells, discarding the shells and swallowing the meat. Eskimo hunters often eat undigested and undamaged clam meat taken from the stomachs of slaughtered walruses after rinsing the clams in sea water.

Among pinnipeds, the walrus is second in size to the elephant seal. One large male weighed 3,432 pounds and a female 1,500 pounds. The male reaches sexual maturity at about six years, the female at five to seven. Little is known about mating behavior, which apparently takes place far out at sea on floating ice in early spring.

In April or May, the female walrus gives birth to a single calf after a gestation period of about one year. (Although several twin fetuses have been recorded, usually only one calf is produced.) She cares for her calf over an unusually long period—about two years—and often carries it on her back as she travels north in the spring—no small effort since a newborn walrus may weigh up to 150 pounds. When the calf is one or two years old, the mother may become pregnant again. According to Eskimo legend, female walruses adopt orphan calves. Perhaps this is true but scientific documentation is yet to be obtained. Some other pinnipeds, particularly the northern fur seal, are known not to tolerate orphans. Other aspects of the walrus's social behavior—such as harem formation and territoriality—are still unknown.

The economic incentive to exploit pinnipeds for oil and hides decreased after the chaotic slaughter of the eighteenth and nineteenth centuries when many marine mammal species were seriously depleted. During the present century, those animals that continue to yield valuable products—such as elephant seals and fur seals—are protected from overexploitation. The Pacific walrus occupies a

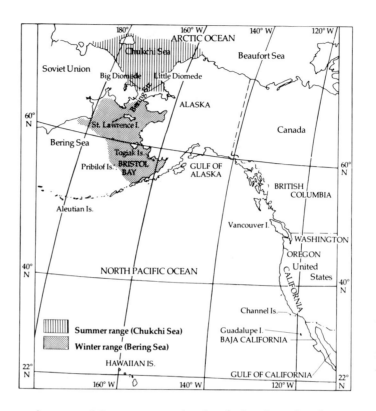

Walrus distribution. Several thousand adult and subadult males remain among the Togiak Islands into the summer.

unique position among pinnipeds in that the demand for its ivory, both carved and unworked (or raw), has increased in recent years.

On 11 May 1958, when the late Stan Fredericksen and I arrived to begin a walrus study at Ignalook Village on Little Diomede, Alaska, the island was icebound. Hunting started a week later and was almost finished when I departed on 14 June; virtually all ice and migrating walruses had passed northward into the Chukchi Sea. Until June, the ice shelf between Little and Big Diomede had remained intact and hunting was conducted off the south tip of the island.

While the ice was breaking up and passing through Bering Strait, the Eskimos hunted from their umiaks throughout the twenty-four daylight hours. Among the one hundred Eskimos living at

Ignalook, there were enough hunters to man four boats. These were wooden framed craft, from twenty to thirty feet long, covered with walrus skins, and powered by outboard engines. Each carried between six and thirteen hunters. Usually they had to travel four to ten miles out to sea, sometimes as much as thirty miles. While we were there, the Eskimos made fifty-seven hunting trips; 245 walruses were killed that season. Of these, 117 were recovered and 128 were lost through sinking.

During our six-week stay, roughly 5,000 to 10,000 walruses passed Little Diomede through the eastern Bering Strait. Between 1,900 and 2,100 were actually seen. The majority usually pass northward through waters off Siberia, west of Big Diomede. Fog often reduced our visibility, but we could hear the walruses bawling.

Research conducted by Alaska biologist John J. Burns during the 1960s and 1970s indicates that the walrus population is increasing. Five aerial surveys between 1960 and 1972 show that when the Bering Sea ice pack is at its maximum, walruses are concentrated primarily in two areas: in the western Bering Sea both north and south of Saint Lawrence Island, and in central Bristol Bay. They are scarce in the northeastern Bering Sea. It is impossible to count all of these animals because their habitat consists of many thousand square miles of ice. In 1972, we counted over nine thousand walruses along a one-mile-wide flight track during a flight covering about five thousand miles. From our data at that time, we calculated the population of the Pacific walrus at more than one hundred thousand animals.

Subsequently, additional surface and aerial surveys have been conducted, motivated in part by the United States Marine Mammal Protection Act of 1972 and by environmental impact studies related to petroleum development and the possible commercial exploitation of Bering Sea clam resources. Some of these were cooperative studies involving biologists of both the United States and the Soviet Union. The best current estimate of the Pacific walrus population is between one hundred sixty thousand and two hundred thousand.

Since prehistoric times, Eskimos of certain Bering Sea islands—namely Nunivak, Saint Lawrence, King, and Big and Little Diomede—have depended on the walrus. Meat and blubber were (and to a limited degree still are) used for human and sled-dog food, and the blubber oil was used for lamp fuel. The skin is still cut in strips for line and rope and split into two sheets to cover their wooden framed boats or umiaks. Although the tusks traditionally provided a smooth surface for sled runners, they are now primarily used in carvings of small arctic figures—including walruses, polar bears, seals, other wildlife, and Eskimos. These are such popular tourist items that many walruses have been killed primarily for their tusks—a practice called "head hunting."

To reduce this wasteful killing before the enactment of the Marine Mammal Protection Act, Alaska state law prohibited the sale of raw or uncarved ivory. Limits were also placed on the number of walruses that could be killed. Trophy hunters were limited to one adult male, and only subsistence hunters could kill more.

During the 1960s more factors favoring walrus conservation developed. As snowmobiles replaced dog sleds, the need for walrus meat as sled-dog food dwindled. Ironically, even trophy hunting, authorized in May 1957, became one of the most important conservation factors. In 1969, John J. Burns wrote that the Eskimos "have reached the point of a rapidly developing trend toward providing services for trophy hunters and photographers that is resulting in reduced harvests and increased monetary return to Eskimo guides. . . . Resident subsistence hunters are very interested in becoming guides since they no longer have to secure the large quantities of meat formerly required. Numerous regulations apply to guides and one of the most important is that guides (and the entire boat crew working for a guide) are not permitted to take game while guiding. . . . Each guided hunt (for trophy or for photos) in essence eliminates one of the traditional boat hunting days in which many walruses were killed. Instead, one bull is taken (or none if a photographer is out), the meat goes to the crew, they also receive a very worthwhile fee, and the hunter gets his trophy."

During the 1960s island Eskimos moved to mainland towns, another conservation factor. King Island, where a large part of the total Alaska kill of fifteen hundred to two thousand walruses was taken, was deserted by the early 1970s. Today, few hunters return from their new homes in Nome to take part in the traditional spring hunt.

The Marine Mammal Protection Act of 1972 removed the walrus from Alaska state jurisdiction. Under this federal law, trophy hunting was illegal, and walrus taking was permitted only for native subsistence. The Eskimos, to satisfy their economic

Walruses swim and rest together on the rocky shores of Round Island in Bristol Bay, Alaska. In water, walrus skin appears white, while in warm sunlight, the skin turns quite pink because of increased blood circulation. (Karl W. Kenyon)

needs, have increased their take of walruses in recent years as greater demand for ivory carvings has encouraged exploitation of the walrus.

There is, however, a more serious threat to the future of the large walrus population. It began in 1977 with the arrival of an experimental clam dredge in the Bering Sea. In winter months, while the walruses are in the Bering Sea, they apparently depend primarily on clams for subsistence. Captive walruses may consume sixty pounds of clams daily. If one hundred thousand animals (assuming that all animals do not eat every day) require a similar amount, then it is possible that the present walrus herd requires over six million pounds of clams daily.

Modern technological clam dredging has now depleted the clam resources of the western North Atlantic. If this industry transfers its activities to the rich Bering Sea feeding grounds of the Pacific walrus, the walrus population may well suffer serious depletion. To avoid this, the clam industry must be stringently regulated and prohibited from operating in the important walrus feeding grounds.

Today, the walrus's only regular summer hauling grounds in the United States are on the Walrus Islands, a group of seven islands in northeast Bristol Bay, Alaska. In June 1958, we found fifteen hundred to two thousand males, both adult and immature, on only one of these islands—Round Island. Most were hauled up on narrow cobble beaches skirting the base of sheer granite cliffs more than one hundred feet high. The majority were molting; many were completely hairless. When approached quietly upwind, they were not easily alarmed, and we were able to place metal tags on the flippers of twelve resting individuals.

As a result of our 1958 survey, we concluded that the Walrus Islands in Bristol Bay should be set aside as a refuge. Our opinion was strengthened when some Togiak villagers were convicted of wastefully slaughtering walruses at the Round Is-

land hauling ground. In June 1960, the Alaska government designated these islands the "Walrus Islands State Game Sanctuary," but the natives of Togiak are still seeking special hunting privileges there.

Observations in the mid-1970s confirmed that population increase had continued: 3,000 or more walruses were hauling out on Round Island. Also, in 1962 and 1965 a few walruses (100 to 150) were first seen in modern times on the beaches of Amak Island, near the Alaska Peninsula. Another Walrus Island, in the Pribilof group, was formerly also an important summer hauling ground. Soon after its discovery in 1786, however, the walruses that habitually came there were killed. It is gratifying that in the mid-1970s, a few of these animals are returning to their ancestral Pribilof hauling grounds. They have not been molested and several were observed at Saint Paul Island in the summer of 1977.

Legal responsibility for walrus management has become controversial in recent years. The state of Alaska petitioned Congress, under provisions of the Marine Mammal Protection Act, to return jurisdiction over certain marine mammals, including the walrus, to the state. Jurisdiction over only the walrus was returned to the state on 6 April 1976. Also, organizations supporting native claims for certain aboriginal rights have complicated prospects concerning jurisdiction over walrus management. Because of environmental as well as jurisdictional factors, the future condition of the Pacific walrus population is still difficult to predict with certainty.

Pacific Harbor Seal

by Terrell C. Newby

Long before scientists began to study and observe the Pacific harbor seal, Captain Charles Scammon, a nineteenth-century whaling skipper, wrote: "At times, when a number meet in the neighborhood of rocks or reefs distant from the mainland, they become quite playful, and exhibit much life in their gambols, leaping out of the water or circling around upon the surface." Toward man, however, the harbor seal is a shy, retiring creature and is seldom seen by most people.

One of the most common and widely distributed pinnipeds in the North Pacific, *Phoca vitulina* is known by various common names: Pacific harbor seal, spotted seal, common seal, or hair seal. It belongs to the family Phocidae, the true or earless seals.

Two subspecies are found in the North Pacific. *Phoca vitulina largha*, the ice breeding form (see "Ice Seals" chapter), lives in the seasonal ice pack in winter and spring, bearing and nurturing its pups in these waters and then moving toward the coast as the ice pack retreats. It is found from East Cape in the Bering Sea to the coast of China. *P. v. richar-*
dii, the coastal form, lives primarily in the more temperate ice-free waters extending south from the Bering Sea to Cedros Island off Baja California. It is the more sedentary of the two subspecies.

In 1973, the estimated harbor seal population in the North Pacific was seven hundred fifty thousand, with *richardii* comprising the major portion. Since the passage of the United States Marine Mammal Protection Act of 1972, there has been a gradual increase in numbers, with the current populations appearing high and stable. For example, the harbor seal population in Washington State, estimated in 1970 at twenty-one hundred, reached fifty-five hundred in 1977. In British Columbia, the harbor seal has been protected since 1970; about thirty-five thousand inhabit the coastal mud flats, sandbars, and reefs of this province.

Throughout its range, the harbor seal is now experiencing a time of protection and peace. It is hunted by only certain natives, with minimal impact in the Arctic. Commercial fishermen, however, do exert some pressure, for seals can be legally destroyed (by means of an exclusion permit in the

On Otter Island in the Aleutians, a harbor seal caught napping raises its foreflipper in surprise. (Karl W. Kenyon)

United States) when they conflict with a fishery. In addition, more subtle predators—in the form of effluent poisons—are now taking their toll on some harbor seal colonies.

The harbor seal frequents rivers and marine estuaries along the coast. Members of the Lewis and Clark expedition in the nineteenth century mistook this seal for an otter when they saw it at The Dalles, Oregon, 180 miles inland on the Columbia River. Even today, it is commonly seen during the winter some 25 miles up the Columbia. In California, the harbor seal has turned up in the American River, 130 miles northeast of San Francisco.

Along the Pacific coast and in Washington State's Puget Sound, one might find them hauled out at low tide on sandspits and coastal rocks. Small reefs around such islands as the San Juans in Washington State and the Gulf Islands in British Columbia provide sites for low tide haulings and ventures. Seeming to select a particular protected location for their hauls—one with unobstructed access to water—harbor seals usually spend equal amounts of time on land and sea. Still, the hauling ground is their home—the hub of their life activities. Here they use the low tidelands for rest cycles, birth, and care of the young.

Man, of course, is the principal disrupter of the harbor seal's habitat. San Francisco Bay provides a typical example. Although the bay is highly urbanized and developed, the harbor seal still survives at three sites: a rookery on Castro Rocks under the Richmond–San Rafael Bridge; at Strawberry Spit, a seasonal area in the North Bay; and at Mowry Slough in the South Bay, where they are most numerous. Strawberry Spit is a typically disturbed colony. In 1973, after much public protest, a 360-unit condominium was built on the spit. To protect the seal colony, a chain link fence was constructed and a five-mile-per-hour speed limit was established along the adjacent waterway. In spite of these protective measures, the seal population has

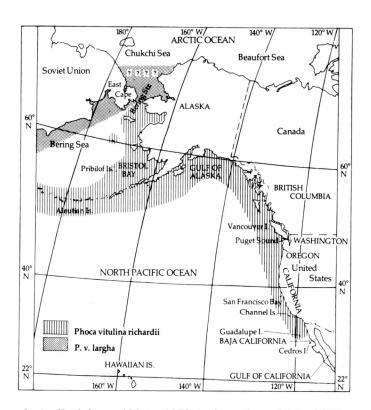

Pacific harbor seal distribution

dwindled from 100 in 1973 to less than 50 in 1977. Joggers and dogs have caused the most damage by traveling around the fence at low tide and going into the seal preserve.

In 1970, Paul A. Paulbitski, one of the first biologists in the area to study these seals, estimated a total of three hundred seals seasonally in San Francisco Bay. Because of their sensitivity to disturbance, he predicts a major reduction in this population if the pressure continues. It would be a pity if this occurred considering how precariously this animal has maintained its existence in such a polluted urban environment.

A typical adult harbor seal of either sex measures from sixty-seven to seventy-five inches and weighs up to 250 pounds. Coloration varies from near white to black, but most often is bluish gray

On Gertrude Island in Washington's Puget Sound, a general haul out shows the characteristic tail flexing of the resting harbor seal. (Terrell C. Newby)

with black spots and irregular white rings and loops. Because of its rings and coloration, the *largha* has been confused with the ringed seal of the Arctic. The ringed seal is smaller, however, and completely dependent on the sea ice.

The harbor seal has been known to dive to depths of almost two hundred feet for short periods and can remain underwater for as long as twenty-three minutes, although most dives average five to six minutes. When diving, it conserves oxygen by constricting all peripheral blood vessels, thus limiting the blood supply to only the vital organs—heart, lungs, kidneys, brain, and intestines. During a dive, its heart slows from an average eighty-five beats to fifteen or twenty beats per minute. High levels of myoglobin (oxygen binders in the blood) in seal muscle protect the animal from tetany (muscle-oxygen deficiency) during these dives.

This diving characteristic has an added benefit. I have observed that the harbor seal can "sleep" on the bottom in shallows when unable to use hauling sites because of disturbance. Underwater, it conserves energy with a reduced heart beat for periods of up to six minutes, surfacing to breathe for about one minute. During one aerial survey, I observed over sixty seals sleeping on the bottom of a shallow cove near McNeil Island, Washington.

Although reproduction studies of the Pacific harbor seal are far from complete, some information is available. The *largha* subspecies forms pairs in March for the duration of a breeding season that ends in April or May. Their single white-coated pup is born the following March or April. The

"Helen K," a blind female harbor seal, rests with her pup on the shores of Gertrude Island. This seal has been recognized by researchers since 1965. (Terrell C. Newby)

richardii, on the other hand, are polygamous. From April until September, they are found in large concentrations where single pups are born. These pups, however, are born with their adult coloration, having shed in utero their white lanugo coats. This lanugo fur is always associated with the afterbirth, which is not consumed by the mother but by gulls and other carrion consumers.

In Washington State, harbor seal birth periods are unique. There are three distinct pupping periods within less than one hundred miles. The two-week pupping season begins in May on the outer coast, in July in northern Puget Sound, and in August in southern Puget Sound. Although several theories have been advanced for this peculiar ecological situation—ranging from food availability at time of weaning to change in photoperiods—no data support the theories, and the mystery remains.

At birth, the harbor seal pup is a skinny, pathetic-looking creature. It emits plaintive cries that may cause the compassionate beachcomber to mistake it for an orphaned animal. Unfortunately, pups are sometimes whisked away from their mothers by well-meaning but untrained persons.

At birth, pups of both subspecies weigh twenty to twenty-six pounds and are thirty-three to thirty-eight inches long. During their four- to six-week nursing periods, they more than double their birth weight because of the high butterfat content (forty-two percent by volume) in the female's milk.

After the birth of the pup, the female *richardii* form nursery areas apart from the main colony for about two weeks. The *largha*, on the other hand, do not form large breeding colonies but are characterized by a family group of a male, female, and pup. These family groupings, found along the ice edge, may be separated from one another by distances of a few feet to many miles.

While nursing, the pup plays with its mother, riding on her back, nipping at her flippers, and chasing her in the water. The female harbor seal is a devoted parent; though she may temporarily abandon her young if disturbed, she will soon return to retrieve the pup. So strong is the mother-pup bond that I have seen one female drag her dead pup around for as long as three days.

Soon after weaning, the adult seals breed. Males of both *largha* and *richardii* subspecies become sexually mature at four to five years, females at three to four years. Just prior to copulation, there is a great deal of excited play, during which the female takes fierce bites of the male's neck and shoulders while the two animals roll, cavort, and occasionally jump completely out of the water. During the breeding season, one commonly observes numerous males bearing the wounds of this love play. Actual copulation takes place in the water.

After conception, delayed implantation retards embryonic development. This is characteristic of pinnipeds and some terrestrial mammals (bears, mink, and badgers) and is a little understood process. Simply stated, the following steps occur: the fertilized egg (zygote) remains in the blastula (ball) state of development for a period of time (in the case of the harbor seal, for two months); then the egg plants itself in the uterine wall and begins full development. Actual fetal growth requires between nine and ten months, which makes a total gestation of eleven months.

Life expectancy for the harbor seal is about thirty years, although there are few recorded "known age" animals. I have determined age in seals that have died naturally beyond twenty years. Of the harbor seals in captivity, Dub-Dub at the Point Defiance Aquarium in Tacoma, Washington, lived for a record thirty-three years before his death in 1972.

Common parasites of harbor seals are anisakid roundworms and acanthocephalons (banjo worms). Occasionally they are also plagued by high infestations of anopluran lice. The latter have been found in epidemic proportions in a small population of harbor seals in southern Puget Sound and are usually associated with heartworms. Harbor seal worm infections contribute in some areas to a high incidence of worm infections in fish. This occurs especially in codfish, which consume worm eggs that are present in seal feces. Respiratory infections and blindness also take their toll on harbor seals.

In 1970, Douglas Arndt and I reported another health problem that has become increasingly evident in recent years—possible PCB and DDT poisoning. The harbor seals on Gertrude Island, Washington, were found to have a high incidence of birth defects in thirty-seven percent of the pups born in 1972. PCB levels found in the blubber and liver tissues of these seals have been as high as 400 parts per million (ppm). One stillborn was found to contain 38.5 ppm PCB in its liver. PCB concentrations between 0.6 and 3 ppm are known to cause mammalian reproductive dysfunction, metabolic anomalies, microsomal enzyme inhibition, and mortality. Although these chemicals are now banned from use by the United States Toxic Substance Control Act of 1976, they are extremely slow to break down in the environment and will undoubtedly be around for many years.

Man threatens the harbor seal's existence in another way. This seal has been at odds with commercial and sport fishermen because it damages fishing gear when competing with man for such fish as herring, smelt, and whitefish. It is most maligned for its taste for an occasional salmon, although research shows that salmon account for only two to five percent of the seal's diet. The harbor seal does not concentrate on any one prey species but is an opportunist, taking the item that requires the least expenditure of energy. Its favorite foods are sole, flounder, sculpin, hake, cod, herring, squid, octopus, and an odd clam or snail. Yet because it damages fishing nets and eats some fish that are also popular with people, the harbor seal has literally "come under the gun." Between 1940

and 1960, for instance, about seventeen thousand seals were killed for bounty in Washington State and some fifty-two thousand in British Columbia. Extensive hunting pressure over the past years has caused this timid sea mammal to abandon such traditional hauling grounds as Washington State's Nisqually Delta where in the 1940s there were nearly two hundred seals; today there are none breeding. Although the killer whale is the harbor seal's natural enemy, it is obviously man—with his poisons and rifles—who is the most significant predator of this retiring animal.

"What good are harbor seals?" people often ask me. "All they do is lie around and stretch." I can only answer this way:

It is nearly four o'clock on a summer morning in Puget Sound. The blue gray waters are calm, the surface ruffled by an occasional breeze from the southwest. I move a small boat toward Gertrude Island, the last remaining stronghold of the harbor seal in southern Puget Sound. My trip is timed for arrival on low tide—for access to the maximum number of seals. Rounding the northern tip of Gertrude, I am treated to the sweet fragrance of the little island's fir trees and the intermittent sounds of gulls and ducks at the water's edge.

About one hundred feet from the seals, I land and quietly secure the boat. Then I crawl up to a point from which I can count some 120 individuals. The plaintive call of a new pup breaks the stillness: "Maaa. . .aa," it says, or "Kru. . .oo." The females lift their heads, searching for ever present dangers, while gulls nearby consume a placenta, reminder of an earlier birth. It is a scene filled with life at its fullest, and my heart throbs in tune. There is "Frank," sleeping at his post, his scarred old head resting on a rock as if it were a pillow of finest down. Near the water's edge is "Helen K," a blind female, again with a fat, sassy pup—her fifth. All around seals are stretching, yawning, growling, grunting, sliding in the water, and moving across the beach.

A harbor seal oversleeps while the tide changes. This hauling position is not uncommon to seals using rocky reefs along Pacific Grove, California. (Terrell C. Newby)

Out in the harbor, males and females are engaged in courtship display. One animal jumps clear of the water in whale fashion. In the mid-distance, a pup tries to nurse from an old male. It is tolerated, then rebuked when the annoyed male snaps. The pup crawls away, calling for his mother. For the moment, all are at apparent peace with their environment.

At the end of my visit, I walk Gertrude's beaches, searching for scat and for animals that may have died. One poor creature, a badly deformed pup with no tail and truncated flippers, lies dead under driftwood at the high tide line. I can only wonder what insidious man-made chemicals may be contributing to the cause of such a monstrosity. The remains are gathered for further study. Back toward the spit, a head or two can be seen in the water, watching my movements. Then, with an alarm slap to the surface, my friends depart. I too leave, somehow hoping that what I have received from the seals can be shared with others so we can gain a better understanding of the relationship between man and animal—each a part of the other in nature's total scheme.

Ice Seals

by John J. Burns

Regions of sea ice of various types—shifting and stable, seasonal and permanent—are the home of four species of northern seals: the ringed seal, bearded seal, spotted seal, and ribbon seal. Each of these seals is adapted to areas within a vast marine system that extends almost one thousand nautical miles north to south from the northern Chukchi Sea (a southern embayment of the Arctic Ocean) to the Bering Sea (a northern embayment of the Pacific Ocean). Exchange between the two seas is through the Bering Strait.

Within this area are constraining boundaries and obstructions formed by the shores of Siberia and Alaska, as well as several large islands; the relatively warm, ice-free, open ocean of the southwestern Bering Sea; and the relatively cold, permanently ice-covered Arctic Ocean. The ice here is not simply one vast, homogeneous habitat type, for weather conditions produce a predictable variety of annually recurring, extensive habitats that change seasonally. As one would expect, the seals that inhabit these areas are adapted to exploit different ecological niches within this system.

Of the four ice-associated seals in the Bering-Chukchi region, only the ringed seal (*Phoca hispida*) can be considered an arctic species. It successfully occupies the thick, extensive ice of the far north and bears its young in arctic weather conditions. It is most abundant in the landfast ice north of the Bering Strait, and also occurs throughout the ice-covered regions, even south to the "edge." For the most part, it maintains a year-round association with the ice.

In winter, the ringed seal is found throughout the ice-covered regions of the Bering and Chukchi seas; it is the only one of the four species to occupy the landfast or shore ice at this time of year. In other seasons, it migrates with the annual advance and retreat of the pack ice. In winter, highest densities occur near shore in the stable landfast ice. The ringed seal's abundance in this zone accounts for its great importance to the coast-dwelling Eskimos of northern Alaska.

This seal's scientific name is derived from the Greek *Phoca*, meaning "seal," and the Latin *hispida*, meaning "rough" or "bristly," which refers to the

A bearded seal, largest of the four ice-associated seals, basks on sea ice in the Bering Sea. Its head is disproportionately small for such a heavy body. The claws on its foreflippers can be used for making breathing holes in the ice. (Lewis Consiglieri)

stiff hairs of its coat.

The coat's color varies, with the most common pattern being a background of silver gray on the flanks and belly, and blue gray on the back. This seal's common name is derived from the light gray rings that encircle most of the irregularly spaced, black spots along the back, upper sides, and, on some individuals, on the belly. Some seals appear uniformly dark gray to black, with gray rings. During the rut, the breeding male develops a dark face.

A very large ringed seal from the Bering Sea may weigh 250 pounds; however, most adults weigh between 140 and 180 pounds, the lightest weight of the four ice seal species. Although similar in size, both sexes are subject to great seasonal fluctuations in weight: they are heaviest in winter and early spring, and lightest in early summer. On the average, about forty-five to fifty percent of their total body weight is comprised of hide and blubber.

Although adult ringed seals may attain a length of fifty-one inches, most are between forty and forty-seven inches long. Girth immediately behind the foreflippers averages eighty-nine percent of the length, which makes this seal appear short and round.

Using the strong claws of its foreflippers, the ringed seal maintains breathing holes through the thick, stable ice. It can also excavate lairs in accumulated snow, a habit that differentiates it from the other ice-associated species. The lairs are used by seals of all ages for resting and pupping. Pups are born in the large-chambered birth lairs, which are continually occupied for several weeks and thus are most common in regions of thick, stable ice. The ringed seal appears to be territorial, and the focal point of the territory of a female with pup is probably the pupping lair. Birth and resting lairs that are formed by the rafting of ice into pressure ridges are also used. In Alaska waters, ringed seals do not normally haul out on land. Those found on beaches are invariably debilitated, the largest pro-

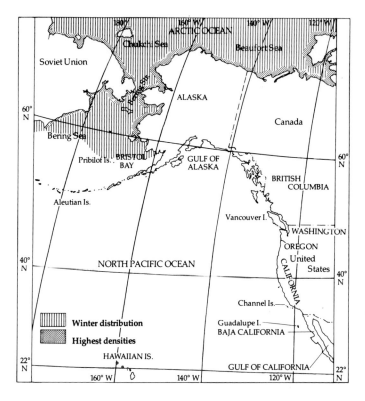

Ringed seal winter distribution—ice-covered regions, with greatest concentrations in fast ice near shore. Summer distribution—north with retreating ice front.

portion being starveling pups that come ashore in early summer.

Ringed seal habitat in the Bering and Chukchi seas occurs in the uniformly shallow water that overlies the extensive Bering-Chukchi continental shelf. This shelf has an average depth of about two hundred feet. However, these seals are by no means restricted to shallow water and, in fact, occur in considerable numbers over deep water such as that in the polar basin.

The ringed seal is probably not a deep diver. Research by J. E. King, a zoologist at the University of New South Wales, indicates that this seal may dive to depths of three hundred feet. A depth of six hundred feet is probably closer to the limit for this species. In very deep water, the ringed seal feeds on organisms in the upper parts of the water column. Maximum diving time, based on field observations, appears to be between fifteen and twenty-two minutes. Experiments conducted at the University of Alaska indicate a maximum of about seventeen minutes in the subadult seals tested.

Depending on the season and the area occupied, this pinniped consumes a variety of foods. In deep water, it subsists mainly on polar cod and zooplankton. In other areas, small fish and shrimps are important. Major prey items include amphipods, mysids, euphausiids, shrimps, crabs, and small pelagic or nektobenthonic schooling fish such as saffron and polar cod, capelin, and sand lance.

The ringed seal is long-lived, attaining a maximum age of thirty-six to forty years. One male reportedly reached the age of forty-three. Physical maturity is probably attained at nine to eleven years in both sexes.

The female ringed seal is sexually mature at six to eight years, the male at seven to nine years. They are monogamous and breeding occurs every year from April to early May. The breeding male has a strong odor, best described as smelling like gasoline, and so is referred to locally as a "gasoline seal." Its meat has a disagreeable taste and is almost unpalatable.

The total gestation period is some 11 months, including a 3.5-month period of delayed implantation. The pups are then usually born in early April. They weigh between eight and ten pounds, measure about twenty-three inches in length, and are covered with a dense white coat of lanugo, or baby fur, which they retain during the nursing period. This period lasts from four to six weeks, apparently depending on the stability of the ice in which the birth lair is constructed. After the lanugo coat is shed, the pup's color resembles that of an adult.

The pups stay in the birth lair until they are weaned. At normal weaning, the young seal weighs between twenty and thirty pounds. If the birth lairs are destroyed by an unusually early ice breakup,

the newborns are apparently abandoned by their mother, and the incidence of starveling pups on the beaches is quite high in such years.

Four to six weeks after giving birth, the female ringed seal is again impregnated. In most years, eighty to ninety percent of the adult females are pregnant, although the incidence of pregnancy occasionally has been less than seventy percent. Although the cause or causes of this variation are unknown, they appear to be related to severe ice conditions that result in reduced production of food.

The arctic fox, the polar bear, and man are this seal's most significant predators. The arctic fox preys heavily on pups in their birth lairs, and is reported to be the major cause of natural mortality of these seals in their early life. Predation by foxes in specific areas has been reported in excess of forty-

The ringed seal, smallest of the ice seals, is so named because of the light gray rings that encircle spots on its sides and back. (John J. Burns)

five percent of the newborns, and the mortality is known to vary greatly in relation to the marked "cyclic" abundance of the arctic fox.

Polar bears also prey extensively on ringed seals throughout the year. Although the polar bear feeds on the bearded seal, walrus, beluga whale, birds, carrion, and other items, the relationship between this bear and the ringed seal is probably such that the polar bear would not exist as a species if this seal did not also exist. Polar bears catch ringed seals of all ages, hunting them in open water leads, in lairs, at breathing holes, and when they are basking on the ice. Their seasonal movements in the Bering and Chukchi seas are related to changes in the sea ice cover and to the distribution of ringed seals. Although the impact of this predation is unknown, it is certainly significant.

Several behavioral attributes of these seals have probably evolved, at least in part, as a result of this continuous predation by bears. This behavior includes the ringed seal's preference for hauling out on flat ice where it can view the surrounding area, the frequency with which it raises its head and looks around (every fifteen to forty-five seconds) when basking, and its use of lairs.

Other less significant predators of the ringed seal include the walrus, raven, red fox, wolverine, wolf, and, near settlements, dogs.

The harvest of ringed seals by subsistence hunters in Alaska has been steadily declining in recent years. Current annual harvests approximate four to five thousand per year—down from eight to fifteen thousand during the 1960s. This reduction is due to several things, including change in the Alaskan Eskimo's diet; the availability of such other native foods as caribou, whale, walrus, and moose; the virtual disappearance of sled dogs; and increased job opportunities. The present low, human harvest of the ringed seal is expected to increase, however, because of more restrictions on the other food sources just mentioned.

There is no commercial harvest of ringed seals in the Bering or Chukchi seas, probably because hunting vessels cannot operate in the regions of heavy ice where these seals are most abundant. Recent annual harvests by Siberians and Alaskans, in combination, have been seven to nine thousand per year.

Aerial censuses in limited areas of landfast ice in the Chukchi Sea have revealed an approximate seal density of 8.4 to 10.8 per square mile. The best estimate of population size in the Bering and Chuk-

An adult male bearded seal shows the whiskers from which it receives its name. Unlike other ice seals, the adult bearded seal is not obviously spotted or banded. (Francis H. Fay)

chi seas is between 1 and 1.5 million.

Oil and gas development on the outer continental shelf may pose the most significant threat to the ringed seal and other marine mammals of the region. Five areas off northern Alaska, within the ringed seal's habitat, are proposed for lease: Bristol Bay, Saint George Basin, Norton Basin, Hope Basin, and the nearshore Beaufort Sea.

Although oil development will probably not result in significant direct mortality to seals, it seems probable that the indirect effects of chronic, low volume releases of petrochemicals, and the expected occasional major spill may have detrimental effects on the animals eaten by the ringed seal. Eggs and larvae of the two cod fish important to this seal are highly susceptible to petrochemical pollution, as are the various kinds of zooplankton that the animal consumes. Of the four seal species discussed in this chapter, the ringed seal's food web includes the greatest number of prey species likely to be adversely affected by oil and gas extraction and transport as accomplished with current technology.

Like the ringed seal, the bearded seal (*Erignathus barbatus*) has a circumpolar distribution and a wide range within the drifting ice areas. It also maintains a year-round association with sea ice, moving north in summer and south in winter. However, a small proportion of the population—mainly juveniles—does occur away from the ice in open water, and young bearded seals do commonly enter mouths of some rivers, usually shortly before the rivers freeze in the fall.

Unlike the ringed seal, the bearded seal is mainly a subarctic species and is restricted to relatively shallow water and to regions where the sea ice is in motion. Although it can use the claws of its foreflippers to make breathing holes in ice, as the ringed seal does, most bearded seals do not live in areas of extensive, heavy, drifting ice.

The bearded seal's winter distribution extends

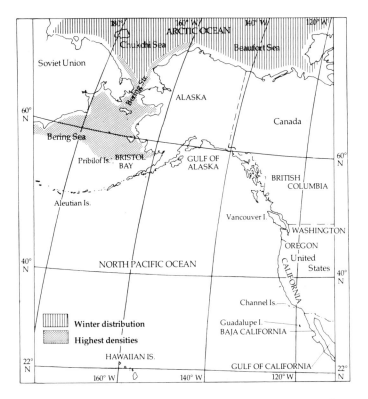

Bearded seal winter distribution—drifting ice zone. Summer distribution—north with retreating sea ice.

into the arctic regions, mostly in association with "flaw zones," where heavy offshore ice is influenced by winds, currents, and coastal features. These zones generally parallel the coasts of Alaska and Siberia. The center of this seal's winter abundance is, however, as far as the ice edge of the central and southern Bering Sea, where favorable ice conditions are much more extensive than in the Chukchi Sea. During winter and spring, bearded seals are widely, although not uniformly, distributed throughout the drifting ice of this area. They do not show the marked selectivity of the other three species for specific ice habitats.

This seal's scientific name refers to two of its distinctive features: *Erignathus*, derived from the Greek, refers to its rather deep jaw; *barbatus*, from the Latin *barba* meaning "beard," is descriptive of its numerous whiskers.

Unlike other seals of this region, adult bearded seals are not obviously spotted or banded, and they vary in color. Some are tawny brown, some light gray, others dark brown, with slightly darker coloration usually evident on their backs. Subadult seals sometimes have large, faint, irregular-shaped spots. These seals also quite commonly have a rusty or reddish brown color on the face and foreflippers. The origin of this pigmentation is unknown; it probably comes from their environment rather than from pigmentation of the hairs, for this seal spends much of its time feeding on the sea floor.

The bearded seal is essentially a benthic or bottom feeder, eating mainly epibenthic organisms—animals that live on the surface of the sea floor. It also consumes organisms that live in the bottom sediments. Major prey items include a variety of crabs, hermit crabs, shrimps, clams, benthic fish, and schooling demersal (near-bottom dwelling) fish. Because of this seal's feeding habits, it is restricted to waters of less than about five hundred feet. The extensive continental shelf of the Bering and Chukchi seas is thus an excellent feeding ground, and comprises the largest continuous habitat of bearded seals in the world—a population estimated at about three hundred thousand.

The bearded seal is the largest of the ice-associated pinnipeds in the Northern Hemisphere. Its body is long and thick, and its head appears disproportionately small. During winter and early spring, when these seals attain maximum weight, adults may weigh as much as 770 pounds. However, most adults weigh between 425 and 550 pounds, with females weighing slightly more than males. Hide and blubber account for thirty-three to thirty-seven percent of the total body weight. Although large seals may reach ninety-three inches in length, most adults are eighty-six to ninety-one inches long. Girth immediately behind the foreflippers is approximately seventy-three percent of

standard length. Seasonal weight loss between April and June may be as much as thirty percent; it is associated with nurturing of pups, molting, and reduced feeding activity. These seals attain full growth when they are about ten years old. Being moderately long-lived, their life-span is usually only twenty-five years, although records show a maximum age of thirty-one years.

The male bearded seal reaches sexual maturity at six to seven years of age, the female at five to six years. Most females breed annually; the incidence of pregnancy is about eighty-three percent, a rate that has remained stable for many years in the Bering and Chukchi seas. In the Beaufort Sea, reduced pregnancy rates have been reported in recent years.

From March through June, the adult male bearded seal is highly vocal. Its "song" is a stereotyped, long, descending warble that frequently lasts more than a minute and is apparently associated with courtship. It is heard most often from mid-April through May.

The male is probably a promiscuous breeder, and mates with females primarily during May. The total gestation period is some eleven months, with a two-month period of delayed implantation, which occurs mainly during mid- to late July. The peak birth period, which takes place later than in the other three species, occurs in the last two thirds of April.

Bearded seal pups are born on the ice and are usually dark brown with a light face mask and one or more broad, light-colored bands across the head or back. Their dark, comparatively long, fine hair is shed by three weeks of age. At birth, the pups are large, weighing around seventy pounds and averaging fifty-two inches in length. Their mothers each have four mammary glands (unlike the ringed, spotted, and ribbon seals, which have two) from which they nurse the pups for twelve to eighteen days. During this time, the average pup's length increases to fifty-eight inches and its weight triples, mostly in the form of blubber. Weaning is abrupt—it appears that the females simply abandon their pups.

Newborn pups can and often do enter the water shortly after birth. They are seldom found in the immediate vicinity of afterbirth; apparently their mothers coax them to swim to adjacent floes to avoid it. Because the pups can swim at birth, they are able to escape from the polar bear, which shares the same habitat.

Major predators of the bearded seal are the polar bear and man. The distribution, habits, and size of the bearded seal are such that predation by the arctic fox is probably insignificant. Other occasional predators include the walrus and, in summer, probably the killer whale.

Some ship-based commercial hunting of bearded seals is conducted by the Soviets; however, most animals are taken by land-based subsistence hunters from Siberia and Alaska. In recent years, the combined harvests from the Bering and Chukchi seas have been on the order of two to four thousand per year.

At present, the bearded seal does not seriously compete with man for fish and shellfish of commercial significance. However, an intensified shrimp and crab fishery in the northern Bering Sea and the prospect of a developing clam fishery may reduce this region's carrying capacity for the bearded seal. Gas and oil development on the outer continental shelf will probably have only a minor effect on the direct mortality of bearded seals, but the indirect effects on their food web, comprised mainly of invertebrates with highly susceptible larval stages, could be serious.

Whereas the bearded seal is a subarctic species and the ringed seal is an arctic species, the spotted and ribbon seals are both species of the north temperate zone and are only seasonally associated with sea ice. They seldom penetrate the heavier

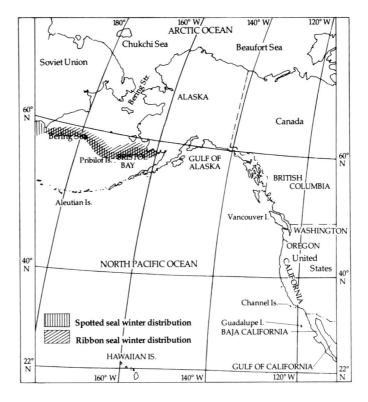

Spotted and ribbon seal distribution. Spotted seal winter distribution—along ice front. Summer distribution—coastal areas where this species hauls out on land. Ribbon seal winter distribution—ice front of Bering Sea. Summer distribution—pelagic, remaining primarily in Bering Sea.

ice and their distribution is restricted to the North Pacific region. Because they do not remain with the ice during summer and fall, the total number of ice-associated pinnipeds is substantially reduced when the ice occupies the most restricted area of any period in the annual cycle. During the ice-free summer months, the ribbon seal adopts a pelagic existence, remaining mostly in the Bering Sea, while the spotted seal lives mainly in coastal areas.

The spotted seal occurs in only the North Pacific, mainly in the Okhotsk, Bering, and Chukchi seas. Small numbers have been recorded in the Beaufort Sea and some probably range into the East Siberian Sea. The estimated number of spotted seals in the Bering-Chukchi population is 280,000 to 330,000 of which about 80,000 are of the Karaginski

The spotted seal is distinguished by a doglike snout, already well-developed in this four- to six-week-old pup. It has already shed its birthcoat, which has been replaced by the adult pelage of irregular dark spots on a grayish background. (John J. Burns)

Bay stock on the Siberian coast. As with the other three ice-associated species, a more accurate population estimate is needed.

The spotted seal (*Phoca vitulina largha*) is closely related to the harbor seal of southern Alaska, Washington, Oregon, and California. A difference of opinion currently persists about the specific or subspecific status of this seal. Until the question is adequately resolved through studies presently underway, I will consider the largha seal a subspecies: *Phoca vitulina largha*. Its specific name, *vitulina*, is derived from the Latin *vitulus*, meaning "calf," because this animal was known in Europe as the "sea dog" or "sea calf." The subspecific name, *largha*, is derived from the native Tungus name for the spotted seal of the western Okhotsk Sea.

The common name "sea dog," used by early Europeans, is descriptive of the long, doglike snout of the spotted (and harbor) seal and also of the growls and other doglike noises this seal sometimes makes. Several Inupiat (northern Eskimo) legends describe how the first spotted seals originated from a group of Eskimo sled dogs that drifted away on the ice. The legends also relate that some individual spotted seals can come up on shore, turn themselves into dogs, and learn about the ways of the Inupiat—how they are treating those seals that have given themselves to the Eskimos to use (whether or not the meat is kept in a clean cache, and whether the hides are properly cared for and used for appropriate garments). These animals then return to the sea, as seals, with this information.

A "typical" spotted seal has many small, dark, irregular-shaped spots on a background color of brownish yellow. These spots are most numerous on the back and upper sides. However, there is considerable variation in the background coloration, ranging from gray white to gray blue. Small, light-colored rings are sometimes present, especially on juvenile animals.

The adult spotted seal's size is between that of the ringed seal and bearded seal. Exceptionally large seals may be as heavy as 270 pounds, but most physically mature adults of both sexes weigh between 180 and 240 pounds. The standard length for adults is 56 to 67 inches. As in the other ice seal species, there is great seasonal variation in weight. On the average, thirty-three to thirty-eight percent of the total body weight is comprised of hide and blubber.

The maximum longevity of this seal is about thirty-five years. It attains physical maturity at age seven or eight, and sexual maturity at three to four years in the female and four to five years in the male. Breeding occurs annually in late April and early May. These seals are monogamous, forming pairs in late March and remaining together until after breeding. As in the other ice-associated species, pregnancy lasts for eleven months, including a delayed implantation period of 3.5 to 4 months. Between eighty-five and ninety-five percent of all adult females become pregnant in any given year.

Birth occurs on the ice floes in late March and April, mainly during the first two weeks in April. Instead of using lairs, as does the ringed seal, the spotted seal seeks the shelter of ice hummocks and crevices if they are present.

Newborn pups weigh eighteen to twenty-six pounds and are about thirty-three inches long. At birth they are covered with a dense lanugo coat, which is a grayish white to off-white color. Faint grayish spots are sometimes evident. Nursing for three to four weeks, a pup can attain a weight of up to eighty pounds. However, most weigh between fifty-five and seventy pounds at weaning. The white lanugo is shed in three to four weeks (at weaning), when the blubber layer is thick enough to provide adequate insulation. The pups do not swim during the first few weeks of life, although they do flounder through the water or slush ice between adjacent ice floes. Near weaning time, they begin to enter the water, but they are so buoyant that they cannot dive well.

Weaning is abrupt, as it is with the other ice seals. The weaned pup spends a great deal of time on the ice, slowly developing the swimming skills—it becomes a proficient swimmer during the first few weeks of independence—and feeding skills required for life on its own. The fat reserve accumulated during nursing is important for survival during this important period of adjustment, for the pup loses a considerable amount of weight at this time. By mid-May the newly independent pup has dropped to between forty-five and fifty-five pounds.

The spotted seal is only seasonally dependent on the sea ice, which it uses when it is resting, bearing and nurturing pups, and molting. It is associated with ice from late fall to early summer. In the Bering and Chukchi seas during late winter and early spring, when the ice cover is at its maximum, the entire spotted seal population is concentrated in or near the "front," which consists of small floes usually less than thirty feet wide, separated by water or slush ice and subject to rapid dispersal or compaction by winds and ocean currents. This is the ice zone in the Bering Sea that extends from the southern ice margin to the heavier ice farther north. Width of the front varies from less than fifteen to more than eighty miles. During April, spotted seals have been found in all areas of the front. However, highest densities occur in Bristol Bay near the Alaska coast and in Karaginski Bay on the Siberian coast.

As the sea ice recedes north and disintegrates in late spring, these seals move north and toward the coasts. Few of them are associated with the ice during late summer and early fall, as they are widely distributed along the coast. They enter the bays and rivers, and haul out on land in any suitable location. In effect, they replace the ringed seals, which go north with the ice in summer.

As the sea ice forms in late autumn, spotted seals occupying the more northerly parts of their range move south, into the Bering Sea. This process continues throughout the early winter—more spotted seals moving away from the coast and associating with the front of the southward advancing ice cover.

The range of these seals in the Bering and Chukchi seas coincides with the continental shelf. Within this area, the spotted seal, which is not a deep diver, feeds mainly on fish, including capelin, pollock, herring, smelts, sand lance, saffron cod, and sculpin. During summer and fall spotted seals concentrate near rivers where anadromous fish, including salmon, go to spawn. Several other species of fish are eaten, as well as shrimps, octopuses, and occasional small crabs and other organisms.

Little is known about the influence of predators on the spotted seal. The ice front is south of the range of the polar bear and the ice-wandering arctic fox. This seal has obviously evolved in regions relatively free of predation by bears and foxes in that the pups are exposed on the ice floes and are incapable of escape from a bear. Sea gulls are numerous where the pups are born, and may kill a few of the deserted or debilitated ones. Pups that apparently have been crushed between ice floes have been found. In some years more than the normal number of starveling pups stranded on beaches have been reported—a phenomenon that may relate to stormy weather or unavailability of food during the initial period of independence. Marine predators, such as the killer whale and Greenland

shark, are thought to take a few. Eskimos report that sea lions play with spotted seal pups, sometimes killing them.

The take of these seals by man is relatively low at present. Commercial harvests by the Soviets have decreased from around fifty-five hundred in 1971 to less than three thousand in 1976. Shore-based subsistence hunters in Alaska and Siberia take an additional three thousand per year.

Intensive commercial fishing in the winter range of the spotted seal is directed at some of its food species, including pandalid shrimps, pollock, and herring. The impact of this fishery on the seal is unknown. Two major outer continental shelf leases are also within the important winter range of the spotted seal: the proposed Bristol Bay and Saint George Basin leases. In addition, indirect effects of

The characteristic striking bands of color on the ribbon seal are most pronounced in mature males, as shown here. The foreflippers of these seals appear to be more flexible than in other species; they are used for pulling the seal across the ice. (John J. Burns)

oil and gas development could adversely affect this seal through further reduction of important prey species.

The ribbon seal (*Phoca fasciata*) is the only species of those discussed here that shows marked sexual dimorphism in coloration. Its scientific name is descriptive of a striking appearance: *Phoca*, as has been stated, is from the Greek word for seal, and *fasciata* is from the Latin *fascia*, meaning "band" or "ribbon," which refers to the striking ribbonlike markings of most adults. *Histriophoca*, this seal's subgeneric name, is from the Latin *histrio*, meaning "stage-player," and the Greek *phoce*; thus the name refers to this seal's strikingly colored coat. As the common and scientific names indicate, the most striking and obvious characteristics of this seal are its distinctive coloration and markings. Adults usually show a series of four light bands on a darker background. One band completely encircles the neck (sometimes extending forward to include the posterior portion of the head). Another encircles the posterior portion of the torso at or behind the navel, and there is one on each side, broadly encircling the foreflippers. The width of these bands is quite variable, and the pattern of coloration changes with age.

Ribbon seal pups are born as white-coats and shed this lanugo at about four weeks. The underlying coat of hair does not show the ribbons. During the first year, the pelage is silver gray on the lower flanks and belly, and blue black on the upper flanks and back. In their first year of life, ribbon seals resemble young hooded seals (a species of the North Atlantic Ocean). After the molt at age one, the ribbon seal is reddish brown to almost black (reddish brown before the molt, almost black immediately after it) with indistinct light bands. These light bands increase in contrast with each succeeding molt until the adult coloration is achieved at about age three. The female shows the same changes and pattern of markings. However, the contrast is much

A recently weaned and molted female ribbon seal pup shows the beginnings of markings that will become more defined with age. (John J. Burns)

less distinct because of a considerably lighter background coloration.

The ribbon seal is of medium size with both sexes weighing about the same. The largest I have examined was a pregnant female that weighed 326 pounds and measured 70.75 inches. Most adult seals, however, are considerably smaller. During late winter, the average adult weight is about 210 pounds and the length is around 61 inches. By late June (after the birth, nursing, and molt periods), the average adult weight is down to around 161 pounds. The adult ribbon seal is, by comparison with the other species, rather slender. Its hide and blubber amount to twenty-seven to thirty-five percent of its total body weight; its girth is about sixty-eight percent of standard length during late May or June.

The growth rate of ribbon seals is rapid in comparison with the other ice-associated species. Proportional length of age classes, compared with the average for seals older than seven years, is sixty-one percent for weaned pups, seventy percent at age one, eighty-six percent at age two, ninety-two percent at age three, and ninety-eight percent at age six. Physical maturity is attained by about age seven. The oldest seals in my samples were twenty-three and the maximum in extensive samples obtained by Soviet investigators was twenty-six. Although the average life-span is more on the order of twenty years, the maximum age may be as old as thirty.

Males and females are seldom seen together, even in the annual breeding season, which occurs in late April to mid-May. Unlike the monogamous spotted seal, the male ribbon seal probably breeds with several females. The total gestation period is 11 months; implantation occurs in September, after a delay of about 3.5 months. Births occur mainly during the first half of April, but some pups are born as late as 10 May.

Birth occurs on the ice floes in conditions similar to that of the spotted seal. Unlike the ringed seal, the ribbon seal does not use a lair, but instead takes advantage of whatever protection may be found on the "home" floe. Newborn ribbon seal pups weigh an average of twenty-three pounds and are about 33.9 inches long. Their dense coat of almost white lanugo is usually shed in three to four weeks. The pups are frequently left unattended, even during the first week of life. The lanugo-coated pups may move from one floe to the next, but do not swim (in the same sense that the older seals do) until they are about four weeks old. The nursing period lasts three to four weeks, during which the pups attain an average weight of about sixty-five pounds and a length of about 36 inches.

At the time of weaning, some pups weigh as much as eighty-five pounds and are forty inches long. Weaning is abrupt, and there is a significant loss of weight during the first few weeks of independence. In late May and early June, the average weight of pups is forty-eight pounds.

The ribbon seal's food habits are not well known because almost all available specimens have been collected from March through June. During that period, major prey items include pollock, capelin, and eelpouts. Other fish consumed include pricklebacks, snailfish, sculpin, and saffron cod. Ribbon seals examined during February had eaten pollock and polar cod. In addition to fish, these seals also eat shrimps, octopuses, and probably squid.

All evidence indicates that the ribbon seal is a good diver. Physiological studies indicate that it has the highest oxygen storage capacity of the four species discussed here. I have seen a large female in a tank of water on board the research vessel *Alpha Helix* remain underwater for twenty-seven minutes. She came to the surface when startled by the noise of a heavy object that fell on deck near the tank. The maximum diving time is unknown but may be considerably longer than this.

One of the ribbon seal's unique attributes is its large air sac. The posterior "rings" of the trachea are not complete and are broadly connected by a tissue membrane on the ventral surface. A slitlike opening, approximately three fourths of the distance down the trachea, opens into the air sac. This sac occurs in both sexes, but is considerably more developed in males. It overlies the ribs on the right side of the body, extending posteriorly along the side. The function of this interesting structure is unknown. It may assist in providing additional buoyancy for resting in the open ocean and/or contribute to the production of the underwater sounds made by this seal.

Another unique characteristic is its manner of rapidly moving across ice floes. Rather than wriggling the way the ringed, spotted, and bearded seals do, it "runs" with its neck extended forward and its head held close to the ice surface. The foreflippers are extended alternately as the seal pulls itself forward. This movement is assisted by the side to side motion of the neck and head and by a similar but exaggerated movement of the posterior torso. For lack of a better descriptive term, this mode of locomotion can be described as "slithering," as compared with the "wriggling" or inchworm gait of the other species.

The ribbon seal, like the spotted seal, is only seasonally associated with the ice. It uses the ice for resting, molting, giving birth, and nurturing its pups. The ribbon seal occurs only in the North Pacific region, with centers of abundance in the Okhotsk and Bering seas. A small proportion of the Bering Sea population enters the Chukchi Sea during summer.

During late winter and spring ribbon seals, like spotted seals, are most abundant in the ice front. However, though they are distributed throughout the front, they are more common in the northern part of this zone and in the area west of about 170 degrees west longitude. Nothing is known about their migrations. All indications are that most ribbon seals remain in the Bering Sea during the ice-free months, adopting a pelagic existence. They can be seen in the ice front during winter and spring and, except for relatively few observations during the ice-free period, their whereabouts are unknown. They do not pass north through the Bering Strait in any great numbers and are rarely seen near the coast. I have no records of ribbon seals found on the beaches of northern Alaska.

This seal is the least abundant of the four ice seal species, with an estimated population of 100,000, which is near the level that existed before intensive commercial exploitation (100,000 to 114,000). Soviets began commercial hunting in the Bering Sea in 1961. Between 1961 and 1967, an average of 13,000 ribbon seals were taken per year.

The effect was a noticeable reduction of the population. In 1968, the take was reduced to 6,290 and to 3,000 the next year. It has remained at about 3,000 through 1976. With the reduction in take, the population has increased from an estimated 60,000 in 1967 to about 100,000 at present.

There is essentially no coastal-based subsistence hunting for these seals, as they normally do not occur near shore. Occasionally, during mild winters when the ice does not move (or form) far south, they are hunted in the Bering Strait region when other, more preferred species are not available. (The order of preference by most subsistence hunters is the bearded seal, followed by the ringed, spotted, and ribbon seals.) The average annual ribbon seal harvests in Alaska amount to less than two hundred per year. The maximum harvest occurred during the exceptionally mild winter and spring of 1967 when about fifteen hundred were taken. In that year, the ice edge barely reached Saint Lawrence Island.

Little is known about the predators of the ribbon seal. The pups, born outside of the normal range of the polar bear and arctic fox, are probably victims of sharks and killer whales during the months when they are at sea in ice-free waters.

Outer continental shelf development may occur in two regions where the ribbon seal winters and bears pups: Bristol Bay and Saint George Basin. As with the other species of seals, little direct mortality is anticipated. The most significant and detrimental effects would probably be through reduced abundance of important prey species.

Northern Elephant Seal

by Robert L. DeLong

The northern elephant seal (*Mirounga angustirostris*), once driven to the brink of extinction by commercial sealing, has experienced a spectacular recovery. By 1900, as few as 100 of these pinnipeds remained on an isolated beach at Guadalupe Island off Baja California. Today, after years of protection, the population has increased to as many as 50,000. Elephant seals now breed on eight islands off Mexico and California.

The breeding rookeries of Baja California contain well over half of the total elephant seal population. The Guadalupe Island population is the largest—between fifteen and twenty thousand—followed by the San Benitos population—between five and ten thousand. In California's Channel Islands, a large population breeds on San Miguel and a smaller one on San Nicolas. In northern California, the Año Nuevo Island rookery, which was reestablished in 1961, now numbers about two thousand animals. The only mainland rookery for elephant seals was formed recently on Año Nuevo Point, adjacent to the island. This point is part of the Año Nuevo State Reserve, where visitors may join a guided tour to view the new rookery. The southeast Farallon Island rookery, off San Francisco, was established in 1972, when two pups were born; in 1976 sixty pups were born there.

The northern elephant seal is the largest of the Northern Hemisphere pinnipeds, and of pinnipeds worldwide is surpassed in size by only the Southern Hemisphere elephant seal. The adult male has a large pendulous snout, measures up to sixteen feet long, and may weigh over two tons. The female is smaller, weighing a ton and measuring about ten feet in length. Size dimorphism—with the male large and female small—is unusual in the earless seals, family Phocidae, of which the elephant seal is a member, but is common in all sea lions and fur seals of the family Otariidae.

Another characteristic that elephant seals share with the fur seals and sea lions is a polygynous social system, in which each mating bull associates with a group of reproductive females. Each December, large adult males begin arriving at the rookery islands off the coast of California and Baja California. There they fight for a position on the

On California's San Nicolas Island, molted and weaned elephant seal pups gather in a typical dense aggregation. (Robert L. DeLong)

beach and a position in the male social structure, a dominance hierarchy in which the more dominant males displace the less dominant. Once the dominance relationships are established, conflicts are generally settled by information exchanged in male-male vocalizations and stereotyped threat postures.

Female elephant seals begin to arrive in late December, and form compact aggregations on the beach. Until the female group exceeds forty or fifty, only the most dominant adult male associates with the females. But when the female aggregation swells above fifty, the single male can no longer move around its perimeter to exclude other males. At this point, a second—and possibly a third—male gains access to the female aggregation. And so progresses the growth of the rookeries through early January. On large rookeries, such as those on Guadalupe, the San Benitos, and San Miguel, female aggregations merge, one into the next, until it becomes impossible to distinguish among them.

About a week after arriving on land, each female bears a single pup weighing about sixty-five pounds. The pup is nursed for about twenty eight days, and frequently triples its birth weight during that time. At about the time of weaning, the pup molts its black natal pelage and grows a sleek, gray coat. Large groups or pods of weaned pups accumulate on the rear fringes of rookeries, away from the aggressive adult females and males. Weaned pups occasionally venture back into the rookery to seek additional milk, but are usually driven away by the sometimes fatal bites of nursing females. Occasionally, a female will tolerate two or more pups attempting to suckle; orphaned and weaned pups accumulate around such tolerant females.

At about the time of weaning, the adult female comes into estrus and mates with one or more of the socially dominant males. She then leaves the rookery island to feed and recover some of the weight lost during her month-long fast while she

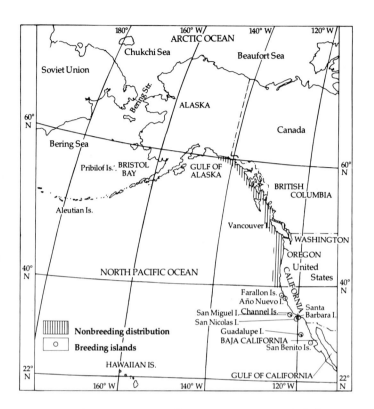

Northern elephant seal distribution

was also feeding a rapidly growing pup. Adult males begin to depart in late February, but some remain on land during March after the breeding season, apparently just to rest; they return to sea in late March.

The transition from fasting on land to feeding in the open ocean necessitates an incredible physiological change. While ashore the animal relies entirely on the metabolism of fat stored in its blubber for both energy and water. When it goes to sea and feeds, its digestive system, which has been essentially turned off, begins to function again. The physiological and physical changes associated with the transition from land fasting to marine feeding have not been studied, but they represent a fascinating adaptation that allows the long stay on land necessary for reproduction.

By early March most of the pups are weaned. They spend the day on land and much of the night in the water, perfecting their swimming skills and possibly beginning to feed. In late March, they begin to leave the rookery island, and in the following months are found on Pacific coast beaches from Mexico to Alaska. The pups come ashore for varied reasons; some are diseased, some injured, and others just appear weak and hungry. In the summer of 1976, a dead pup found on an Oregon beach was reported to have died from a Pacific ocean perch lodged in its throat. Many of these pups that come ashore in a weakened condition are now being picked up by personnel from oceanariums and aquariums and nursed back to health. They are then either released into the wild or supplied to institutions that have permits to display elephant seals.

Healthy pups, however, go to sea and many do not return to the rookery island until the following April, when they come ashore to molt. From tagging studies conducted by Professor Burney LeBoeuf and other researchers at the University of California at Santa Cruz, the pups appear to move north along the coast, spending some time on islands, then continuing north along the continental slope off Oregon, Washington, British Columbia, and Alaska.

The females return to land to molt after about two months at sea. The elephant seal is one of the few seals that experiences an epidermal molt (after the natal molt). The pelage and some epidermis is sloughed off in patches, and the hair is replaced with a fresh, gray coat. During the molt, which requires several weeks to complete, the elephant seals

Adult male elephant seals, ready for territorial battle, assume their characteristic threat posture—rearing back their heads and dropping their elephantlike proboscises. (W. J. Houck)

Elephant seals mate on California's San Miguel Island. (W. J. Houck)

stay quietly ashore for long periods, some not moving for days except to flip sand onto their backs to aid in keeping cool. The bulls return to land to molt in July and August, then go to sea again until the next breeding season in December.

The food habits of northern elephant seals are not well known, but available information indicates that they feed on deepwater, bottom-dwelling marine life such as ratfish, swell sharks, spiny dogfish, cusk eels, various rockfish, and squid. While on a research cruise from the Scripps Institution of Oceanography (in La Jolla, California) to Guadalupe Island with Professor Carl Hubbs, I observed a subadult elephant seal surface with a small blue shark in its mouth. The shark was alive and the seal was shaking it. I interpreted this to be a feeding attempt by the elephant seal, but our approaching vessel forced the seal to dive with the shark still held crosswise in its mouth.

Elephant seals dive deep for much of their food. Three subadults were accidentally hooked on sable fish setline gear. The gear was in six hundred feet of water, thirty-five miles off Florence, Oregon, indicating that they feed well offshore and commonly descend to at least that depth. Their diving behavior has not been studied in detail, so modal and extreme depths of dives are not yet described.

Animals that move north after the breeding season seem to be the young of that year and subadult and adult males. Historically, the Makah Indians of northwestern Washington State took some elephant seals in coastal waters each spring while they were engaged in hunting northern fur seals. April, May, and June are still the months when elephant seals are seen along the Washington, British Columbia, and Alaska coasts. There are three published records of elephant seals in Puget Sound, Washington; every year since 1968, one or two sightings—generally of adult males—have been reported to the United States National Marine Fisheries Service in Seattle. Sightings of male

elephant seals are recorded from the west side of Vancouver Island, British Columbia, through Hecate Strait and up the inland passage of southeastern Alaska. Only two sightings have been reported from the Gulf of Alaska, which probably represents the northern limit of this animal's range.

Natural enemies of the elephant seal—which included aboriginal and modern man—today are limited to large sharks, particularly the white shark, and the killer whale. Although these large predators undoubtedly take a modest number of seals, predation does not seem to be checking the rapid population growth that the northern elephant seal is enjoying throughout most of its range.

The elephant seal, along with the monk seal, experiences a unique epidermal molt whereby the skin is replaced from below. The darker markings around the eyes and snout of this seal are newly molted areas. (Robert L. DeLong)

Hawaiian Monk Seal

by Karl W. Kenyon

Monk seals are the most primitive of living seals. The Hawaiian monk seal (*Monachus schauinslandi*) was separated from its ancestral population about fifteen million years ago and has remained unchanged since that time, according to a 1977 study of fossil remains by paleontologists C. A. Repenning and C. E. Ray. Thus, the Hawaiian monk seal is virtually a "living fossil."

Throughout the world, three species comprise the genus *Monachus*. The Hawaiian variety is found on the coral atolls and islets of the northwestern or Leeward Hawaiian Islands. Its nearest living relative is the Mediterranean monk seal (*Monachus monachus*), a species noted by Aristotle in the third century B.C. and the first pinniped ever described. The only other species, the Caribbean or West Indian monk seal (*Monachus tropicalis*), was last seen in 1952. After exhaustive correspondence with scientists working within its former habitat, plus an extensive aerial survey in 1973 of all places where this seal had been authentically reported in the past 100 years, I concluded that the Caribbean monk seal must have become extinct shortly after it was last observed.

The Hawaiian monk seal differs from other earless seals in certain ways. Because of its isolation on remote oceanic islands, it evolved free of terrestrial enemies, and thus did not develop the need to flee. Instead, like certain species of island-breeding seabirds, it is genetically tame and easily approached by humans. An observed increase in pup mortality when nursing mothers are subjected to repeated human disturbance, however, indicates that this activity has serious physiological consequences.

The isolated tropical and subtropical coral atolls and islets of the Leeward Hawaiian Islands are the only habitat of this rare species, which was officially designated as endangered in 1976. Except for Midway and Kure atolls, all of these lands comprise the protected Hawaiian Islands National Wildlife Refuge. Stretching northwestward, this twelve-hundred-mile chain consists of sand islets that are protected from oceanic storms by coral reefs. Low growing shrubs—*Scaevola* and *Messerschmidia*—and perennial grasses—*Eragrostis*—crown many of these islands, providing a breeding ground for literally

A Hawaiian monk seal rests in the shade of a Scaevola *bush in the Leeward Hawaiian Islands. The scar on its body is the result of shark attack, not uncommon among these seals. Such shark scars enable researchers to identify individual monk seals. (Karl W. Kenyon)*

millions of seabirds, while the sandy shores are nesting spaces for the green turtle. Certain beaches also provide pupping areas for the monk seal—usually a sandy beach backed by vegetation and, most important, adjacent to shallow protected water.

The monk seal breeds regularly in five areas along the Leeward chain: French Frigate Shoals, Laysan Island, Lisianski Island, Pearl and Hermes Reef, and Kure Atoll. A sixth breeding population at Midway Atoll disappeared between 1958 and 1968, probably because nursing mothers were frequently disturbed by personnel from the large naval station there. Although since 1968 a few pregnant females have come ashore and given birth to pups on the isolated sandspits at Midway, the amount of human disturbance is apparently enough to prevent the reestablishment of a substantial breeding colony. A new small breeding group may be developing at Necker Island: one pup was born there in 1975, another in 1976, and three adult females that appeared to be pregnant were seen there in 1977. However, the limited beaches on this rocky islet preclude its becoming a significant colony.

Intermittent observations of seals have been made as far back as 1957, but only since 1976 have the United States National Marine Fisheries Service and the United States Fish and Wildlife Service been involved in an intensive cooperative study of the Hawaiian monk seal. In 1957, we found 1,012 seals and in 1958 as many as 1,206. Our surveys of the breeding islands in 1976 and 1977, however, yielded lower counts of 695 and 625 seals respectively. Human disturbance of nursing mother seals is undoubtedly an important factor in the declines at Midway Island and at Kure Atoll, site of a United States Coast Guard loran station. A population decline at Pearl and Hermes Reef is not so easily explained. Our counts there in 1957 and 1958 produced 290 and 338 seals respectively. The 1976 and 1977 counts indicate a precipitous decline: 26 and 43

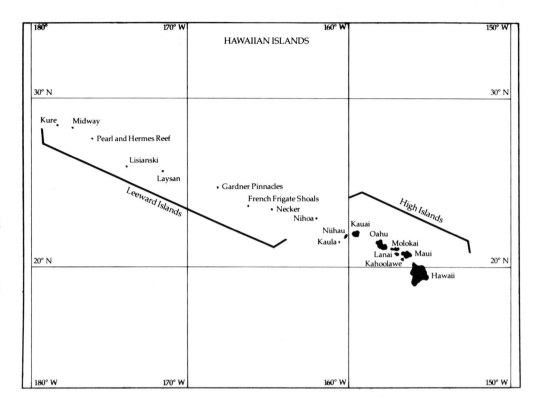

seals respectively, with juveniles and pups abnormally scarce.

What has caused this apparent population loss? Two possibilities have been suggested: (1) shark attack, because we see many seals bearing shark bite scars, and have found seals dead on beaches after being attacked by sharks; and (2) ciguatera, a disease that occurs in terrestrial mammals and originates in a benthic dinoflagellate protozoan whose toxin is concentrated and stored in the flesh of fish. Although these possible causes of mortality are under investigation, the precise reason for this decline on Pearl and Hermes Reef is still a mystery. During this same period, the French Frigate Shoals field counts have shown a gratifying increase from a low of 35 in 1957 to a high of 223 in 1977.

Allowing for seals that were at sea during our

Hawaiian monk seals are found in the Leeward Hawaiian Islands. They are rarely observed in the main "high islands."

The monk seal is born with a black birthcoat, which it sheds a few weeks later. Here it nurses from its mother, who will not seek food for herself during the pup's first five or six weeks of life. (Dale W. Rice)

surveys, we estimate that the total number of Hawaiian monk seals alive today probably does not much exceed one thousand animals. Even at that, this population is more prosperous than its Mediterranean relative, which may number as few as five hundred.

The pupping season for the monk seal is prolonged. Although a few young may be born as early as late December, the peak of the season occurs between late March and May, with the last few pups born in July. When the mother monk seal comes ashore to bear her single black pup, she is enormously fat and may weigh about 600 pounds. For some six weeks, she lives off her stored blubber while nursing her pup. During this period, she does not seek food for herself, while the nursing pup increases its birth weight from about 35 pounds to 140 pounds. At this time, the pup also molts its black birthcoat and grows a new one of pearly gray. The pup's early development is dependent on the fatness of the mother at its birth; a pup from a very fat mother may, at weaning, be considerably larger than a pup from a less fat mother—a critical early survival factor.

Regurgitated stomach contents or spewings found on beaches indicate that monk seals feed on a variety of reef fish, octopuses, and crayfish. Observations of tagged monk seals show that they may travel many miles at sea from one island to another. Thus, they must be able to find food in the open sea as well as in the shallow lagoons surrounding their breeding beaches. So much time is spent at sea that monk seals, when seen on beaches, appear to have green fur. This color is caused by certain algae that grow among the pelage fibers.

Feeding behavior was not observed until the spring of 1977. At French Frigate Shoals, we found that several adult monk seals habitually dived for food in a channel some thirty feet deep near the northwest end of Tern Island. The seals fed at all hours and their feeding dives usually lasted between ten and fifteen minutes.

The monk seal shares with the elephant seal a unique type of molt in which the outer layer of epidermis is shed along with the old pelage. In the first postnatal molt, however, only the hair, and not the epidermis, is shed. The adult male completes the molt in late winter and early spring; the female does not begin to molt until after she has weaned her pup.

Much is still left to be learned about the life history of this most primitive of seals. Meanwhile, great care must be taken to protect mothers and pups from undue disturbance during the critical nursing period.

In recent years, commercial fishing interests and officials of the state of Hawaii have been attempting to promote fishing among the Leeward Hawaiian Islands. Because monk seals are curious and would no doubt become entangled in fishing gear, fishing operations would pose a direct threat to the welfare of these seals. Mortality of the young also would surely increase if fishermen went ashore on breeding islands and disturbed nursing mother seals. Moreover, the effect of removing the seal's food organisms from the reefs and waters surrounding its breeding islands is unknown. A similar situation has occurred before: fishermen appear to have been the primary cause for the Caribbean monk seal's extinction. Let us hope that the future of the Hawaiian monk seal will be better secured.

Other Marine-Adapted Species

Polar Bear, Sea Otter, Steller Sea Cow

*I*n addition to the cetaceans and pinnipeds, a few other mammals have adapted to the marine environment. In the eastern North Pacific and Arctic, there are three: the polar bear, sea otter, and the now extinct Steller sea cow.

The polar bear is included because of its close association with the polar ice pack where icebergs and broken pan ice make swimming necessary. A close relative of the brown bear, this largest of land-based carnivores is a product of the late Pleistocene epoch in North America, and is more marine-adapted than the rest of its ursid kin. The polar bear's life is dependent on the breaks and leads in the ice where the ringed seal, its favored prey, emerges for a breath of air. To find food, the polar bear will not hesitate to swim—however slowly—as far as twenty miles, using slow strokes of its strong forelimbs and trailing its hind legs.

Smallest of the marine mammals, the sea otter is also the most recent mammal to adapt completely to the sea, having first appeared in the North Pacific about one and one-half million years ago. In addition, it is the largest and only marine-adapted member of the weasel family. Flipperlike, webbed hind feet and a short, horizontally flattened tail enable the sea otter to dive for sea urchins or abalone around rocky coasts and kelp forests of the North Pacific. It swims on its back, making alternating strokes with its hind flippers on the water's surface. Underwater its hind feet and tail function like the cetacean's flukes. No layer of blubber protects the sea otter from the chilly waters; instead it is insulated by a blanket of air trapped in its dense fur.

The Steller sea cow, although now extinct, was once adapted to the sea. The sole northerly member of the order Sirenia (which comprises the only herbivorous sea mammals), the sea cow's remaining relatives are the dugong and manatee of tropical coastal waters. The sea cow was a giant, slow-moving grazer that fed on seaweeds around the Commander Islands in the North Pacific. It swam with paddlelike forelimbs and a large, horizontally flattened tail that was similar to the flukes of a whale. Discovered in 1741, the sea cow was exterminated by Russian fur hunters about 1768, thus becoming the only North Pacific sea mammal in historic times to become extinct.

D. H.

Polar Bear

by Jack W. Lentfer

Harry Brower, an Eskimo trapper from Point Barrow, Alaska, was checking his arctic fox trapline on the tundra southeast of Point Barrow in late March when he crossed fresh *nanook* (or polar bear) tracks. He followed them a few hundred yards to a hole in deep, drifted snow on the cutbank of a meandering stream. This polar bear den was about twenty-five miles inland, as far from the coast as Eskimos usually find them. Harry was quite certain that this was a female with one or two cubs still too small to survive outside the den, and he did not wish to disturb them. His main concern, as he continued on his trapline, was that a cub might become caught in one of his traps.

He returned a few days later and was able to tell from tracks that the den contained a female polar bear with a single cub. Knowing that the female had not eaten since forming the den five months previously and that she had been lactating for three months, he had brought a large piece of whale blubber, which he left near the den. By his next visit, which was on a bright, mild day of twenty below zero degrees Farenheit in early April,

Harry had a plan. He had more whale blubber on his sled and was able to get the female to leave her cub and follow his snowmobile and sled for a short distance. When the bear stopped, Harry unhooked the sled and drove off. The bear then approached the sled and started feeding, and Harry quickly picked up the fifteen-pound cub and drove off; the cub's penetrating, persistent bawling caused the mother to chase the snowmobile. Knowing that it was the time of year when bears normally leave maternity dens and go to the drifting sea ice to hunt ringed seals (their principal food), Harry headed toward the coast, some twenty miles away, with the cub in his lap and its mother in pursuit. He left them when they were completely clear of his trapline. He knew that the mother could form a temporary resting den in snow in the lee of a pressure ridge now that the maternity den was no longer available.

Few people have the kind of contact with polar bears that Harry Brower experienced, but people throughout the world have a special interest and concern for the welfare of this large, white carni-

A female polar bear is followed by her cub. Except for family groups of females and young, the polar bear is solitary during most of the year. (Jack W. Lentfer)

vore that survives in an inhospitable and largely unknown environment. The polar bear can be considered a marine mammal because it spends a great portion of its life associated with the sea and sea ice, and subsists almost entirely on arctic marine food chains. Appropriately, its scientific name is *Ursus maritimus*, which means "sea bear." From an evolutionary standpoint, however, the polar bear is more closely related to the brown bear than to marine mammals. Comparative studies of skulls and teeth and other fossil evidence indicate that the polar bear and the brown bear originated from a common ancestor, possibly in Eurasia in the early Pleistocene era. In zoos, matings of polar and brown bears have produced fertile offspring, which also indicates a close genetic relationship.

Similar to the brown bear in size and weight but generally more elongated and less robust, the adult male polar bear is from eight to eleven feet long and weighs eight hundred to fourteen hundred pounds. The adult female commonly weighs between four hundred and six hundred pounds.

This mammal is well adapted for survival in the arctic marine environment. A white coat camouflages and aids in stalking seals. Dense fur and a blubber layer provide insulation from cold air and cold water, and short, densely furred ears and heavy fur (which surrounds and protects foot pads) also conserve heat. Compared with the teeth of other bears, polar bear teeth are more suited for biting than grinding—an adaptation made in their evolution from omnivore to carnivore. An extremely well-developed sense of smell aids in finding food and in bringing bears together during the breeding season, which is important in the arctic because of the sparse distribution of food and bears.

The polar bear prefers areas where sea ice is kept in motion by winds and currents, and where open water and newly frozen ice facilitate seal hunting. These areas are found around the rim of the

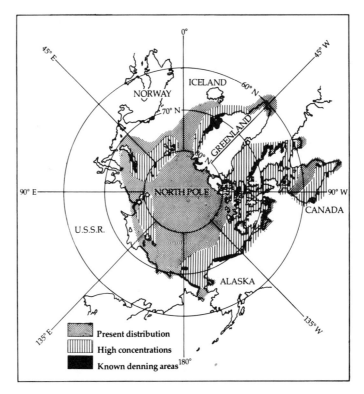

Polar bear distribution

polar basin within about two hundred miles of land masses. In the summer, bears move to the north within this zone as the ice recedes from coastal areas. They are also sparsely distributed on the heavy ice toward the center of the polar basin.

Except for family groups of females and young, the polar bear is solitary during most of the year. From April through June—its breeding season—the male actively seeks females by following their tracks on the sea ice. The bear is polygamous, and a male probably remains with a female a relatively short time and then seeks another female.

The gestation period is about eight months. For several months the embryo probably does not develop, but then grows quite rapidly immediately before birth through the process known as delayed implantation. In October and November the preg-

nant females seek out denning areas. A denning female may form a den by making a depression in the snow and then letting the drifting snow cover her. As the snow depth increases, she forms a chamber about five feet in diameter and three to four feet high. Although her metabolic processes are slowed during the winter, she is not completely dormant. In many cases, she may tunnel through the snow and form a new denning chamber during the winter, possibly when ice in the first denning chamber reduces the insulating value of the snow or the exchange of gases through the snow.

In December, polar bear cubs are born, usually in litters of two, often in litters of one, but rarely in litters of three. They weigh between one and two pounds and are about ten inches long. With short hair and no blubber layer for temperature regula-

tion, they are completely dependent on the protection of the den and their mother for the first three months of life. The female and her cubs break out of the den in late March or early April when the cubs weigh between fifteen and twenty pounds. They make short trips outside the den for several days to allow the cubs to acclimate to outside temperatures and gain experience in traveling. They then desert the den site and search for sea ice areas where they can feed on seals. Studies in Alaska indicate that the young remain with their mother for about twenty-eight months.

Although polar bears other than pregnant females may occupy temporary dens, pregnant females are the only polar bears that normally occupy winter dens for extended periods. Snowfall, ambient temperatures, topography, and wind are

A litter of two is most common among polar bears. These twins were sighted on sea ice north of Point Barrow, Alaska. (Jack W. Lentfer)

all factors that contribute to successful denning because the bears require snowdrifts that do not thaw during the denning period. Other requirements are the presence of seals nearby and ice conditions that help the bears catch seals during predenning and postdenning periods.

Polar bears concentrate their denning on offshore islands and certain portions of the mainland. There are also records of bears denning on drifting sea ice. However, the drifting ice may be less suitable than land for denning because it can transport the bears through areas where ice movement is a threat to dens, or to areas where feeding conditions are poor when the bears emerge from their dens.

Studies conducted in Alaska show that the female polar bear breeds for the first time between 3 and 7 years of age, with the average age being 5.4 years. The female can produce litters every third year, but not all do so. The average interval between litters is 3.6 years, and the average litter size is 1.63. The reproductive rate is 0.45 young per adult female per year. This indicates a fairly low reproductive potential and a need for close monitoring and control of activities that may reduce populations. Some polar bears may live as long as twenty-five to thirty years.

Polar bears off the Alaska coast feed primarily on ringed seals and, to a limited extent, on bearded seals; both species are associated with sea ice throughout the year. In other locations, bears also feed on harp and bladdernose seals. When other food is not available, they occasionally eat carrion (including whale, walrus, and seal carcasses), and small mammals, birds, eggs, and vegetation.

The polar bear catches seals in various ways. It may wait at breathing holes or at the edge of open water leads, or stalk seals that are sunning on top of the ice during favorable weather. (The story is often told that a bear stalking a seal on top of the ice will cover its black nose with a paw as it sneaks

forward.) The bear also breaks into ringed seal dens, formed in snowdrifts on top of the ice, in April and May when the seals are giving birth. Young seals are vulnerable at this time because they cannot swim for a period after birth.

An interesting relationship exists between the polar bear and the arctic fox. The arctic fox survives on sea ice by feeding on remains of seals that the bear has killed. This may be a more stable food source than lemmings and other terrestrial food, which support the segment of the fox population that remains on land during the winter.

Approximately sixty percent of Alaskan bears harbor the pork worm or trichina, which they apparently ingest by eating seals and other marine mammals, garbage, or possibly carcasses of other bears, and which can cause trichinosis. This illness is similar to that contracted from eating infected pork, so Eskimos thoroughly boil polar bear meat before eating it. Because of its high vitamin A content, polar bear liver is toxic if eaten. Low levels of environmental contaminants (including DDT, PCB, and mercury) have also been found in most of the Alaskan bears examined for these substances.

World population estimates of polar bears are based on limited data and broad assumptions, and should be considered as general estimates. They range from ten thousand by the Soviets to twenty thousand by the Norwegians. Mark and recapture studies and studies of comparative size of animals indicate that bears form somewhat discrete subpopulations throughout the polar basin.

Five countries, each with a somewhat different management philosophy, have polar bears under their jurisdictions: the Soviet Union, Norway, Denmark, Canada, and the United States. The Soviet Union believes that its polar bears have been reduced in number and has prohibited hunting since 1956. Only a few cubs are taken and only for zoos. Until recent years, Norwegian sealers killed bears as predators, Spitsbergen trappers used baited set

The polar bear blends well into its environment. Only its black eyes and nose are visible against the white background, providing good camouflage for stalking seals. (Jack W. Lentfer)

guns to obtain hides to sell, and trophy hunters hunted the bears from Norwegian boats in the summer. The current feeling in Norway is that these uses should no longer be permitted or should be closely regulated. Norway stopped set gun and trophy hunting in 1971 and enacted a five-year moratorium in 1973. In Greenland, which is governed by Denmark, taking is limited to Eskimos or long-term residents who use the meat primarily for subsistence and the skins for personal uses. The annual take is 125 to 150 animals. In Canada, polar bears have traditionally been taken by Eskimos for subsistence and for sale of the skins. Harvests in recent years have been regulated by establishment of hunting districts with quotas. The annual kill there is now about 600.

In Alaska, the only location where the United States has polar bears under its jurisdiction, there have been various management practices and authorities over the years. Traditionally, polar bears were important in the subsistence economy and culture of Alaskan Eskimos. After commercial whaling began in the 1850s, the sale and barter of skins became especially important. Skins were used for robes and clothing, and meat was used for food. Eskimo ceremonies and dances were related to the taking of bears, and a hunter's prestige was enhanced considerably by his success in killing bears. Prior to the late 1940s, nearly all Alaska polar bear hunting was by Eskimos with dog teams, with a harvest of about 120 animals per year.

Trophy hunting of polar bears with aircraft began in the late 1940s. Most hunters took bears with the aid of a relatively few pilot-guides operating from Eskimo coastal villages. The use of airplanes for hunting continued after Alaska became a state and assumed game management authority in 1960. State hunting regulations became more restrictive as pilot-guides became more efficient in taking bears and more people desired to hunt. Between 1961 and 1972, an average of 260 polar bears were taken annually.

To control illegal killing by a few pilot-guides, Alaska stopped polar bear hunting with aircraft in 1972. Regulations were adopted to provide more aesthetically acceptable sport hunting from the ground. The environmental protectionist movement was strong enough by this time that elimination of hunting with aircraft was not enough to stop polar bears from being included in the United States Marine Mammal Protection Act of 1972. This act transferred management authority from the state to the federal government and enacted a moratorium on the taking of marine mammals by anyone other than Alaskan natives, who could take them without restriction provided waste did not occur. This was much more liberal than the previous state management program, which imposed bag limits on polar bear subsistence hunters and provided complete protection for females with young.

The state of Alaska has requested return of management for certain marine mammals, including polar bears, under provisions of a program that would allow animal numbers to remain within the range of what is considered the optimum sustainable population. The proposed state management program provides for subsistence hunting and for recreational hunting, both to be done from the ground only. Females with young and bears in dens will receive complete protection, and there will be quotas by areas and bag limits for all hunters.

The five polar bear nations have provided for international management of polar bears in the Agreement on Conservation of Polar Bears. The agreement is based on the premise that nations have the ability to manage populations on and adjacent to their coasts. It creates a de facto "high seas" sanctuary for bears by not allowing them to be taken with aircraft, large motorized boats, or in areas where they have not been taken by traditional means in the past. The agreement states that nations shall protect the ecosystems of which polar bears are a part and emphasizes the need for protection of habitat components such as denning and feeding areas, and migration routes. The agreement also states that countries shall conduct national research, coordinate management and research for populations that occur in more than one area of national jurisdiction, and exchange research results and harvest data. Resolutions appended to the agreement request establishment of an international hide marking system in order to control traffic in illegal hides, protection of cubs and females with cubs, and prohibition of hunting in denning areas when bears are moving into these areas or are in dens.

Until recently, hunting appeared to pose a major threat to polar bears, but more restrictions and research providing a better understanding of populations have largely eliminated this concern. An increase in other human activity in the Arctic is now of concern, however. One of the greatest potential threats is the increase of human activity associated with oil, gas, and coal exploration and development that could adversely affect denning of polar bears. Human activity could cause female bears coming ashore to den in October and November to move back onto drifting sea ice and den there. The drifting ice, however, may provide a less stable platform than land or shore-fast ice and thereby reduce denning success. It could also carry bears to areas where feeding conditions would be poor when they emerge from dens. Human activity may also frighten bears away from more desirable sites on land, and cause them to den in less favorable locations. Disturbances after cubs are born may cause females to leave dens before cubs are developed enough to survive the severe midwinter environment.

Other adverse effects could result from major oil spills and from the chronic effects of small discharges of oil and contaminants associated with drilling. Oil could reduce the insulating value of the bears' fur, cause adverse effects if ingested, and affect organisms in the short arctic marine food chain, thereby affecting the bears. This problem is intensified because there is no known method to contain or clean up oil under the ice. The danger of spills in the Arctic is extremely high because drifting ice could damage offshore drilling and pumping equipment, and ships used to transport oil. Extremely high pressures, as encountered in the eastern Beaufort Sea oil formation, could increase the possibility of blowouts and uncontrolled discharge of oil.

Another effect would result from the direct interaction of bears with people. There will be more encounters as more people spend more time in bear habitats and as the bears are attracted to camps and settlements because of their curiosity, and by garbage. Bears in most of these encounters will not survive.

The problem in Alaska may be especially critical because there is the potential for fossil fuel development along most of Alaska's north coast and offshore. As plans for development proceed, managers must consider biological resources along with energy resources, and provide adequate protective measures.

Natural occurrences may also affect populations. Long-term warming trends would decrease the number of areas available for denning and other activities. Years of little snowfall could reduce denning success. Changes in the food chain supporting bears could also affect bears.

Much effort has been devoted to polar bear research since 1965 when representatives of the five polar bear nations met in Fairbanks, Alaska, to report on the status of polar bears in their countries and to define informational needs. The international Polar Bear Specialist Group, formed after the Fairbanks meeting, meets every two years to exchange findings and coordinate research efforts. The research activity receiving the greatest emphasis has been a mark and recapture program conducted by each of the five nations. Between fifteen hundred and two thousand bears have been captured and marked since 1966. Capturing and recapturing provide data on distribution and movements, breeding biology, and reproductive and mortality rates. Information from marking has been supplemented by a limited amount of information from radio-tracking, now done by satellite. Studies have been made concerning delineation of critical habitat areas, especially those used for denning; productivity of some denning areas, especially in Canada; physiology related mostly to thermoregulation and bioenergetics; levels of environmental contaminants; food habits; and estimates of population size and predictions of what effects disturbances of different magnitudes may have on populations.

Our future research should be directed more toward gaining an understanding of the relationship of the polar bear to its environment. Studies of arctic marine food chains, sea ice, ocean currents, and the effects of disturbance on bears will further ensure survival for *nanook*—the great white sea bear.

Sea Otter

by Karl W. Kenyon

The sea otter (*Enhydra lutris*), valued for its fur and its unique characteristics, was hunted almost to extinction during the eighteenth and nineteenth centuries. Thanks to strict protection and careful management, the species has increased greatly during the past seventy years and has been reestablished through transplants along eastern North Pacific coasts.

All marine mammals, including the sea otter, are descended from land mammals that went to sea. The sea otter is related to the river otter, weasel, and skunk of the family Mustelidae. Although other members of this family may enter salt water, the sea otter has never been recorded in freshwater rivers or lakes. It is also the smallest marine mammal, the adult male weighing up to 100 pounds and the female about 72 pounds. The maximum recorded length is fifty-eight inches from the tip of the nose to the tip of the tail. Its tail is flattened and about one quarter of the body length.

Although well adapted to shallow coasts, the sea otter does not share with the whales and the seals the specializations for survival in other marine areas. It must obtain food from the bottom in relatively shallow water, and therefore cannot travel or migrate long distances at sea as do seals and whales. It also differs from both seals and whales in not having a layer of blubber; it depends instead on its dense fur for insulation against the chilly marine environment. Therefore, the sea otter is particularly vulnerable to polluted waters. If oil or other foreign matter soils its fur and destroys the millions of tiny air pockets among the dry underfur fibers, water reaches the skin and the otter soon dies of exposure. Because its body temperature is similar to man's, cold water directly on its skin is as disastrous as long-term exposure to cold sea water would be to the unprotected human swimmer.

The barrier between life and death is the sea otter's two-layered, dry underfur. The sparse guard hair is about one and one-half inches long and the dense underfur about a quarter of an inch shorter. It grows in bundles, each bundle containing one guard hair and approximately seventy underfur roots. Studies by marine mammalogist Victor B. Scheffer have shown that the sea otter's fur is

A mother sea otter gives her pup almost constant attention until it is about a year old. (Karl W. Kenyon)

nearly twice as dense as that of the fur seal. Our calculations indicate that a large sea otter may have nearly a billion fur fibers.

Care of the fur is of primary importance. In order to maintain it in clean, waterproof condition, the sea otter grooms itself many times a day. Visitors to zoos often assume that the sea otter has external parasites because they misinterpret this constant grooming for scratching. Instead, the sea otter is probably unique among mammals because no external parasites (fleas or lice) have ever been found in its fur.

The forepaws are specialized for grooming and grasping food rather than for swimming. The front (but not the hind) claws are catlike—retractile, so that slippery food can be grasped; the extended claws may also aid in grooming.

Early hunters considered the sea otter's fur of prime quality in all seasons. Recent studies have shown why—the molt of these animals is prolonged. Unlike other mammals, no thinning or massive shedding is noticeable in any season. The fur shed by "Gus" at the Point Defiance Aquarium in Tacoma, Washington, was collected from the drain of his pool over a twenty-four-hour period each week for a year by aquarium director Cecil Brosseau. On examining the shed pelage samples, I found that, although the amount of fur shed in August was much more than in February, some shedding took place the year-round. Thus, the sea otter is able to maintain its warm, dense fur while, at the same time, changing its coat in a prolonged molt.

In general, the sea otter's coat may be dark brown or nearly black. Guard hairs may be light or dark. Alaska game biologist John Vania (who grades sea otter pelts for commercial sale) told me that, despite the general similarity in color, it is difficult to match pelts to be sold in lots of three or four skins of nearly identical appearance. With age, the pelage of the head and chest may become quite grizzled and, in general, males tend to have lighter colored heads than females.

The sea otter requires a large food intake—about twenty to twenty-three percent of its body weight in meat per day. Gus, the large male at the Tacoma aquarium, weighed about seventy-five pounds and consistently ate fifteen pounds of filleted fish and squid daily. Given this large intake and the sea otter's restriction to shallow water zones, crowds of these animals may seriously deplete food organisms. At Amchitka, Alaska, we found that fish, primarily sluggish bottom forms, were an important food item.

The sea otter's teeth are unique among carnivores. They do not have sharp cutting edges; even the canines are rounded. The postcanines have flattened, rounded cusps, which are well adapted to crushing the invertebrates that are a primary food. Because the sea otter must scoop much of its food from the shells of clams, snails, and sea urchins, the lower incisors protrude so that soft parts may be scooped from shells. Unlike any other member of the order Carnivora, the sea otter has only two pairs of lower incisors; all other carnivores have three.

When the sea otter feeds, it dives to the bottom, collects food with its forepaws, and stores it under the left foreleg in order to carry it to the surface. This habit indicates that the sea otter is right-handed. Under each foreleg and extending across the chest is a pouch of loose skin. In this pouch, the otter may carry up to twenty-five sea urchins and a number of clams, depending on their size.

Sea otters prefer to feed in shallow water when possible. During our aerial surveys, we rarely saw otters in water as deep as 180 feet. The majority were seen in depths of 120 feet or less. A 1975 observation by marine mammalogist Terrell C. Newby, however, indicates that otters are capable of much deeper dives. Newby recovered the remains of an adult male sea otter from a crab trap that was set at 318 feet.

The sea otter's beautiful, dense fur coat—its only insulation from chilly North Pacific waters—is visible in this adult male. (Karl W. Kenyon)

When feeding, the sea otter has the unique ability to use a stone as an anvil on which to break the shells of large clams and mussels. Susie, a female from Amchitka that lived at Woodland Park Zoo in Seattle, Washington, used stones to break the concrete edge of her pool, so the stones had to be removed. She also used a stone to hammer the cover of her drain so that she could reach into the mysterious dark hole beneath. Although we did not notice sea otters using stones as anvils or hammers in Alaska, animals caught in Alaska used stones as soon as they were given them in captivity. This habit is often observed among sea otters on the California coast. The only explanation for wild otters not using the stone in Alaska is that the organisms on which they feed are usually small enough to be crushed by their teeth.

The sea otters' mating period may last approximately three days, at which time the mated pair center their activities around a chosen rock. Mating takes place in the water near the rock and the animals feed close together nearby. During food dives, the male follows the female closely and emerges an instant after she does to eat beside her as they float on their backs at the surface. At night, they haul out together and sleep alongside each other on the chosen rock.

The female terminates the mating period. On several occasions I watched the breaking of the pair bond. Apparently the male otter, requiring more food than the smaller female, left her on the chosen rock while he gathered food and ate nearby. As his feeding activity carried him perhaps two hundred feet from the rock, the female watched him intently. Suddenly she left the rock and swam rapidly away underwater while the male was beneath the surface diving for food. After the male noted her absence, he hurriedly explored the chosen rock and other rocks in the vicinity. Never did I see a male find his mate once she deserted him.

Sea otter pups may be born during all months of the year. Our field counts of young and studies of reproductive tracts indicate, however, that the majority of young in the Aleutian area are born in the late spring and summer months. Studies of reproductive tracts also show that there is a period of delayed implantation during which the fertilized ovum rests. The exact lengths of the unimplanted period and period of fetal development are not known, but the total gestation period may be as long as eight months to a year.

Because of the long periods of both gestation and dependency, intervals between births may be about two years. Although there are records of more than one fetus in the reproductive tract of a female sea otter, we have never seen more than one young with a mother. It would probably be impossible for a mother to raise more than one pup at a time because she must give her pup almost constant attention—carrying it on her chest while she swims on her back and meticulously grooming its fur at frequent intervals—from the time it is born until it is about a year old. This excellent maternal care probably ensures a high rate of survival despite the otter's low reproductive rate.

At birth, the sea otter pup has a long, warm coat of dense woolly fur, which is brownish with a pale yellow tinge. Within several weeks, the yellowish guard hairs grow to nearly two inches, giving the pup a distinct yellowish look.

The pup's eyes are open at birth; it weighs about five pounds, and is helpless. While the mother dives for food, the pup is warm and sleeps on the water, buoyed up by the blanket of air in its fur. If it awakes during the mother's absence beneath the surface, the pup may squirm about and make swimming motions, but it cannot swim. When the pup first tries to dive at several weeks of age, its buoyant air layer keeps it from submerging. It needs many weeks of practice before it gains strength and diving skill and learns to reach bottom, and when it does, it usually brings up worthless items such as pebbles, small sea urchins, or brightly colored starfish, which are of little or no food value. As it reaches a body size of twenty to twenty-five pounds, it may obtain some of its own food, but it is primarily dependent on sharing its mother's food. Early in life the pup receives most of its nourishment from its mother's two abdominal nipples, but at an early age it also receives small solid items of food from its mother's paws.

The mother sea otter is somewhat solitary, although several mothers and young may feed in one area and bring their young ashore on the same rocks. Mothers with young are not nearly so gregarious as certain groups of males, which may come ashore and sleep close together on some habitually used beach.

The sea otter has relatively few predators. A Soviet biologist has recorded an observation of a killer whale attacking sea otters. I have seen killer whales and sea otters in the same areas but have never seen any indication that the killer whales disturbed the otters. Bald eagles may rarely take baby sea otters while the mother is gathering food beneath the surface. There are few observations, however, of such a thing occurring, and I have frequently seen baby sea otters and eagles in the same areas. In California, fragments of the tooth of great white or man-eating sharks have been found in the lacerated bodies of several dead sea otters. In general, however, the sea otter's primary historical predator is man.

The protection of sea otters and their increased numbers, however, have brought about some reversal of the situation. In some locales, the sea otter

A female and juvenile sea otter are surprised along the kelp-lined, rocky shores of the Aleutian Islands, where sea otters regularly haul out to groom and dry their fur before sleeping. (Karl W. Kenyon)

may be viewed as the predator. In California, at present, a heated controversy rages between "The Friends of the Sea Otter" and "The Friends of the Abalone" because a growing sea otter population is entering areas where the otters compete with both commercial and sport fishermen for pismo clams and abalone.

Sea otters not only use a stone to break mollusks on their chests, but are also capable of pounding the shell of an abalone with a stone until it breaks, after which they may carry the abalone to the surface and eat it. Most biologists who have studied the sea otter believe that if a healthy sea otter population and a healthy abalone population are to be maintained in the same area, studies and management programs will be necessary for these species. Otherwise, a large sea otter population will join eventually with the abalone fishermen in depleting the abalone resource. Then the otters will move to other areas or starve, and the abalone fishermen will have to seek other occupations.

At the time of its discovery in 1741, the sea otter ranged from central Baja California, north along the coast and among the islands of North America to a northernmost limit in Prince William Sound, Alaska. From there it ranged southwestward along the Alaska Peninsula through the Aleutian, Commander, and Kuril islands to northern Japan. Populations in the Pribilof Islands were exterminated soon after these islands were discovered in 1786. During a century and a half of wholesale exploitation, the sea otter vanished from much of its original range. Because of the great value of the fur, men spent years seeking out the last surviving sea otters in isolated areas.

By 1911, when the sea otter was given protection, scientists believed that the population had been so drastically reduced that the survival of the species was doubtful. Little was seen or heard of the sea otter between 1911 and the mid-1930s. During this period, scattered sightings were reported to

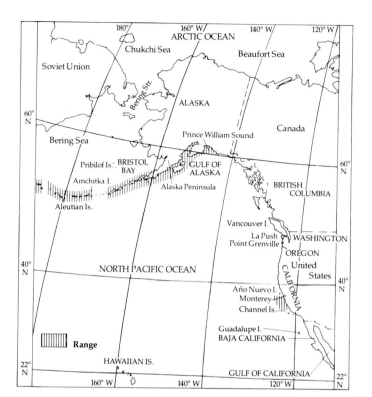

Sea otter distribution

the United States Bureau of Fisheries and a few skins were confiscated. These records indicated that several tiny seed populations of sea otters in the outer Aleutian Islands and along the Alaska Peninsula remained. Undoubtedly the harsh environment and many outlying reefs protected these animals from hunters.

By the mid-1940s several growing sea otter populations were surveyed. One at Amchitka Island, Alaska, was particularly prosperous and numbered some thousands of animals during the mid-1940s. Besides the Alaska population, a remnant population on the California coast survived, as did a small group in the Commander and Kuril islands.

As early as the mid-1940s, certain Aleutian Island populations began to overcrowd their habitat, exceeding the maximum numbers that food could support. Field observers reported numbers of animals dying on beaches. Assuming at first that these "die-offs" were the result of a disease, biologists began systematic studies of the sea otter at Amchitka Island.

During the course of several seasons of work in the mid-1950s, I found that most of the dead otters were either large juveniles or older animals with seriously worn teeth. Healthy young adults seldom appeared dead on the beach. Studies in other less crowded areas indicated that winter mortality was slight. Examination of the animals that died in the crowded Amchitka population showed that they were emaciated and had no body fat.

The stomachs and intestines of the animals dying on Amchitka beaches contained only the remains of small sea urchins. Analysis of the food value of organisms available to sea otters at Amchitka showed that certain of the invertebrates were valueless as food: the otters were dying of starvation. Strong animals in their prime were able to catch fish, and more than fifty percent of the food found in such animals that we collected contained fish. The animals dying on beaches were the young, newly separated from their mothers, and those with worn-out teeth, weakened by age, and unable to capture more nutritious but elusive prey.

Aerial surveys conducted between 1959 and 1965 covered most of the otters' former habitat in Alaska—a distance of some two thousand linear miles. We counted nearly eighteen thousand otters and calculated that at that time there were about thirty thousand total. Our studies showed also that certain otter populations were increasing at a rate of about five percent per year. From these studies and population data from the Soviet Union, we estimated that the world population in the mid-1960s was between forty thousand and fifty thousand animals—the majority of them in Alaska.

Continuing surveys of the Alaska population by Alaska game biologist Karl Schneider indicate that many populations are still growing. By the mid-1970s, the Alaska population probably numbered between one hundred thousand and one hundred twenty thousand animals. In early 1970, the largest assemblage of otters ever photographed contained over one thousand animals. This group was in the Bering Sea north of the Alaska Peninsula. There are no kelp beds in this area, but the animals gather there to feed on the rich bottom fauna of the shallow Bering Sea.

In 1969 and 1970, the California Department of Fish and Game surveyed their otter population. They found that it had grown from about one hundred animals in the mid-1930s to well over one thousand. Continuing surveys placed the 1977 population at eighteen hundred to two thousand animals. These were found within a linear distance of about 170 miles along the coast between Año Nuevo Island (north of Santa Cruz) and Point San Luis (near San Luis Obispo), California.

There are a number of myths about sea otters. Some people believe that sea otters will "play catch" with a ball or a wad of kelp. Others believe that they need kelp beds in their habitat. Although sea otters appear to prefer kelp beds, where they wrap themselves with kelp while sleeping to prevent drifting, they do not require kelp beds. In certain places in the Bering Sea large numbers of sea otters thrive year-round where there are no kelp beds at all. They appear to sleep quite comfortably on the open sea.

According to another myth, sea urchins are essential to their diet. Although adult sea urchins with large egg masses are highly nutritious and furnish excellent sea otter food, small sea urchins and those with undeveloped egg masses are almost useless as food. Thus, animals died of starvation while consuming quantities of small urchins at Amchitka. When starving sea otters taken from beaches were fed fish in our Amchitka Island enclosure, they quickly regained health and refused to eat the

sea urchins.

Yet another myth is that kelp is a sea otter food. Although sea otters may eat kelp from time to time—partly because it is stuck to other food items—it passes through the entire gastrointestinal tract and shows no signs of digestion. Sea otters are also unable to digest the meat of birds and seals, some of which we fed experimentally to them in captivity.

Residents or visitors in inland waters, such as around Washington State's San Juan Islands, often report that they have seen sea otters. After investigating many such "sightings," we found that in every case the reports concerned river otters, which are abundant in salt water among the San Juan and other islands north to Alaska. The differences between the two species are easily observed. The sea otter always eats while floating high on its back in the water. It never goes out onto the rocks to eat as the river otter frequently does. Also, the river otter has a relatively long tail (more than one half its body length), heavily thickened at its base, while the sea otter has a relatively short (about one third

its body length), flattened tail. It seems unlikely that sea otters ever frequented the San Juan Islands: in early times, explorers recorded that they could not get sea otter skins from natives of the inland waters but had to get them from Nootka Sound, Vancouver Island, British Columbia, and other areas on the outer coast.

In order to restore the sea otter to its former range, it was obvious to wildlife biologists that transplants would be required in some areas. The transportation of sea otters over long distances, however, poses problems: otters kept in dry bedding easily suffer from heat prostration and die. If they survive the trip, their fur may be soiled by food and excrement so that when they are placed in water, they become soaked to the skin, causing chilling and death.

Our first (and sometimes unsuccessful) efforts to transport a group of sea otters from Alaska to Seattle began in 1955. At that time the trip from Amchitka to Seattle took from twenty-four to seventy-two hours. Although death en route or soon after arrival was frequent, one otter—Susie—

Sea otters rest in kelp beds at Monterey, California. In these areas, they may wrap themselves with kelp fronds to prevent drifting while asleep. (Bud Antonelis)

lived in the Seattle zoo for six years and, thanks to her, our knowledge of these sea mammals increased.

With the development of faster aircraft and improved traveling pens that contained water, the translocation of sea otters to areas where they had become extinct became practical. Between 1965 and 1969, a total of 413 otters were flown from Prince William Sound to southeastern Alaska. This new population is thriving; many young were seen on surveys in the mid-1970s.

In 1969, 1970, and 1972, a total of eighty-nine otters were transplanted to the outer coast of Vancouver Island, British Columbia. In 1977, a count of sixty otters, including pups, indicated that this colony will probably survive.

A shipment of thirty otters was liberated at Point Grenville on the Washington coast in 1969. Because these animals had become badly soiled during the flight from Amchitka, their survival was poor. Another attempt was made in July 1970. The transplant shipment came directly from Amchitka to La Push, Washington, in about seven and one-half hours. Fortunately, the Washington Department of Game was well prepared. A holding pool was ready when the aircraft landed with thirty adult otters. As the animals groomed and fed in their floating enclosure, we could see that they were in excellent condition. When these animals were liberated five days later they were quite content. On a survey in June 1977 wildlife biologist Ron Jameson and I were able to find eighteen otters, including four pups. Thus there is hope that this colony may survive.

A total of ninety-three otters were flown from Amchitka in 1970 and 1971 and were liberated on the Oregon coast. Jameson has watched this group intently since their release. Although his observations of young have been encouraging, the total counts are discouraging: in 1973 he found twenty-three; in 1975 there were thirteen; in 1976 there were twelve; and, sadly, in 1977 we could find only four. In October 1976, I observed one indication of what may be happening. On a beach near Port Orford, Oregon, I found the body of an adult male otter. Its abdomen had been torn open, and many parallel gashes, typical of shark attack, were found on other parts of his body. We are thus pessimistic about the survival of Oregon's colony.

Because of its small size, limited range, and possible environmental threats caused by increasing human activity, the California sea otter population is now designated as "threatened." This official classification under the United States Endangered Species Act of 1973 became effective on 14 January 1977. A proposal to translocate a number of these otters to the California Channel Islands or to an unoccupied range along the coast also has been made. Such new colonies would reduce the population losses that might be caused by a massive oil spill. As of mid-1978, no decision has been made on possible future action.

Today we view a sea otter population that has recovered from near extinction in 1911, to overabundance in some areas, and developing, healthy populations in others. Crowded island populations in the north have been experimentally cropped under the watchful eyes of Alaska's wildlife biologists. It also has been demonstrated that new populations may be established, although the future of some is still uncertain.

The evolution of man's attention to the sea otter is now complete. It began with wasteful exploitation (1741 to 1911), proceeded to absolute protection (1911 and 1962), and finally culminated in management and study programs that are continuing. The species once thought to be doomed is now safely reestablished.

Steller Sea Cow

by Delphine Haley

The Steller sea cow (*Hydrodamalis gigas*) is the only North Pacific sea mammal to become extinct in historical times. Discovered in 1741 by the shipwrecked crew of explorer Vitus Bering, this giant marine herbivore was literally devoured to death because of its beeflike meat and sweet tasting oil. For twenty-seven years following its discovery, the sea cow was a major food source for Russian hunters seeking furs and oil across the North Pacific. It was found only in the shallow waters off Bering and Copper islands in the Commander Islands, some one hundred miles east of Russia in the Bering Sea. There, slow moving and unafraid, it grazed on seaweeds until its disappearance around 1768. The Steller sea cow is included here because of its unique adaptations and the role it played in the region's history, and because, although presumed extinct, there is still the rare unconfirmed claim that the creature still lives.

Georg Wilhelm Steller, the Bering expedition's naturalist and surgeon, was among the first to notice the sea cow. It resembled an overturned boat drifting beyond the tides, until it moved, revealing a huge form about twenty-five feet long. Spindle-shaped, the body ended fore and aft with a disproportionately small, bristly muzzled head and a large, laterally lobed tail. To Steller we are indebted for the only scientific description of the sea cow, one of many species that bear his name.

The Steller sea cow, along with the dugong and manatee, is a member of the order Sirenia. Although the sirenians superficially resemble the modern whale and seal, they are actually descended from an ancient Egyptian fossil animal, *Moeritherium*, a pig-sized, primitive ungulate that led a hippolike existence in the upper Eocene some fifty million years ago. Oddly enough, its modern descendants, aside from the aquatically adapted sirenians, are the hyrax and the elephant.

Sirenians share a fusiform shape, heavy boned frame for stability, horizontally flattened tail, tough wrinkled hide, bristly hairs around the lips, and a preference for vegetation-filled coastal waters and estuaries. They lack both an external ear and a dorsal fin. Two groups—the manatees (Trichechidae) of the tropical Atlantic and Caribbean and the dugong

The Steller sea cow is measured for the first time. This reconstruction of the sea cow was made by Georg Steller's biographer, Leonhard Stejneger. It was based on a length of thirty feet for the animal, using human figures some six feet tall.

(Dugongidae) of the Indian Ocean and African and Indo-Malaysian waters—are the present-day representatives.

The sea cow, a dugongid, was the only recent family member to adapt to cold waters. To accomplish this, it evolved distinguishing traits of its own, which—thanks to Steller's descriptions—are known to us. The sea cow was by far the largest sirenian, at about twenty-five feet in length. Its weight is confusing, for Steller recorded it at "200 pud," or 4.5 tons, and "1200 pud," or 26.8 tons. (Marine mammalogist Victor Scheffer, using a clay model of the sea cow, and assuming the animal's specific gravity to be the same as that of seawater, has calculated that an individual some twenty-five feet long would weigh seven tons.) Four inches of fat—nine in some places—provided insulation from the cold, and an inch-thick hide furnished protection from the abrasions of ice and surf-pounded rocky coasts. Its elephantlike hide—hairless, black, and sometimes marked with white spots and zones—consisted of a rough outer cuticle, particularly around the head, eyes, ears, breasts, and under the forelimbs. The hide was uneven, full of grooves, wrinkles, and funnel-shaped lesions or pits gnawed out by a parasitic amphipod later named *Cyamus rhytina*. Sea gulls were known to sit on the sea cows' backs and feed on these parasites.

Steller's descriptions of the sea cow and other North Pacific sea mammals were published posthumously in 1751 by the Saint Petersburg Academy of Science under the title *De Bestiis Marinis*. Even in translation, his notes convey the immediacy of discovery. He was quick to relate the creature to the one called "manatee" by the Spaniards in America and "sea cow" by the English and Dutch. Consciously or not, he noted its ungulate qualities:

These animals, like cattle, live in herds at sea, males and females going together and driving the young before them about the shore. They are occupied with nothing

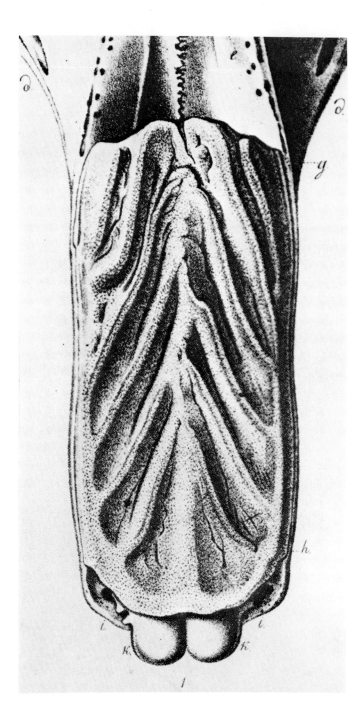

Two of these horny, flat chewing plates took the place of teeth in the Steller sea cow. One was fastened to the palate, the other to the inside of the lower jaw, and both fitted together efficiently for mashing seaweeds. (J. F. Brandt, Symbolae Sirenologicae, 1849)

else but their food. The back and half the body are always seen out of the water. They eat in the same manner as the land animals, with a slow forward movement. They tear the seaweed from the rocks with the feet and chew it without cessation . . . During the eating they move the head and neck like an ox, and after the lapse of a few minutes they lift the head out of the water and draw fresh air with a rasping and snorting sound after the manner of horses.

The sea cow had several strange physical features. Instead of teeth, two flat bones—one attached to the palate, another to the lower jaw—served as chewing plates. (Subsequent examination of the plates identified them as horny, tubercle-filled structures.) Indented with wavy canals, the chewing plates fitted together for efficient mashing of the seaweed. The sea cow's lips were "double and divided into internal and external lips," the protruding exterior upper lip being fourteen inches wide and fringed with thick bristles. In spite of its stupendous size, the sea cow's lidless eyes were no larger than those of a sheep. Nor was there any trace of an external ear; instead, within the wrinkles of the skin there was an opening "hardly large enough for the insertion of a pea." The forelimbs were about two feet long, and were used in moving about in the shallows or supporting the enormous body on slippery rocks. Most peculiar to Steller were the clawless forefeet, which he said resembled horses' hooves except that they were "furnished underneath with many short and closely set bristles like a scratch brush."

Before leaving Bering Island, Steller was able to dissect a sea cow. The specimen, a female, measured twenty-four feet in length and twenty feet at its greatest circumference. Its heart weighed 36.5 pounds; the stomach stretched six by five feet and was so stuffed with seaweed that four strong men with a rope could scarcely move it. The length of the intestinal tract from pharynx to anus was 497 feet, or twenty times the animal's length.

Altogether, he listed forty-seven measurements as he charted a physiological map of the external and internal organs. A brief description of the bones, which Steller found surpassed those of land animals in size and thickness, was also included. The detailed description now serves as a written reconstruction of a lost species—a fleshing out of the few pieced-together skeletons found in museums today.

The scientist noted the sea cows' behavior as he watched them each day during his ten-month stay on Bering Island. He described their liking for shallow, sandy places along the shore, particularly at the mouths of freshwater streams where sometimes they came in so close that he stroked their backs with his hand. They pastured in family groups—a male, female, and a "little tender one," the adults always keeping the calf in front or, when traveling in a group, guarding it in the midst of the herd. Steller believed them to be monogamous; mating usually occurred in early spring and most of the single newborns appeared in autumn after a presumed gestation of more than a year.

The sea cow's docile disposition and slow-moving habits, its low reproduction rate and limited distribution were its undoing. Added to this was its single-minded taste for certain seaweeds, making it oblivious to all danger. One could safely row a boat into the midst of a herd while the animals grazed with heads underwater. Furthermore, even if badly injured, the sea cow would do nothing more than move away from the shallow water and return later, apparently unmindful of its injury.

Aware of these habits, the Bering crew set out in calm seas of May to capture and kill the delicious food source floating offshore. After a few unsuccessful attempts, they hooked a sea cow from a boat and pulled it in by rope, a feat requiring the efforts of forty men on land. En route the beast struggled and sighed; sometimes other sea cows tried to rescue the captive by pressing on the rope or upsetting the boat with their backs. Once landed, the immense animal was hewn and carved into sections. The resulting sea cow steaks were described as "exceedingly savory"; even more delicious to the malnourished crew was the fat, which tasted like sweet almond-oil.

Six weeks after the first sea cow was killed, the crew set out in a rebuilt boat for their Russian homeland. They took with them a supply of fat and salted meat and also news of a fortune to be made in furs from sea otter, fox, and seal—with the sea cow as a food source. For the next twenty-seven years, the sea cow was slaughtered by successive expeditions. According to Steller's biographer, Leonhard Stejneger, the animal was rarely killed outright but instead sought the high seas and died there—only one out of five killed were actually consumed. In 1768, explorer Martin Sauer recorded the killing of the last sea cow.

What caused the rapid disappearance of a species that Steller described as "occurring in large numbers all year round"? Stejneger, after one and one-half years on Bering Island, determined that, if the fifteen river mouths where the sea cows congregated were visited by herds of only fifteen or twenty animals, they would have seemed abundant, even though the true total may not have been more than a few hundred. He estimated the population in Steller's time at probably less than fifteen hundred and concluded that those animals seen after 1768 were probably stray female narwhals. As for the cause of the rapid disappearance, in an article in *The American Naturalist* (1887) he wrote:

There can hardly be any doubt that these animals were the last survivors of a once more numerous and more widely distributed species, which had been spared to that late date because man had not yet reached their last resort. It is, then, pretty safe to assume that this colony was not on the increase, and that, under the most favorable circumstances, the number of surviving young ones barely balanced the number of deaths caused by the dangers of the long winters. Under this supposition,

every animal killed by a new agency—in this case by man—represents one less in the total number.

Sea cow sightings since 1768 have been the subject of much dispute, yet they persist—fueled perhaps by the wish that somehow Steller's beast has managed to survive. Expeditions in 1772 and 1783 failed to find any sea cows. This probably came as no surprise for in 1755 a petition had been filed with Kamchatka authorities by Peter Jakovleff, a mining engineer, requesting that sea cow hunting be restricted because the animals had already disappeared from Copper Island and would soon be gone from Bering Island.

Some investigators extended the sea cow's demise beyond 1768. Among them was Norwegian explorer A. E. Nordenskjöld, who visited Bering Island for five days in 1879. While there, he spoke with three older natives who stated that they had seen animals of this description as late as 1854. Russian naturalist Benedict Dybowski also extended the date. During six years (1879 to 1885) spent on Bering Island, he was told by natives that the great sea cow still survived when the permanent settlers arrived, which would extend its existence to 1830.

Even in recent years, there are reports of sea cows in the North Pacific. In July 1962, a Soviet research vessel near Cape Navarin northeast of the Kamchatka Peninsula came within three hundred feet of six very large, unfamiliar animals feeding offshore. They were dark-skinned with relatively small heads. Each had a bifurcated upper lip, which, perhaps because of its thick whiskers, seemed to project beyond the lower lip. The animals, which were twenty-seven feet long, maintained a tight formation, swam slowly, and dived at regular intervals for short periods, emerging high out of the water. A similar animal was seen in the same vicinity the next day. In an article in the Soviet scientific journal *Priroda*, the authors (A. A. Berzin, E. A. Tikhomirov, and V. I. Troinin) state

that this sighting was only the most recent of several that had been reported in the region. To show that such reports were not impossible they added that since the 1950s two completely new marine mammal species had been discovered—the ginkgo-tooth whale and the Gulf of California porpoise.

As anticipated by the authors, the sea cow sighting was challenged—again in *Priroda* (1965)—by Soviet zoologist V. G. Heptner, who labeled it only another in a series of Loch Nesslike stories. He noted a gap of 194 years between the last trustworthy sea cow sighting (1768) and the Cape Navarin report (1962), and asked: Could such a visible animal, one whose back was usually exposed and on which sea gulls often perched, an animal that grazed near shore and left behind heaps of seaweed piled on the beach, have been overlooked all this time? Since Soviet times, he added, the faunal components of the region have been thoroughly known; even earlier, when Russians and Americans hunted in the region, the sea cow was never mentioned.

In 1977 the sea cow surfaced again in an article of *Kamchatsky Komsomolets*, a newspaper in Petropavlovsk, Kamchatka. It described a sighting by fishermen in Anapkinskaya Bay, a region southwest of Cape Navarin. The author, Vladimir Malukovich of the Kamchatka Museum of local lore, interviewed one of the fishermen, who described an "unknown animal on a tidal belt" that was neither seal nor sea lion. The translation reads: "Its skin was dark, its extremities were flippers, its tail forked like a whale. A slight outline of round ribs was noticeable. We approached the animal, touched it and were surprised as its head bore an unusual form and its snout was long." When shown a drawing of the Steller sea cow, the fisherman stated that this was the animal—the same tail, foreflippers, and head—and he was surprised to learn that it presumably no longer existed. The author added that paleontological data collected by local students had also yielded bones that *appeared* to be those of a sea cow dead only ten years.

Aside from such reports, the sad fact remains that there is no hard proof that the Steller sea cow survived, at least for very long past 1768. Evidence to the contrary is insubstantial—as illusive as the North Pacific mists. However unwittingly, it looks like man struck the last blow and Steller's giant browser perished—literally the victim of human appetite and greed.

This section of a chart attributed to Swen Waxell, an officer on Bering's 1741 expedition to North America, depicts sea mammals of the Bering Sea: the sea cow (A), sea lion (B), and fur seal (C). The original sea cow drawings commissioned by Steller were lost.

Conservation

of Marine Mammals

by Victor B. Scheffer

"There seemed many great auks," wrote the poet John Fowles, "till the last one was killed." Within the past twenty years—through the media of television, newspapers, magazines, books, aquarium shows, and camera safaris—many of us have become widely informed about the mammals of the sea and of the dangers that threaten their existence. What we have learned has led us to be concerned for their welfare and perhaps to prevent them from suffering the fate of the great auks. Witness the unique United States Marine Mammal Protection Act of 1972 and the work of the International Whaling Commission. And witness the many citizen groups that now devote part or all of their energies toward the conservation of seals, sea otters, dolphins, and whales. For some species, our concern may have come too late; for most others, there is hope.

I believe that our rising concern for these creatures is powered less by a foreseen demand for their skins, meat, bones, and oil than by the other values that they offer as examples of living organisms. Long ago, their land ancestors were forced to meet the challenges of a strange and unfriendly environment—the ocean. To those primitive, hairy, four-footed beasts (as yet unknown in the fossil record) the ocean must have seemed a chilly, fluid, vast, three-dimensional, and salty place. Yet within five or ten million generations, they adapted.

Strange in form and habit, the marine mammals have become to us symbols of adjustment, of fine-tuning to their respective environments. Eminently, they have opened our eyes to the far limits of power, beauty, and grace that life can reach. This contribution is to all the peoples of the earth and not only to the whalemeat eaters, food processors, and fur and tusk hunters. The marine mammals are a shared and universal good, "a common heritage of mankind."

Some may counter, "Very well, but why not kill a few of these creatures for their fats and proteins, their furs and tusks, in order to keep whalemen and other hunters employed, while sparing the rest of the sea mammals for their amenity values?" There are historical reasons for doubting that such divided management (which is still being

"Strange in form and habit, the marine mammals have become to us symbols of adjustment, of fine-tuning to their respective environments. Eminently, they have opened our eyes to the far limits of power, beauty, and grace that life can reach. . . . " (Photo by Karl W. Kenyon)

applied to sperm whales, for example) will work. Let me give one case in point. When the gray whales of the North Pacific were nearing extinction in the 1930s, they were protected from hunting and soon began to increase. They now number eleven thousand. The right whales of the North Pacific were given similar protection but did not recover. They still number fewer than three hundred. So elusive are the unknowns and the unknowables in marine ecosystems that zoologists can only guess at the reasons for the dissimilar population trends of the right whales and the grays.

Beyond these reasons for conserving marine mammals, my real argument is emotional or, if you wish, sentimental. I believe, quite simply, that sentiment is one of the best reasons for saving not only some of these animals but all of them.

Mariner Jacques Cousteau once said of the killing of newborn Canadian harp seals (white-coat pups), "The harp seal question is entirely emotional. We have to be logical . . . Those who are moved by the plight of the harp seal could also be moved by the plight of the pig, with which we make our bacon." Many of us would disagree. Our mental image of a seal pup is quite unlike that of a fattened pig and we see no reason to confuse the two. We gently agree with T. S. Eliot who wrote, "Human kind cannot bear very much reality." We know that both seal and pig are animals but we reserve the right to spare the one and to kill the other. We make a deliberate choice between two values that cannot be compared—one that can be framed in "rational" words and one that must remain unframed in wordless feelings.

People's preferences with respect to wildlife uses are, I think, an extension of their attitudes toward humaneness. At the core of humaneness is the idea of *kind-ness*, or the idea that we and the other animals are basically of one kind. We are all caught up together in a sort of spiritual biomass. Thus, for the reason that you and I are part of the living animal world we have the right to insist, not only that animals be spared distress (pain and fear) but that they be used in ways acceptable to large numbers of thoughtful men and women.

The responsibility for conserving and maintaining a sort of useful abundance of sea mammals in a World Ocean now modified by man will call for the technical skills of the professionals known as wildlife managers. They must listen both to the biologists who tell us how marine mammals *could* be used to satisfy our needs, and to the sociologists and other samplers of public opinion who tell us how they *should* be used. Though I must confess my inability to deal adequately with the problem of how one learns what the general public wants from, and for, the whales, seals, and other marine mammals, I myself believe that what men and women are saying today about them is "Let them be." A useful marine mammal, they say, is one out there somewhere in the wild—free, alive, hidden, breathing, perpetuating its ancient bloodline.

The more desperate becomes our own struggle to live within finite resources of energy and materials, the more we admire the ability of the marine mammals to live within theirs. If we are to survive, we will care for the whales and the pinnipeds and their wild companions. If we perish through our own cleverness, the end of the wild things will have been an early warning of our folly.

Classification of Eastern North Pacific Marine Mammals

Order Cetacea
  Suborder Mysticeti (Baleen Whales)
    Family Balaenopteridae
      Balaenoptera musculus (blue whale)
      Balaenoptera physalus (fin whale)
      Balaenoptera borealis (sei whale)
      Balaenoptera edeni (Bryde's whale)
      Balaenoptera acutorostrata (minke whale)
      Megaptera novaeangliae (humpback whale)
    Family Eschrichtiidae
      Eschrichtius robustus (gray whale)
    Family Balaenidae
      Balaena glacialis (right whale)
      Balaena mysticetus (bowhead whale)
  Suborder Odontoceti (Toothed Whales)
    Family Physeteridae
      Physeter macrocephalus (sperm whale)
      Kogia breviceps (pygmy sperm whale)
      Kogia simus (dwarf sperm whale)
    Family Ziphiidae
      Berardius bairdii
        (giant bottlenose whale)
      Ziphius cavirostris (goosebeak whale)
      Mesoplodon densirostris (densebeak whale)
      Mesoplodon stejnegeri
        (Bering Sea beaked whale)
      Mesoplodon ginkgodens
        (ginkgo-tooth whale)
      Mesoplodon carlhubbsi (archbeak whale)
    Family Delphinidae
      Phocoenoides dalli (Dall's porpoise)
      Phocoena phocoena (harbor porpoise)
      Phocoena sinus
        (vaquita or Gulf of California porpoise)
      Tursiops truncatus (bottlenose dolphin)
      Lagenorhynchus obliquidens
        (Pacific white-sided dolphin)
      Delphinus delphis (common dolphin)
      Lissodelphis borealis
        (northern right whale dolphin)
      Grampus griseus (Risso's dolphin)
      Stenella coeruleoalba (striped dolphin)
      Stenella attenuata (spotted dolphin)
      Stenella longirostris (spinner dolphin)
      Steno bredanensis (rough-toothed dolphin)
      Pseudorca crassidens (false killer whale)
      Globicephala macrorhynchus (pilot whale)
      Orcinus orca (killer whale)
    Family Monodontidae
      Delphinapterus leucas (beluga)
      Monodon monoceros (narwhal)

Order Carnivora
  Family Otariidae (Eared Seals)
    Callorhinus ursinus (northern fur seal)
    Arctocephalus townsendi
      (Guadalupe fur seal)
    Eumetopias jubatus (Steller sea lion)
    Zalophus californianus
      (California sea lion)
  Family Odobenidae (Walrus)
    Odobenus rosmarus (walrus)
  Family Phocidae (Earless Seals)
    Phoca vitulina richardii (harbor seal)
    Phoca vitulina largha (spotted seal)
    Phoca hispida (ringed seal)
    Phoca fasciata (ribbon seal)
    Erignathus barbatus (bearded seal)
    Mirounga angustirostris
      (northern elephant seal)
    Monachus schauinslandi (Hawaiian monk seal)
  Family Ursidae
    Ursus maritimus (polar bear)
  Family Mustelidae
    Enhydra lutris (sea otter)

Order Sirenia
  Family Dugongidae
    Hydrodamalis gigas (Steller sea cow)

Further Reading

The following have been selected from reading lists provided by the authors.

General

Andersen, H. T., ed. 1969. *The biology of marine mammals*. New York: Acad. Pr.

Daugherty, A. E. 1972. *Marine mammals of California*. 2d ed. rev. Sacramento, Calif.: St. of Calif., Resources Agency, Dept. Fish and Game.

Harrison, R. J. *Functional anatomy of marine mammals*. Vols. 1 (1972), 2 (1974), and 3 (1977). London and New York: Acad. Pr.

Harrison, R. J. and Ridgway, S. H. 1976. *Deep diving in mammals*. Durham, Engl.: Meadowfield Pr.

Harrison, R. J. and King, J. E. 1973. *Marine mammals*. London: Hutchinson U. Lib.

Howell, A. B. 1930. *Aquatic mammals: their adaptations to life in the water*. Springfield, Ill. and Baltimore, Md.: Thomas. (Reprinted 1970 in paperback. New York: Dover.)

Mitchell, E. D. 1966. Faunal succession of extinct North Pacific marine mammals. *Norsk Hvalfangst-Tidende* 1966 (3):47–60.

Pike, G. C. and MacAskie, I. B. 1969. *Marine mammals of British Columbia*. Fish. Res. Board Can. Bull. 171.

Rice, D. W. 1977. *A list of the marine mammals of the world*. NOAA Technical Report. NMFS SSRF-711.

Ridgway, S. H., ed. 1972. *Mammals of the sea—biology and medicine*. Springfield, Ill.: Thomas.

Scammon, C. M. 1874. *The marine mammals of the north-western coast of North America: together with an account of the American whale-fishery*. San Francisco: John Carmany and Co. (Reprinted 1968 in paperback. New York: Dover.)

Scheffer, V. B. 1976. *A natural history of marine mammals*. New York: Scribner.

Wood, F. G. 1973. *Marine mammals and man: the Navy's porpoises and sea lions*. Washington, D.C.: Robert B. Luce.

Cetaceans

Allen, G. M. 1941. Pygmy sperm whale in the Atlantic. *Field Mus. Nat. Hist. (Publ.) Zool. Ser.* 27:17–36.

Andrews, R. C. 1916. *Monographs of the Pacific Cetacea. II.—The sei whale (Balaenoptera borealis Lesson)*. New York: Memoirs of Am. Mus. Nat. Hist. (New Series), vol. I, part 6.

———. 1916. *Whale hunting with gun and camera*. New York: D. Appleton.

———. 1914. *Monographs of the Pacific Cetacea. I.—The California gray whale (Rhachianectes glaucus Cope)*. New York: Memoirs of Am. Mus. Nat. Hist. (New Series), vol. I, part 5.

———. 1909. Observations on the habits of the finback and humpback whales of the eastern North Pacific. *Bull. Am. Mus. Nat. Hist.* 26:213–26.

Audubon 77 (January 1975).

Barnes, L. G. 1976. Outline of eastern North Pacific fossil cetacean assemblages. *Syst. Zool.* 25:321–43.

Beale, T. 1839. *The natural history of the sperm whale*. London: John Van Voorst. (Reprinted 1973. London: Holland Pr.)

Beddard, F. E. 1900. *A book of whales*. New York: G. P. Putnam.

Berzin, A. A. 1972. *The sperm whale*. Jerusalem: Israel Program Scientific Translations. (Translated from Russian.)

Bigg, M. A. and Wolman, A. A. 1975. Live-capture killer whale (*Orcinus orca*) fishery, British Columbia and Washington, 1962–1973. *J. Fish. Res. Board Can.* 32:1213–21.

Bodfish, H. H. 1936. *Chasing the bowhead*. Cambridge, Mass.: Harvard U. Pr.

Brown, D. H.; Caldwell, D. K.; and Caldwell, M. C. 1966. Observations on the behavior of wild and captive false killer whales, with notes on associated behavior of other genera of captive delphinids. *Los Angeles Cty. Mus. Contrib. Sci.* No. 95:1–32.

Burgess, K. 1968. The behavior and training of a killer whale *Orcinus orca* at San Diego Sea World. *Int. Zoo Yearb.* 8:202–5.

Busnel, R. G. 1973. Symbiotic relationship between man and dolphins. *N.Y. Acad. Sci.* 35:112–31.

Caldwell, D. K. and Caldwell, M. C. 1972. *The world of the bottlenosed dolphin*. Philadelphia: Lippincott.

Caldwell, D. K.; Caldwell, M. C.; and Rice, D. W. 1966. Behavior of the sperm whale *Physeter catodon* L. In *Whales, dolphins, and porpoises*. Norris, K. S., ed. Berkeley and Los Angeles: U. Calif. Pr.

Carroll, G. M. 1976. Utilization of the bowhead whale. *Mar. Fish. Rev.* 38:18–21.

Chandler, R.; Goebel, C.; and Balcomb, K. 1977. Who is that killer whale? A new key to whale watching. *Pac. Search* 11:25–28.

Chittleborough, R. G. 1965. Dynamics of two populations of the humpback whale, *Megaptera novaeangliae* (Borowski). *Aust. J. Mar. Freshwater Res.* 16:33–128.

Cook, J. A. 1926. *Pursuing the whale: a quarter-century of whaling in the Arctic*. Boston and New York: Houghton Mifflin.

Darling, J. 1977. The Vancouver Island gray whales. *Waters* (J. Vancouver Aquar.) 2:5–19.

Davis, R. 1974. Sea wolves of the Northwest [killer whales]. *Defenders Wildl.* 49(4):288–92; 49(5):397–402.

Evans, W. E., ed. 1974. The California gray whale. *Mar. Fish. Rev.* 36:1–65.

Fay, F. H. 1974. The role of ice in the ecology of marine mammals of the Bering Sea. In *Oceanography of the Bering Sea.* Hood, D. W. and Kelly, E. J., eds. Fairbanks: Inst. of Arctic Biol., U. Alaska.

Gilmore, R. M. 1976. The friendly whales of Laguna San Ignacio. *Terra* 15:24–28.

———. 1962. *Bubbles and other pilot whales.* Del Mar, Calif.: Barley Brae Printers.

———. 1961. *The story of the gray whale.* 2d ed. rev. San Diego, Calif.: Pioneer Printers.

Graves, W. 1976. The imperiled giants. *Natl. Geor. Mag.* 150:722–51.

Griffin, E. I. 1966. Making friends with a killer whale. *Natl. Geor. Mag.* 129:418–46.

Gulland, J. 1972. Future of the blue whale. *New Sci.* 54:198–99.

Handley, C. O. 1966. A synopsis of the genus *Kogia* (pygmy sperm whales). In *Whales, dolphins, and porpoises.* Norris, K. S., ed. Berkeley and Los Angeles: U. Calif. Pr.

Hubbs, C. L. 1951. Eastern Pacific records and general distribution of the pygmy whale. *J. Mammal.* 32:403–10.

Hubbs, C. L.; Perrin, W. F.; and Balcomb, K. C. 1973. *Stenella coeruleoalba* in the eastern and central tropical Pacific. *J. Mammal.* 54:549–52.

Jonsgård, Å. and Lyshoel, P. B. 1970. A contribution to the knowledge of the biology of the killer whale *Orcinus orca* (L.). *Norw. J. Zool.* 18:41–48.

Kasuya, T. 1977. Age determination and growth of the Baird's beaked whale with a comment on the fetal growth rate. *Sci. Rep. Whales Res. Inst. Tokyo* No. 29:1–20.

Kellogg, R. 1928. The history of whales—their adaptations to life in the water. *Q. Rev. Biol.* 3(1):29–76; 3(2):174–208.

Kleinenberg, S. E.; Yablokov, A. V.; Bel'kovich, B. M.; and Tarasevich, M. N. 1969. *Beluga (Delphinapterus leucas): investigation of the species.* Jerusalem: Israel Program Scientific Translations. (Translated from Russian.)

Leatherwood, S. 1975. Some observations of feeding behavior of bottle-nosed dolphins (*Tursiops truncatus*) in the northern Gulf of Mexico and (*Tursiops* cf *T. gilli*) off Southern California, Baja California, and Nayarit, Mexico. *Mar. Fish. Rev.* 37:10–16.

Leatherwood, S. and Walker, W. 1978. The northern right whale dolphin, *Lissodelphis borealis,* in the eastern North Pacific. In *Behavior of marine animals.* Vol. 3, *Natural history of whales.* Winn, H. E. and Olla, B. L., eds. New York: Plenum.

Leatherwood, S.; Evans, W. E.; and Rice, D. W. 1972. The *whales, dolphins and porpoises of the eastern North Pacific: a guide to their identification in the water.* NUC TP 282. San Diego, Calif.: Naval Undersea Center.

Mackintosh, N. A. 1965. *The stocks of whales.* London: Fishing News (Books).

Mackintosh, N. A., and Wheeler, J. F. G. 1929. Southern blue and fin whales. *Discovery Rep.* (Cambridge U. Pr.) 1:257–540.

McIntyre, J., ed. 1974. *Mind in the waters: a book to celebrate the consciousness of whales and dolphins.* New York: Scribner. San Francisco: Sierra Club.

McNulty, F. 1974. *The great whales.* Garden City, N.Y.: Doubleday.

Mansfield, A. W.; Smith, T. G.; and Beck, B. 1975. The narwhal, *Monodon monoceros,* in eastern Canadian waters. *J. Fish. Res. Board Can.* 32:1041–46.

Marquette, W. M. May 1977. *The 1976 catch of bowhead whales (Balaena mysticetus) by Alaskan Eskimos, with a review of the fishery, 1973–76, and a biological summary of the species.* Seattle: U.S. Dept. Commerce, NOAA, NMFS, Northwest and Alaska Fish. Center (processed report).

Masaki, Y. 1976. Biological studies on the North Pacific sei whale. *Bull. Far Seas Fish. Res. Lab.* (Shimizu, Japan) No. 14:1–104.

Miller, T. 1975. *The world of the California gray whale.* Santa Ana, Calif.: Baja Trail.

Mitchell, E. 1975. *Porpoise, dolphin and small whale fisheries of the world.* IUCN Monograph No. 3. Morges, Switz.

———. 1973. The status of the world's whales. *Nat. Can.* 2:9–19.

———. 1968. Northeast Pacific stranding distribution and seasonality of Cuvier's beaked whale, *Ziphius cavirostris. Can. J. Zool.* 46:265–79.

———. 1965. Evidence for mass strandings of the false killer whale (*Pseudorca crassidens*) in the eastern North Pacific Ocean. *Norsk Hvalfangst-Tidende* No. 8:172–77.

Moore, J. C. 1966. Diagnoses and distributions of beaked whales of the genus *Mesoplodon* known from North American waters. In *Whales, dolphins, and porpoises.* Norris, K. S., ed. Berkeley and Los Angeles: U. Calif. Pr.

Morejohn, G. V. 1978. The natural history of Dall's porpoise in the North Pacific Ocean. In *Behavior of marine animals.* Vol. 3, *Natural history of whales.* Winn, H. E. and Olla, B. L., eds. New York: Plenum.

Nemoto, T. 1959. Food of baleen whales with reference to whale movements. *Sci. Rep. Whales Res. Inst. Tokyo* No. 14:149–290.

Nickerson, R. 1977. *Brother whale: a Pacific whalewatcher's log.* San Francisco: Chronicle Books.

Nishiwaki, M. and Oguro, N. 1972. Catch of the Cuvier's beaked whale off Japan in recent years. *Sci. Rep. Whales*

Res. Inst. Tokyo No. 24:35–41.

Norris, K. S. 1974. *The porpoise watcher: a naturalist's experiences with porpoises and whales.* New York: Norton.

Norris, K. S. and Prescott, J. H. 1961. Observations of Pacific cetaceans of California and Mexican waters. *Univ. Calif. Pub. Zool.* 63:291–402.

Ohsumi, S. 1965. Reproduction of the sperm whale in the north-west Pacific. *Sci. Rep. Whales Res. Inst. Tokyo* No. 19:1–35.

Omura, H. and Sakiura, H. 1956. Studies on the little piked whale from the coast of Japan. *Sci. Rep. Whales Res. Inst. Tokyo* No. 11:1–37.

Omura, H.; Fujino, K.; and Kimura, S. 1955. Beaked whale *Berardius bairdi* of Japan, with notes on *Ziphius cavirostris. Sci. Rep. Whales Res. Inst. Tokyo* No. 10:89–132.

Omura, H. S.; Ohsumi, S.; Nemoto, T.; Nasu, K.; and Kasuya, T. 1969. Black right whales in the North Pacific. *Sci. Rep. Whales Res. Inst. Tokyo* No. 21:1–78.

Perrin, W. F. 1975. Distribution and differentiation of populations of dolphins of the genus *Stenella* in the eastern tropical Pacific. *J. Fish. Res. Board Can.* 32:1059–67.

Perrin, W. F. and Walker, W. A. 1975. The rough-toothed porpoise, *Steno bredanensis*, in the eastern tropical Pacific. *J. Mammal.* 56:905–7.

Pryor, K. W. 1975. *Lads before the wind: adventures in porpoise training.* New York: Har.-Row.

Reeves, R. R. 1976. Narwhals: another endangered species. *Can. Geogr. J.* 92:12–19.

Rice, D. W. 1968. Stomach contents and feeding behavior of killer whales in the eastern North Pacific. *Norsk Hvalfangst-Tidende* No. 3:35–38.

Rice, D. W. 1967. Cetaceans. In *Recent mammals of the world, a synopsis of families.* Anderson, S. and Jones, J. K., eds. New York: Ronald Pr.

Rice, D. W. and Wolman, A. A. 1971. *The life history and ecology of the gray whale (Eschrichtius robustus).* Stillwater, Okla.: Am. Soc. Mammal. Spec. Publ. No. 3.

Rice, D. W. and Fiscus, C. H. 1968. Right whales in the south-eastern North Pacific. *Norsk Hvalfangst-Tidende* No. 57:105–7.

Samaras, W. F. 1974. Reproductive behavior of the gray whale, *Eschrichtius robustus*, in Baja California. *Bull. South. Calif. Acad. Sci.* 73:57–64.

Scheffer, V. B. 1976. Exploring the lives of whales. *Natl. Geor. Mag.* 150:752–67.

———. 1970. The cliché of the killer. *Nat. Hist.* 50:26–28.

Scheffer, V. B. and Slipp, J. W. 1948. The whales and dolphins of Washington State with a key to the cetaceans of the west coast of North America. *Am. Midl. Nat.* 39:257–337.

Schevill, W. E., ed. 1974. *The whale problem: a status report.*

Cambridge, Mass.: Harvard U. Pr.

Sergeant, D. E. 1973. Biology of white whales (*Delphinapterus leucas*) in western Hudson Bay. *J. Fish. Res. Board Can.* 30:1065–90.

———. 1969. Feeding rates of Cetacea. *FiskDir. Skr. Ser. HavUnders.* 15:246–58.

———. 1962. *The biology of the pilot or pothead whale Globicephala melaena (Traill) in Newfoundland waters.* Fish. Res. Board Can. Bull. 132.

Sergeant, D. E. and Brodie, P. F. 1975. Identity, abundance, and present status of populations of white whales, *Delphinapterus leucas*, in North America. *J. Fish. Res. Board Can.* 32:1047–54.

Slijper, E. J. 1977. *Whales and dolphins.* Ann Arbor: U. Mich. Pr.

———. 1962. *Whales.* New York: Basic Books.

Townsend, C. H. 1935. The distribution of certain whales as shown by logbook records of American whaleships. *Zoologica, Scientific Contributions New York Zoological Society* 19:3–50.

Watkins, W. A. 1977. Acoustic behavior of sperm whales. *Oceanus* (Woods Hole Oceanographic Institution) 20:50–58.

Zimushko, V. V. and Lenskaya, S. A. 1970. Feeding of the gray whale (*Eschrichtius gibbosus*) at foraging grounds. *Ecology* No. 3:205–12. (Translated from Russian.)

Pinnipeds

Bartholomew, G. A. 1952. Reproductive and social behavior of the northern elephant seal. *Univ. Calif. Publ. Zool.* 47:369–472.

Bartholomew, G. A. and Boolootian, R. A. 1960. Numbers and population structure of the pinnipeds on the California Channel Islands. *J. Mammal.* 41:366–75.

Bigg, M. A. 1969. *The harbour seal in British Columbia.* Fish. Res. Board Can. Bull. 172.

Brooks, J. W. 1954. *A contribution to the life history and ecology of the Pacific walrus.* Alaska Coop. Wildl. Res. Unit (College Alaska) Spec. Rept. No. 1.

Burns, J. J. 1970. Remarks on the distribution and natural history of pagophilic pinnipeds in the Bering and Chukchi seas. *J. Mammal.* 51:445–54.

———. 1967. *The Pacific bearded seal.* Juneau: Alaska Dept. Fish and Game.

Cowan, I. M. and Carl, G. C. 1945. The northern elephant seal (*Mirounga angustirostris*) in British Columbia waters and vicinity. *Can. Field-Nat.* 59:170–71.

Fay, F. H. 1957. History and present status of the Pacific walrus population. *Trans. No. Am. Wildl. Conf.* 22:431–45.

Fay, F. H. and Stoker, S. W. 1977. *The role of the Pacific walrus in the trophic system of the Bering Sea.* U.S. Marine Mammal

Commission contract report MM5AC024.

Fiscus, C. H. and Baines, G. A. 1966. Food and feeding behavior of Steller and California sea lions. *J. Mammal.* 47:195–200.

Fisher, H. D. 1952. *The status of the harbour seal in British Columbia, with particular reference to the Skeena River.* Fish. Res. Board Can. Bull. 93.

Harrison, R. J., ed. 1968. *The behavior and physiology of pinnipeds.* New York: Appleton-Century-Crofts.

Hubbs, C. L. 1956. Back from oblivion. Guadalupe fur seal: still a living species. *Pac. Discovery* 9:14–21.

Imler, R. H. and Sarber, H. R. 1947. *Harbor seals and sea lions in Alaska.* U.S. Fish and Wildl. Serv. Spec. Sci. Rept. 28.

Kenyon, K. W. 1972. Man versus the monk seal. *J. Mammal.* 53:687–96.

———. 1960. The Pacific walrus. *Oryx* 5:332–40.

Kenyon, K. W. and Rice, D. W. 1961. Abundance and distribution of the Steller sea lion. *J. Mammal.* 42:223–34.

Kenyon, K. W. and Rice, D. W. 1959. Life history of the Hawaiian monk seal. *Pac. Sci.* 13:215–52.

King, J. E. 1964. *Seals of the world.* London: British Mus. (Nat. Hist.).

LeBoeuf, B. J. 1972. Sexual behavior in the northern elephant seal, *Mirounga angustirostris. Behavior* 41:1–26.

Mansfield, A. W. 1967. *Seals of arctic and eastern Canada.* 2d ed. rev. Fish. Res. Board Can. Bull. 137.

McLaren, I. A. 1966. Taxonomy of harbor seals of the western North Pacific and evolution of certain other hair seals. *J. Mammal.* 47:466–73.

———. 1958. *The biology of the ringed seal (Phoca hispida Schreber) in the eastern Canadian Arctic.* Fish. Res. Board Can. Bull. 118.

Odell, D. K. 1977. Structure of northern elephant seal population breeding on San Nicolas Island, California, in 1971. *Anim. Behav.* 25:208–14.

Ognev, S. E. 1935. *Mammals of the U.S.S.R. and adjacent countries.* Vol. 3, *Carnivora (Fissipedia and Pinnipedia).* Washington, D.C.: Smithsonian Institution and National Science Foundation. (Translated by Israel Program Scientific Translations, Jerusalem, 1962.)

Peterson, R. S. and Bartholomew, G. A. 1967. *The natural history and behavior of the California sea lion.* Am. Soc. Mammal. Spec. Publ. No. 1. Stillwater, Okla.: Am. Soc. Mammal.

Repenning, C. A.; Peterson, R. S.; and Hubbs, C. L. 1971. Contributions to the systematics of the southern fur seals, with particular reference to the Juan Fernandez and Guadalupe species. In *Antarctic Pinnipedia.* Burt, W. H., ed. Washington, D.C.: Antarctic Res. Ser. 18:1–34.

Scheffer, V. B. 1958. *Seals, sea lions and walruses: a review of the Pinnipedia.* Stanford, Calif.: Stanford U. Pr.

Scheffer, V. B. and Slipp, J. W. 1944. The harbor seal in Washington State. *Am. Midl. Nat.* 32:373–416.

Spalding, D. J. 1964. *Comparative feeding habits of the fur seal, sea lion, and harbour seal on the British Columbia coast.* Fish. Res. Board Can. Bull. 146.

Venables, U. M. and Venables, L. S. V. 1955. Observations on a breeding colony of the seal *Phoca vitulina* in Shetland. *Proc. Zool. Soc. Lon.* 125:521–32.

Other Marine-Adapted Species

Golder, F. A. 1925. *Bering's voyages.* Vol. 2. New York: Am. Geogr. Soc. (Includes Steller's journal of 1743, translated and in part annotated by L. Stejneger.)

Harington, C. R. 1968. *Denning habits of the polar bear (Ursus maritimus Phipps).* Can. Wildl. Ser. Rept. Series 5.

Kenyon, K. W. 1971. Return of the sea otter. *Natl. Geor. Mag.* 140:520–39.

———. 1961. *The sea otter in the eastern Pacific Ocean.* Washington, D.C.: USFWS, North American Fauna Series No. 68. (Reprinted 1975 in paperback. New York: Dover.)

Lentfer, J. W. 1972. Polar bear–sea ice relationships. In *Bears— their biology and management.* Proc. Second Internat. Conf. Bear Res. and Manage. IUCN Publ. New Series 23:165–71.

Manning, T. 1971. *Geographical variation in the polar bear (Ursus maritimus Phipps).* Can. Wildl. Ser. Rept. Series 13.

Ogden, A. 1941. *The California sea otter trade, 1784–1848.* Berkeley and Los Angeles: U. Calif. Pr.

Ognev, S. I. 1931. *Mammals of eastern Europe and northern Asia.* Vol. 2, *Carnivora (Fissipedia).* Washington, D.C.: Smithsonian Institution and National Science Foundation. (Translated by Israel Program Scientific Translations, Jerusalem, 1962.)

Perry, R. 1966. *The world of the polar bear.* Seattle and London: U. Wash. Pr.

Stejneger, L. 1936. *Georg Wilhelm Steller, the pioneer of Alaskan natural history.* Cambridge, Mass.: Harvard U. Pr.

———. 1887. How the great northern sea-cow (*Rytina*) became exterminated. *Am. Nat.* 21:1047–54.

Steller, G. W. 1899. The beasts of the sea. In *The fur seals and fur-seal islands of the North Pacific Ocean.* Jordan, D. S., ed. Washington, D.C.: Govt. Printing Ofc. Part 3, Art. 8. (Translation by Miller, W. and Miller, J. E. of *De bestiis marinis* 2:289–398.)

———. 1751. *De bestiis marinis.* Vol. 2. Nov. Comm. Acad. Sci. Imp.

Index